Successful Time Management

Wiley Self-Teaching Guides teach practical skills from accounting to astronomy, management to mathematics. Look for them at your local bookstore.

Other Wiley Self-Teaching Guides on Business Skills:

Accounting: A Self-Teaching Guide, by Neal Margolis and N. Paul Harmon

Effective Meetings: A Self-Teaching Guide, by Clyde W. Burleson

Listening: The Forgotten Skill, A Self-Teaching Guide, Second Edition, by Madelyn Burley-Allen

Making Successful Presentations: A Self-Teaching Guide, by Terry C. Smith

Managing Assertively: A Self-Teaching Guide, Second Edition, by Madelyn Burley-Allen

Managing Behavior on the Job: A Self-Teaching Guide, by Paul L. Brown

Quick Business Math: A Self-Teaching Guide, by Steve Slavin

Selling on the Phone: A Self-Teaching Guide, by James Porterfield

Successful Time Management

A Self-Teaching Guide

Second Edition

Jack D. Ferner

John Wiley & Sons, Inc.

New York • Chichester • Brisbane • Toronto • Singapore

To my parents, Dorothy and John

Copyright © 1995 by John Wiley & Sons, Inc.

Library of Congress Cataloging-in-Publication Data:

Ferner, Jack D.
    Successful time management / Jack D. Ferner. — 2nd ed.
        p. cm. — (A self-teaching guide)
    Includes index.
    ISBN 0-471-03392-8 (acid-free paper)
    1. Time management—Handbooks, manuals, etc.   I. Title.
HD69.T54F47   1994
650.1—dc20   94-20691

Contents

Preface

This book is the product of many struggles with the management of time—my own struggles as well as those of hundreds of people I have talked with in seminars, workshops, and casual conversation. I have been struck by the pervasiveness of the problems and the elusiveness of solutions. The more involved we become, the more responsibility we take on, the worse the problems. Quick solutions, secret formulas, and gimmicks provide only temporary relief.

One person has referred to time management as a "flaky" subject. This may be true if our problem analysis is superficial and we attempt to apply gimmicky solutions. But if time management is approached like any other management subject—with sound principles—then we can develop a solid framework for gaining control of our time.

Like all management problems, time management must be subjected to principles of analysis and planning. We must know where our time goes, what our problems and their causes are, and realistically how long it takes to accomplish certain tasks. Planning is equally important for both long-term goals and daily schedules.

What makes time management particularly troublesome is that it's so personal. Any system we use must be adapted to our own individual style and situation. And it takes a strong personal commitment—good time management must be internalized and become a habit. No one checks up on us, except ourselves. It's easy to let it slide, not to plan, to be a "nice" guy and never say no. It's easy to rationalize that we are different and therefore can't do anything to gain control of our lives. Inevitably, when I address a group on time management, someone will say, "But my job is different; I can't control my time." The reality is that we all have very similar problems. I have heard very few that are unique.

One fact is abundantly clear: The people I have observed who are most successful, who have the time to do the things that are most important to them, are the ones who take the trouble to analyze, plan, and commit to a course of action. They control interruptions, can say no, and delegate effectively.

The choice is yours. If you understand the principles of time management, apply them to your situation, and commit them to habit, you will be able to increase your effectiveness, success, and self-satisfaction. Ignore them and you'll be operating at a disadvantage—like having one hand tied behind your back.

This book presents a framework of management principles, along with many exercises, worksheets, case studies, references, and key ideas, to help you systematically gain control of your time. Some people will use the book to learn an entire system; others will seek one or two key ideas on overcoming procrastination or running more efficient meetings. Whatever your objectives, you should find this book a practical guide.

You can derive the most benefit by going through the entire book and doing most of the exercises in sequence. But if certain areas interest you particularly, go right to them. Consider your priorities: What is your most important objective? How will you get the most help in the least amount of time? Setting priorities is one of the many key time management principles presented in this book.

Another is: Do it now—don't procrastinate. Isn't it time to get started? Good luck!

ACKNOWLEDGMENTS

Many people have contributed to this book. First and foremost are the people from all walks of life who have related to me their successes and frustrations with time management. Bits and pieces of these stories are interspersed throughout the book, adding up to a wealth of human experience.

Also many thanks to Janet Fox, Sharon Booth, and Marty Lentz, who assisted in the writing of certain sections, and to the many others who helped in reviewing and testing the materials. Then there were the three great secretaries, Phyllis Harper, Jerry Russell, and Lynn Ebert, who had to make a readable manuscript out of my scribblings. My special thanks to them.

Finally, I appreciate the cooperation and support of the Babcock Graduate School of Management and Wake Forest University.

Jack D. Ferner

Winston-Salem, N.C.
November 1994

1 Basic Concepts of Time Management

"But I don't have time!" How often have you heard those words? How often do you use them yourself? Consider the following incidents about people who think they don't have enough time.

- You have to explain to your boss why you haven't completed the budget for your department. "Lisa, it's been one crisis after another all week. I just haven't had time to pull the figures together."

- A father tries to explain to his wife why he hasn't made an appointment with his son's teacher to discuss the boy's poor grades. "You know I'm working late every night. I just don't have time to get away from the office."

- A homemaker tries to answer an old college friend's question about why she hasn't kept up with her painting, which she used to enjoy and did very well. "The twins are really a handful. I've pretty much given up on trying to do anything for myself these days. I really miss painting, but there just aren't enough hours in the day."

"If only there were thirty-six hours in the day." That's another well-worn phrase that is often heard from people who are not accomplishing all that is expected of them or that they expect of themselves. Take the case of Chet Craig, a plant manager.

CASE STUDY*

Chet Craig is manager of Norris Company's central plant, one of three plants operated by Norris that produce high-quality color printing for commercial businesses. Upon returning to his office from his afternoon plant tour, Chet answered the ringing phone. It was the secretary of the manager of the Newark plant asking what time he would be arriving there the next day. They were having some quality problems and had finally prevailed on Chet to help them out for a day. Chet rummaged around his in-basket for his plane ticket, but couldn't find it and finally told her he would call back.

He picked a memo and phone message out of the in-basket and started reading them as he walked to the outer office to find Jeanne, his secretary, and see what plane reservations she had made for him.

"Darn, I'm still not ready to make that decision. Better get the Sales, Production, Cost, and Quality Control managers in here and try to figure whether we can make money on that product line with that equipment. It's a big risk!"

Chet finally found Jeanne and told her to set up a meeting first thing in the morning. She reminded him that Universal Waxing Corp. would be in to see him early to go over their lagging delivery schedule. They had insisted on meeting with Chet personally. She gave him his plane ticket, which was for a noon flight. That was earlier than he wanted, and he mumbled, "I'll have to leave for the airport right after I get through with Universal. Well, we'll have to meet this afternoon. Call and see how soon you can get them all down here." It was 2:30. Ralph Valle, the expeditor, came by with a clipboard full of delivery problems. Chet became engrossed in trying to adjust the product schedule to help expedite some key orders. Personnel called to ask about a couple of people they had located to fill a supervisor's job. The warehouse manager stopped by to talk about a personal problem. Chet noticed the time slipping by and finally yelled to Jeanne, asking when the meeting was going to be. She informed him that Williams, the sales man-

To	Chet			
Date	9/19	Time	2:10	A.M. ☐ P.M. ☒

WHILE YOU WERE OUT

M __Your wife, Cheryl, called__

of _____

Phone_____
  Area Code   Number   Extension

TELEPHONED	X	PLEASE CALL	X
CALLED TO SEE YOU		WILL CALL AGAIN	
WANTS TO SEE YOU		**URGENT**	X
RETURNED YOUR CALL			

Message__Your daughter came home today with a note from her teacher that she would like to meet with you both. A serious disciplinary problem. Your wife set up a meeting at 6:45 pm just before the PTA meeting and wants to make sure you'll be there.

Operator __Jeanne__

*As adapted from "The Case of the Missing Time," copyright 1960, Northwestern University.

NORRIS COMPANY
Central Plant, Midvale, Ohio

MEMORANDUM

To: Chet Craig, Plant Manager   **Date:** September 19

From: Phil Potter, Purchasing Agent

Subject: Purchase of the New Six-Color, Ultra-Speed Press
                from Harrington Press Co.

Chet:

Bill Teames called from Harrington Press and said they had another buyer
for the ultra-speed press. As you know, we've been putting them off on a
final decision, and Bill said if they didn't hear from us by tomorrow
morning, they'd sell it to the other buyer, who I think may be a competitor
of ours on the East Coast.

If we don't get this press, it'll be over six months before they have another
available and we'll miss the promotional calendar market. Even worse, we're
pretty sure to get socked with a price increase, which will be about 7½%.

I know it's a big decision; a lot of money to commit to a new product line,
and we're not sure how strong our competitive position is. Nonetheless,
we'd better fish or cut bait. Let me know.

                                          Phil

ager, was with a customer and would let her know when he was free.

At 4:45 the meeting convened. They began talking about the pros and cons of the product line. Jeanne came in at 5:00 with some letters to sign, a couple of phone messages, and to say she was leaving for the day. At 5:20, Chet's wife, Cheryl, called to say he needed to get home so he could have supper and pick up the baby-sitter before going to school for their meeting. He felt beads of perspiration forming on his forehead. He started to tell her he would be late, but then remembered he hadn't even let her know about his trip tomorrow and decided not to say anything. He felt a bit flushed as he hung up and turned to the others, "It's getting late. Does anyone have anything else to add to the subject?" The production manager said he didn't really believe the productivity figures that were used by Harrington in the economic justification. Chet said he would sleep on it and make a decision in the morning. With that, the meeting broke up.

At 11:07 the next morning, Chet scribbled out a requisition for the new press. As he rushed out the door to catch the plane, he shoved it at Jeanne, saying, "Get this down to Phil right away and tell him he had better call Harrington and let them know we want the press."

As he drove to the airport, he thought, "Boy, I hope that new line of promotional calendars works out or I'll end up eating a hundred-thousand-dollar press. Wish I'd had more time!"

Chet literally ran out of time—time he needed to make a very important decision in an effective manner. The reasons? Interruptions, lack of priorities, disorganization, inability to say "no," and ineffective delegation. This book will give you solutions to those problems.

THE 168-HOUR LIMIT

Two axioms of time management address those self-serving clichés, "if only there were more hours in the day," and "I don't have enough time":

First, there are exactly 24 hours in a day . . .
168 hours in a week, and
8,760 hours in a year.
No more, no less.

Second, we all have the same amount of time—rich or poor, powerful or weak, the U.S. President or an insurance salesman, a wife managing a home and family or a retiree.

It isn't a matter of not having enough time, or of somehow being able to beg, borrow, or steal someone else's time. We each have all the time available.

Time management, then, is the process of managing the things we do in that block of 168 hours per week.

At first glance, 168 hours—one week—may seem like a great deal of time. People will often say, "I can do a lot in 168 hours." But if you add up all the things you must do by necessity, ought to do because of commitments, and would like to do to fulfill your goals, 168 hours may not be so long after all. For example, a breakdown follows of how activities typically consume our time.

	Hours/week
Personal work:	
sleep (7 hours a night)	49
eat (2 hours a day)	14
dress (1 hour per day)	7
commute to work (1 hour)	5
other chores required to maintain ourselves, our families, homes, etc. (2 hours per day)	14
Total	89 hours
Working on the job	40–50 hours
Family	
Leisure	
Personal growth—education, reading, hobbies	30–40 hours
Free time	
Total	168 hours/week

Figure 1.1 shows this breakdown in a pie chart. Thus, if half of our time gets used up on personal work and a minimum of another quarter on the job, we have at most 40 hours per week to do all the other activities. But if we choose a challenging career and expand our work week to 50 or 60 hours, where does that time come from? Our families? Our hobby or leisure time? Our evening walk down to the river to fish and relax?

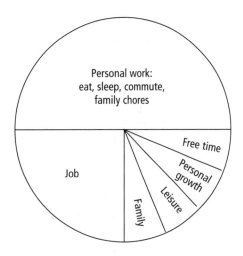

FIGURE 1.1

How we use our 168 hours per week.

The 168 hours is a boundary or constraint. Whatever we do must be done within that 168-hour boundary. Therefore it is crucial to know what we want to do, to set priorities, and to use that time to best advantage.

HOW CAN BETTER TIME MANAGEMENT HELP YOU?

Take a moment and reflect on how you are spending your time and living your life. Ask yourself the questions in Exercise 1.1 and indicate the appropriate responses in the blanks provided.

EXERCISE 1.1

	Most of the time	Some of the time	Seldom
Are you spending your time the way you really want to?		X	
Do you feel harried, obligated to do too many things you really don't want to do?		X	
Do you get a feeling of self-satisfaction and accomplishment from your work?	X		
Do you work long hours? How many? 60 hours.	X		
Do you take work home evenings or weekends?	X		
Is there stress in your work? Do you feel tense and insecure?	X		
Do you have guilt feelings about not doing a better job?	X		
Is your job fun?	X		
Do you enjoy your family?	X		
Are you giving your family as much time as you would like? Quality time?		X	
Do you have time to keep physically fit?		X	
Do you have time to take the vacations and long weekends you would like?			X
Do you have time to engage in a favorite hobby, sport, good book, concert series, or church activity?		X	
Do you feel you must always be busy doing something productive?	X		
Do you feel guilty when you just goof off for awhile?	X		
Do you have enough free time?			X

You probably were able to answer some questions positively—others not. We work hard but don't seem to get anywhere. Constant interruptions keep us from doing important job assignments. Busy careers often put pressure on our marriages. A large family interferes with our personal interests.

Look again at the questions you were unable to answer satisfactorily. Where do you see payoffs from a program in time management? Some people would like to learn to control interruptions at work, others to run a more effective meeting or to procrastinate less. Maybe you'd like more time with your family, or time to take a vacation. Using Exercise 1.2, describe your objectives in learning more about time management.

EXERCISE 1.2   **My Time Management Objectives**

Learn to prioritize
Organize myself
Learn when to quit work & go home
Better judge how much can get done
in a day

This book is intended to be a practical guide for improving time management. As you proceed through it, keep your objectives in mind. Look for ideas that will help you meet these objectives. Come back to page 7 occasionally to review your objectives. Perhaps you can make them more explicit or add to them.

TIME: A SCARCE RESOURCE

In his book *The Harried Leisure Class,** Staffan Linder talks about the "increasing scarcity of time." In economic terms, time can indeed be considered a scarce resource. Economists are concerned with how differ-

---

*New York: Columbia University Press, 1970.

ent societies allocate their resources, such as land, labor, materials, capital, knowledge/technology, information, and enterprise. Allocation of these resources is accomplished by economic entities, which include nations, governments, businesses, social organizations, families, and individuals.

Individuals, of course, have varying amounts of land, capital (money), and the resources just listed. But individuals also have other resources. Have you ever considered your experience, talent, and personality as resources? They are. Some people make a fortune by selling their talent or personality. Think of Bill Cosby, Michael Jordan, and Barbra Streisand. Or, closer to home, think of a minister whose resources may include compassion, an ability to listen, and a talent for writing inspirational sermons. Or a teacher whose resources include the ability to make learning interesting and to articulate thoughts clearly. Or a business leader whose resources include effective leadership ability and the capacity to motivate subordinates to develop their own abilities. Or a mother whose resources are love and patience.

Time controls and limits how we use our other resources. Thus, it is often referred to as our most valuable resource.

Take some time now to write down your personal resources (Exercise 1.3). Remember, this is a personalized workbook, a chance to freely express yourself without someone looking over your shoulder, so give yourself credit for what you are.

EXERCISE 1.3

Resources that you bring to your work (examples: experience, training, motivation, creativity, selling skills, leadership qualities).

That are important to your family (examples: financial, love, moral values).

That are important in your community or school or volunteer work (examples: leadership skills, concern for the handicapped).

That give you the most inward satisfaction (examples: a solid golf swing, an interest in astrology).

Managing our time means managing ourselves and that means managing these resources—our strengths. We will assess our personal resources in more detail in Chapter 4.

GOALS

Inherent in the concept of allocating resources is *purpose.* Governments are established with the purpose of providing service and protection, of making and enforcing laws, and of redistributing wealth through taxation. Companies exist to make products or provide services and thereby make a profit. A neighborhood association is established for the purpose of improving the neighborhood and protecting its residents. The United Way has the purpose of raising money to distribute to social agencies, which in turn have the purpose of improving the quality of life in the community.

Individuals also allocate their resources to their own needs and purposes. In his writing on human motivation, Abraham Maslow theorized that needs are arranged in a hierarchy from basic psychological needs to needs for self-actualization. Maslow's concept is that a person is motivated to satisfy the basic needs before the higher-level needs. When a need is satisfied, it ceases to motivate; the person then moves on to an upper-level need.* The figure below illustrates this theory.

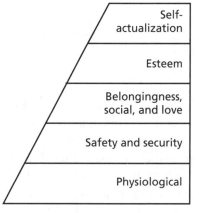

Self-actualization	The need to fulfill oneself by maximizing the use of our abilities, skills, and potential.
Esteem	The need for self-esteem and the esteem of others.
Belongingness, social, and love	The need for friendship, affiliation, interaction, and love.
Safety and security	The need for freedom from threat, security, and safety from threatening events and surroundings
Physiological	The need for food, drink, shelter, warmth, and relief from pain.

*A. H. Maslow, "A Theory of Human Motivation," *Psychological Review,* July 1943, pp. 370–396; and A. H. Maslow, *Motivation and Personality* (New York: Harper & Row, 1954).

You can think of people at all levels in Maslow's hierarchy of needs. People in third-world nations whose physiological needs are not being met—people dying of starvation. Or people in war-torn areas whose safety and security are threatened daily.

This book is for people who wish to accomplish something special, to live happy and productive lives. It's for people who want more than basic needs, who have self-actualization needs—people who are reaching for their dreams. As an example, let's take a look at Mark's goals.

CASE STUDY   As soon as Mark gets out of bed in the morning, he spends 20 minutes on the stationary bike in his bedroom. He passes up the doughnuts at coffee break and eats a light lunch (except for a piece of chocolate pie, which is his weakness). Staying trim and healthy is a personal goal of Mark's, and he has made a habit of doing something toward that goal every day.

Mark goes to his job as director of a drug abuse center. He has held the job for six years and feels secure in it. What he needs from his work is the knowledge that he is doing the best he can, and right now his priorities are to upgrade the training of the counselors who work under him and to enhance community awareness and support for the center. Most of his actions on any given day are tasks that advance those goals.

When he gets home from work, Mark tries to go out and shoot baskets with his 12-year-old son for half an hour or so before dinner. The boy, Andy, is on the third-string basketball team at his junior high and wants to make the varsity team. Mark usually feels pretty worn out when he gets home from work, but he thinks it is very important to stay in touch with his son. Andy isn't very interested in confiding in his parents these days, but he is comfortable going one-on-one with his father on the basketball court.

After dinner, Mark goes to the local high school where he teaches an English class to a group of foreign students two nights a week. He lives near the state university, and every year dozens of graduate students arrive from Mexico and Central and South America. Often their English is poor and they have serious problems with both school and everyday occurrences. Mark had a personal experience of "culture shock" in the Peace Corps, and he has decided that working with these students is the best way he can serve his community.

Mark's goals relate to different facets of his life. He has a personal goal of physical fitness. His work goal is to be a "good manager" of the drug abuse center. That general goal is broken down into subgoals that reflect immediate priorities of the center. He also has a family goal of being a "good father" to his son. Finally, there is a need to serve his community through teaching English to foreign students.

What are your personal goals? In Exercise 1.4, write them down quickly and spontaneously. Remember, all goals don't have to produce great value; they don't have to be lofty. Having more time for leisure—to goof off—can be a worthy goal, too.

	This year	*In the longer term*
EXERCISE 1.4		

Work goals:

Family goals:

Community goals:

Self goals:

Analyzing your goals is crucial if you are to use your time more effectively. We will go into this more deeply in Chapter 5. Appendix III contains resource materials on goal setting.

THE REAL MEANING OF TIME MANAGEMENT

The valuable resource, time, affects the way we use our other resources. It is the only resource that we all have equally. Once used, it's gone forever. And, unlike many of our resources, time cannot be stored until we have a plan for it.

What this means is that we cannot manage time in the same sense that we can manage money, for example. Time management is more exactly the management of the activities we engage in during our time. Time management is self-management. Managing oneself is like managing anything else. It involves certain skills—planning, organizing, implementing, and controlling.

Time management means the *efficient use of our resources, including time, in such a way that we are effective in achieving important personal goals.* Efficiency has been defined as doing things right—effectiveness, as doing the *right* things right.

If you are concerned about how you are spending your time, and serious about improving, take a look at what's involved.

Commitment: There are no gimmicks or shortcuts. Sloppy time management is just like a bad habit. You must be committed to doing something about it—the same as losing weight, stopping smoking, or beating the drug habit.

Analysis: You must have data on where you spend your time, what your problems are, and the causes. Time logs and other forms of analysis are essential.

Planning: You may be saying "I don't have time to plan." But effective management always requires planning, whether you are managing the family budget, your church, a business, or time. An hour of planning will save you many hours of doing the wrong things, fighting crises, avoiding the unimportant.

Follow-up and Reanalysis: A plan won't work very well, no matter how good it is, if you don't monitor results, detect problems, and modify the plan.

Thus, time management is a continuous, ongoing process of analyzing, planning, reanalyzing, and replanning. This is depicted as a circular process in Figure 1.2. It has been subdivided into eight discrete steps.

1. Find out how you use your time now. Use time logs and other means to get an accurate recording.
2. Analyze your time log to identify your problems—activities that are taking up large amounts of time without corresponding value.
3. Practice self-assessment. Occasionally, appraise your abilities, resources, interests, and present situation. Note how appraisal statements ("I am," "I can") match up with goal statements ("I need," "I desire").
4. Set goals that are important to you. Establish their relative importance by means of priority ratings.
5. Develop action plans to achieve your important goals. Define tasks, resource needs, and a time frame.

6. Implement the action plans. Schedule the key tasks into your daily calendar. Use a planning guide, to-do lists, and other aids.
7. Develop techniques and solutions for overcoming specific time management problems such as interruptions, crises, procrastination, or inefficient meetings.
8. Follow up and reanalyze. Keep score for continued improvement.

This book is designed to help you become an effective and efficient user of your time. You will begin by finding out what your time problems are—what is getting in the way of accomplishing your goals. In Chapter 2, you will find a case study—the story of a real person in a real situation—that illustrates a variety of time problems. You will probably find elements of yourself in this case. You will also do a case study of yourself in that chapter. You will keep track of your own time for a week and analyze your time log to determine where your time is going, how much time is wasted (and by whom and what), and how much time really is available for working on your important goals.

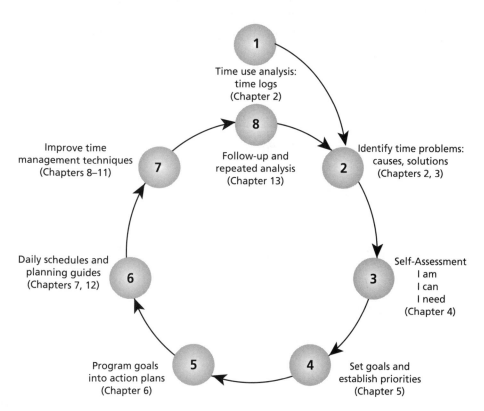

FIGURE 1.2

The process of effective time management.

The second part of the book focuses on goals. You'll start by taking closer stock of your own resources and using this information to set realistic goals for yourself. Most people are concerned not only with making better use of their working hours, but also with achieving certain objectives in their family lives, in their communities, and in their own development. You'll identify your own goals in these four areas and set priorities among them. Then we will move to a step-by-step procedure for making your goals become reality. A case study will show how goal programming works.

The third section of the book will show you how to use time management techniques on a daily basis. You will develop your own techniques to realize your goals and get your time robbers under control. You will learn effective ways to control interruptions, conduct shorter and more productive meetings, delegate work to others, work more efficiently with other members of your team, and control your tendency to procrastinate.

This is a "to-do" book, so the value of doing the exercises included in each chapter cannot be emphasized too strongly. Getting things in writing—making your goals, plans, and tasks visible—is a "principle" of time management.

2 The Time Log: Analyzing How You Use Your Time

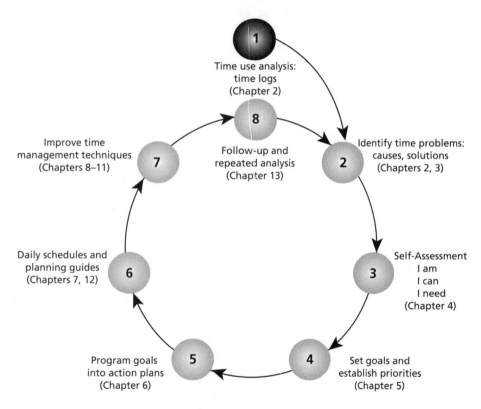

The first step in more effective management of your time is to analyze how you are presently spending it. That means keeping a time log for at least one week.

"Why keep a time log?" people sometimes ask. "I already know where my time goes. Besides, I don't have time. Isn't a time log itself a waste of time?"

Before we answer that question, let's see how well you can estimate where your time goes. Exercise 2.1 is broken into the major categories of time use described in Chapter 1—personal work, job, time with the family, personal growth, leisure, and free time. These general categories are further divided into specific activities. Use the blank spaces to indicate activities that are uniquely important to you.

On the right page of Exercise 2.1 are three columns for each activity. In the first column, write how you spend your time in a typical day. Think of a day this past week, for example. In the third column, indicate how you would like to be spending your time. These then become targets for change. For example, a sales manager who travels a great deal might write, "I'm not spending nearly enough time with my family." Or a working mother: "Five hours a day on housekeeping chores is too much along with my job. I must find ways to cut down." From the office manager of a large car dealership: "Three hours a day on little routine tasks is three times too much. There are a lot of things I can delegate, or don't have to do at all."

Fill in the first and third columns of Exercise 2.1 now. Later in this chapter, you will be asked to keep a detailed time log. After you have done this, you can come back to Exercise 2.1 and fill in the second column—a typical day out of your time log. Then you will be able to compare your actual use of time against your estimate to see how accurate (or inaccurate) your perceptions were. And the targets you identify will be the areas you want to improve in as you learn to manage your time more effectively.

The answer to objections such as "I don't have time to keep a time log" is that without a detailed record of our activities, most of us simply don't know where our time goes. People's guesstimates of how much time they spend at daily tasks usually turn out to be surprisingly inaccurate. We overestimate the time spent on some activities and underestimate the time spent on others. We tend to be defensive about how hard we work and biased about the important tasks we do.

Without the hard record, we are also prone to make excuses about our inability to get things done. "I couldn't get anything done at the office today because of the phone calls, the meetings, the boss coming in every hour . . . ," we say. Or, "It wasn't my fault. Susie got sick, and then the washing machine broke down and the carpool driver didn't show up."

Keeping a time log will help you find out how much of your time is being eaten away by external factors, such as telephone interruptions, and how much time you waste because of obstacles within yourself, such as indecision and failure to delegate tasks.

Knowing, not guessing, how long things really do take will enable you to plan better. For example:

> Karen is working on a statistical report involving an analysis of sales by product, salesperson, and territory. The report is due in her boss's hands at noon. The raw data are in the computer, and Karen struggles late into the evening to do her analysis. Blurry-eyed from staring at the computer screen all day, she departs from the office figuring that it will only take a short time in the morning to summarize the analysis, format it in report form, and get it printed out for her boss. But a fresh look the next day tells Karen the analysis is flawed and she needs to redo it. She tries to make the changes quickly, but it only gets worse. She figures it will take another full day. Desperately, Karen calls her boss to tell him the report will be late. She ends up working late a second night. Her boss is obviously irritated.

Obviously, Karen's assumption that finishing the report would "only take a short time" was off base. Most of us can think of many occasions when misjudging the time it would take to perform some minor task threw off the whole day's schedule, putting us behind on some really important and urgent matter. For example:

> John is in charge of production scheduling. He knows that completing the new schedule will take him well into the evening, even with no interruptions, and it must be ready for the production supervisors when the plant starts up at 8:00 a.m. tomorrow. It's noon, and John decides to take 10 minutes and jump out for a quick bite to eat. When he returns from lunch (which actually took 40 minutes), he checks his voice mail. Nine messages have accumulated while he worked on the production schedule and went out for lunch. He decides to take 10 minutes to return calls (John thinks in terms of 10 minutes). When he looks at his watch, a full hour has passed, and he hasn't been able to reach three of the callers. He just gets going on the schedule again when he's interrupted by one of the callbacks. It is now 2:30, and he hasn't made any progress on the schedule since he went to lunch at noon. The phone rings again. This time the caller wants some information that John has to get from someone else. He promises to call back in 10 minutes.

Just knowing where your time goes and how long it takes you to do things gives you power. Your time log becomes a standard by which you

EXERCISE 2.1	*General category*	*Activity*

1. Personal work

(a) Eating
(b) Sleeping
(c) Dressing
(d) Commuting to work
(e) Family/household chores (specify)

_____
_____
_____
_____

2. On the job

(a) Time I control:
   important projects
   catching up on routine tasks
   goofing off
(b) Time I don't control:
   phone interruptions
   drop-in visitors
   meetings
   the boss
   time with subordinates
   routine tasks
   important projects
   other

3. Time with the family

(a) _____
(b) _____
(c) _____

4. Personal growth

(a) _____
(b) _____

5. Leisure

(a) _____
(b) _____
(c) _____

6. Free time

(a) _____
(b) _____

My estimate of how I spend my time	A typical day out of my time log	My target of how I'd like to spend my day

can measure your progress in using your time more effectively. For example:

> You find you are spending about 3½ hours each day answering and making phone calls. You are determined to cut this down. You decide it would be reasonable to expect to cut out one hour on the phone each day, and you work out some ways to do it. For instance, you assign some routine calls to an assistant. In two months you want to check how you are doing. You start keeping track of your time again, making a time log for one week. You find that you have cut only about 20 minutes off your phone time. You still have a way to go, and you decide to intensify your efforts and check again in a month. You make a little chart to record your progress month by month.

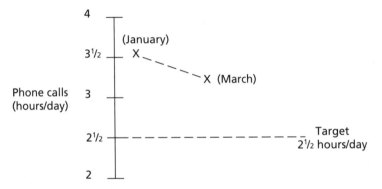

I hope these examples have persuaded you of the value of knowing where your time goes. For your time log, use the calendar provided in Appendix I, pages 231 and 232, for recording how you spend your time for one week. Or use a calendar you have on hand. Whatever works best for you. Keep the calendar with you and make your entries as you go, rather than relying on your memory at the end of the day, because you will tend to forget the details. I find it most useful to divide the hours into 10- or 15-minute increments, since many activities require only a few minutes.

You will have to decide whether to record only your working hours or to include all your waking hours. I think it is worth the extra effort to keep track of all your time, 24 hours a day, for one week. Your job is not your whole life, and it is important to get some perspective on how you divide your time between work, family, recreation, community, and personal activities. Try to make it a typical week, not the only week in the year that you took a business trip, for example.

Be brutally honest in your time log. If your 15-minute coffee breaks turned out to be 40-minute coffee breaks, write it down. If you spend 25 minutes staring into space, write it down. If your ambitious closet-cleaning project degenerated into an afternoon of going through old photo albums, write it down. The time log is for your eyes only and your benefit. The exercise won't be much help if you record what you think you should have done instead of what you actually did.

Meanwhile, let's look at the case study of a busy bank personnel manager who has an active family as well as some commitments to community projects. This case study describes a more-or-less typical day in the life of Kathryn Lennox. You may recognize some problems similar to your own. At the end, you will be asked to identify some of her crucial time management problems, and you will see how she kept a time log and analyzed her important time problems. All of this should prepare you to get the most useful information out of your own time log.

CASE STUDY

Kathryn Lennox

People were always telling Kathryn Lennox they didn't see how she did it. She was personnel manager of Webber Bank and Trust Company, a wife, and a mother of two, and she still found time for a few community activities. "You must really be well organized," her neighbor said the other day, "to get so much done. I wish I knew your secret."

Kathryn appreciated the praise, but her secret was that she wasn't sure she deserved it. She had worked hard for her promotion to personnel manager, but there was so much she wanted to do with the job and with her family that she was afraid she'd shortchange both if she didn't stay on the go every minute. Tom and the kids were beginning to complain that she didn't have time for them anymore. Her efficiency and willingness to help had made her the favorite of many civic groups, and the executive vice president at the bank had said her community work was beneficial because it "contributed to a good public image of Webber Bank."

Kathryn was great with people. She considered herself a good listener, and she enjoyed helping people work out their problems. She was the sort of person everyone seemed to like and trust, and that was both her strength and her weakness.

In college, she had majored in psychology and been very active in campus events. She was elected to many offices and was vice president of the student body her senior year. Her grades were excellent, and, though she hadn't really prepared for a specific career, she knew she wanted to do something with people.

Her first job was as an administrative assistant in the Loan Administration Department of Webber Bank, a bank with six branches, all located in her hometown of Windsor. In her two years she learned quite a bit about banking, though she wished the work were less routine.

She had just about decided to find a more challenging job when she heard from a friend in the personnel office that the bank was looking for qualified women to promote as part of its affirmative action program. She applied for the management trainee program and was accepted.

After two years of rotating through every department in the bank, she was assigned to the personnel department in the main office. She started as a recruiter and then spent five years as assistant manager in charge of benefits and training. When Cecil Hardy retired last year, he had recommended Kathryn to succeed him as personnel manager.

She had met and married Tom while she was

an assistant, and he had encouraged her in her career. He was sales manager for a company that sold programmed texts and video presentations to companies for use in training programs, so their professional interests actually fit together well.

Kathryn had returned to work soon after the births of Jeannette and Christopher, now nine and six. Tom was a devoted father, and, because his schedule was more flexible than hers, he had been willing to take his turn with the children. But he had been complaining lately that he and Kathryn never had time alone together, and last night he questioned whether Kathryn's raise and promotion were worth "sacrificing her family life for." They had had a long talk about it, and she went to sleep feeling that the air was cleared.

When the alarm went off at six, Kathryn jumped out of bed, feeling energetic and determined to get a lot done today so that she could leave work at five without a briefcase full of bank business, and go out with the family for hamburgers and a Disney movie the kids wanted to see.

She showered and dressed and went down to the kitchen to have a cup of coffee and read the paper. She enjoyed this quiet time before the children were awake, and she liked to read the paper before breakfast so she could have time to talk with the children at the table. They were at exciting ages now, full of questions and observations, and spending time with them was fun.

This morning was an exception. Tom came into the kitchen after waking the kids and reported that Jeannette was upset because she couldn't find the top to the outfit she wanted to wear. Just last year they could hardly get her out of her jeans long enough to wash them, and now she had decided to become a fashion model. While Kathryn prepared cereal and fruit, Jeannette and Tom rifled through the dirty clothes hamper in search of the missing blouse. Jeannette found it and burst into tears because she couldn't wear her "favorite outfit" to school. Tom finally calmed her

down and went back upstairs to help her select some other clothes. By then breakfast was ready, and when Jeannette and Tom finally reappeared Chris wasn't with them. "He had crawled back in bed," Tom said. "I dragged him out and told him to step on it."

Jeannette went to the foot of the stairs and yelled that if he didn't hurry he'd miss the school bus. In a few minutes Chris wandered in wearing a dirty shirt and no shoes or socks. He picked at his food and didn't have much to say during the meal, a fact that was nearly obscured by Jeannette's constant chatter on subjects from her afternoon class at the arts council to her latest career ambition to be a circus performer and astronaut in the off-season.

After breakfast, Kathryn raced upstairs with Chris to get him ready for school. He still seemed subdued, and he dawdled so much that she finally had to sit him down and put on his socks and shoes for him.

She finally got the children out the door, searched the den for a magazine article on flex-time that she wanted to take to work, kissed Tom good-bye, grabbed her briefcase, and rushed out the door.

As Kathryn inched along in the rush-hour traffic, she reflected that she would consider the day well spent if she could get going on the Total Quality Management (TQM) program. Getting TQM into the bank was her pet project; she had worked hard for approval, over the objections of a few stuffy vice presidents who were not exactly receptive to change, to put it mildly. But diplomacy was Kathryn's strong point, and she had finally gotten the project approved two months ago. Since then, though, Kathryn hadn't done a thing to implement the project. It seemed that one urgent task after another came up to delay her going ahead with the TQM scheme. She knew it would take time and effort to assemble the training materials, set up meetings for all the department heads, and plan seminars for supervisors, and she just hadn't "gotten her act together" to take the first steps. Tom had even offered to help her at home—TQM was a specialty of his—but she was so exhausted when she got home that bank work was the last thing she wanted to do.

So the project languished, even though Kathryn was convinced that it would be great for employee productivity and morale. But she was full of resolution this morning, and she told herself she'd spend at least an hour planning the project. Just as she walked into the office, her secretary, Pat, handed her a three-inch high stack of mail. She decided to take a moment to plan her day before the drudgery of going through the mail. She knew the employee records system needed overhauling. Cecil was a nice fellow, but he hadn't kept the essential information that was required these days. "Government red tape," he had said, "is a complete waste of time." Now that Cecil was gone, she had to deal with the annoyance of missing or incomplete information. Maybe she should get the Information Systems people to work on this. She made a note to call Glen Harper in I/S.

The employee benefits manual was getting to be an urgent situation. The old manual was completely outdated, but they were still giving it to new employees, and then Jody or Harold (the two assistant personnel managers) had to spend time explaining changes or answering questions. Jody had done some work on the policies, and she seemed enthusiastic about the project, but Kathryn hadn't found time to put it all together and get it approved by her boss (Ken Ward, vice president for Administration). Kathryn reflected that she probably could have rewritten the whole thing in the time she had spent on the phone last month answering questions about the new maternity plan, the changes in medical coverage designed to reduce the escalating costs, and the revised sick leave policy.

Miriam Leak stopped in to tell Kathryn that

two data processing clerks in the Operations Department had called in, one sick and the other with a child who had measles and would be out of school for a few days. Miriam wanted Kathryn to get at least one replacement from a temporary help agency, since there was no way they could get all the work done with two people out.

"Sure," Kathryn said, and, just as she was about to make a note of it, the phone rang. It was Wayne Samuels in Corporate Communications asking for a new secretary. "Last time, I must have neglected to ask for someone who could spell," he said sarcastically, and went on at length about the deficiencies of the school system.

Just as Wayne hung up, the phone rang again, and Helen Shannon asked Kathryn if she had time for a little talk. Helen sounded distressed, so Kathryn told her to come right down. Helen closed the door behind her when she came in and settled down for a long chat. She wanted to transfer out of the Trust Department, she said, because things weren't going well with her boss. Her theory was that he felt threatened by a woman with a master's degree in business administration and thus was always bogging her down with menial, time-consuming work. She had tried talking to him, but he said he didn't know what she was talking about and said that someone had to do the work. He obviously wasn't going to change, Helen said, and unless she could transfer to another department she would begin looking for a job elsewhere.

Kathryn was in her element with this kind of problem. She felt comfortable in the role of counselor, and she spent almost an hour with Helen, listening to her concerns and hearing some of her own similar experiences. After Helen left, Kathryn went to check with Jim Welch, the management recruiter, to see if there were any openings that might suit Helen.

Pat came in with a stack of computer outputs, the revised pay scales for three departments, and told Kathryn that Miriam had called to see if she had found a temp yet. Kathryn looked up the temporary help number and dialed it, but the line was busy. Pat stuck her head in the door again to remind Kathryn that she was five minutes late for the staff meeting on the budget. Those things never start on time anyway, Kathryn thought, as she frantically searched in her desk drawer for the budget papers. She finally found them on her credenza under some memos she needed to reply to and hurried out to the elevator. When she got to the meeting, everyone was still drinking coffee and discussing the upcoming local election. She left the meeting an hour later with some notes on projections she would have to prepare before the next budget session in two days.

Back at her desk, Kathryn saw the mail still sitting in her in-basket. She hastily went through it, redirected several pieces to more appropriate people, and gave Pat half a dozen letters from job applicants for replies. There was a notice from the Crisis Control Ministry, of a board of directors' meeting the following Thursday. Minutes of the last meeting were enclosed, along with an agenda for this one. Kathryn enjoyed her work with the Crisis Control Ministry, and she looked forward to the board meetings because they were well organized and seemed productive. There were two urgent memos and one message, on her E-mail, and she made several calls to take care of those items.

Finally, she pushed all the other papers aside and put a fresh pad and pencil in front of her. Now she was ready to draw up a rough schedule for implementing the TQM program. This would be day one. Soon the whole project would be in line. Kathryn was staring out the window and feeling efficient when she heard a deep voice say, "Hello, Kathy, how's my favorite personnel manager?" It was Cecil Hardy, who could never enter the bank to cash a check without visiting Kathryn, whom he considered his protégée. He was proud of her accomplishments and often bragged that he was the one who "talked her into joining the management training program." Cecil was having a diffi-

cult time adjusting to retirement, and these visits seemed to make him feel better. He told her about his garden, how his wife had complained that she had married him "for better or for worse but not for lunch," and said he was considering getting his real estate broker's license and doing a little work. Kathryn made several gentle attempts to ease Cecil out, but she knew from experience that he was long-winded, so she resigned herself to letting him talk. It was 11:30 before she finally guided him out the door.

In her outer office she saw an assistant department head waiting for their 11:30 appointment. He was leaving the bank to take a better-paying job, but there had been a lot of turnover in that department lately and she suspected that there was more to it than that.

Even though exit interviews were usually done by one of the assistants, she especially wanted to handle this one herself, since she might be able to get some insight into how things were going in that department. During the half hour she had scheduled for the interview, her phone rang three times—Jeannette's Brownie troop leader wanting to tell her about the family outing scheduled for this weekend and ask her what she could bring; a guy in the Operations Department who wanted to go over job descriptions for a new section in his area; and Christopher's school, to tell her that he had a sore throat and was running a slight fever. She cut her interview short and called Mrs. Blankenship, who often baby-sat for them, to ask if she could come over this afternoon to stay with Chris. She could, fortunately, so Kathryn dashed out of the office, telling Pat that Chris was sick and that she would be back that afternoon if it was nothing serious. At the school, she discovered that Chris was a bit under the weather but was already asking if he would have to miss recess. Just one of those things, she thought, and drove the boy home only to find Tom there doing paperwork in the den.

"Just leave him here with me," Tom said. "I

wish you had called first. I thought I told you I'd be working at home today."

Kathryn grabbed a sandwich, called Mrs. Blankenship, and made it back to the office by 1:15, feeling as if she had just competed in a cross-country marathon. There were an unusual number of applicants in the waiting area. The influx always started about mid-May. Kathryn figured Jody and Harold would have a hard time getting to all of them, so she interviewed a couple herself. Then she went down to talk to the manager of Operations about the new project team, what sort of staff would be needed, and how they would fit into the salary grade scale.

When she returned to her desk, there were five phone messages. While she was returning the calls, Jody stopped in and said she had an applicant in her office who looked like a good prospect for one of the new jobs in Operations and wondered if Kathryn would like to take a look at him herself. Kathryn spent 10 minutes with the applicant and a few more minutes with Jody. Then she called back down to the Operations manager to see about scheduling an interview for him with the applicant. The manager had thought of a few more things he had meant to say when they talked earlier (some of which he *had* said earlier) and, after 15 minutes, Kathryn extricated herself from that chat.

She couldn't believe it was 4:40. She asked Pat to bring all her materials on TQM from the files so at least it would be ready for her to get started first thing in the morning. She was tempted to take the work home, but she didn't dare after her conversation with Tom last night and her new resolution to spend more time with the family. While she dictated several letters for Pat to type first thing in the morning, the phone rang twice. A manager in Loan Administration wanted to know if they had found a vacation replacement for her secretary, and Kathryn had to go through a stack of papers on Pat's desk before she could give the woman an answer. Then a supervisor called to ask about the new sick leave

policy. They would really have to get cracking on that manual, Kathryn thought. It wouldn't be at all difficult, but it was just so time-consuming.

Just as she was about to call it a day, Harry Calder, the controller, walked in. His "nocturnal visits," as they had come to be known in the bank, were a joke. He prided himself on working longer hours than anyone else, and his favorite trick was to call or come by just at quitting time for a lengthy chat. Often, in the presence of her boss, he had said, "I dropped by your office the other afternoon [about 6:45, he neglected to add], but I guess you had gone home early."

This time he was concerned about the amount of temporary help the Trust Department had hired this year during the tax season. He wondered what she could do to encourage them to cut down on that. She let him go on for a while, not reminding him that the temporary help had been his idea last year when he complained about the amount of overtime they'd paid the regular staff.

They finally worked out a plan to use some part-time help and some overtime work. Kathryn was always tempted to tell Harry that she'd prefer setting a time in the morning to talk, but he was easily offended, and she'd worked hard to establish a good relationship between the two offices. "Excuse me just a minute," she told Harry, and called the after-school program to tell them she'd be there for Jeannette as soon as she finished a meeting.

"Oh, excuse me," Harry said. "I forget that you working mothers have more to worry about than bank business." Obviously you don't, Kathryn thought to herself. She knew that Harry's wife had recently had twins, and she wondered if he had named them Debit and Credit.

When Harry headed back to his office for who knows how much longer and Kathryn turned off the light in her office, it was nearly 6:15. Too late, she realized that she'd never found a temp for Miriam Leak.

The after-school program director was just closing up when Kathryn picked up Jeannette. It was a good program, and their community was lucky to have a place that provided structured activities and supervised play for children in the afternoons.

She didn't realize how tired she was until she got home and flopped down on the sofa. "What a day," she said to Tom, who brought her a glass of wine and asked her how she'd spent her day. She was surprised to find that she didn't really have anything significant to tell him, except that she'd talked with Helen Shannon and done a lot of interviewing.

"You interviewed until six-thirty?" Tom asked, and Kathryn explained that she had been the victim of some of Harry Calder's "night prowling." "Boy, somebody ought to tell that guy to buzz off," Tom said. "I know," said Kathryn, "but no one ever wins a fight with the controller's office. They'll get you one way or another, and it helps to have Harry on my side at budget time."

The movie was out, since Chris was feeling sick again, so Kathryn took some spaghetti sauce out of the freezer and made a salad. After supper, Jeannette worked on her homework and Chris colored while Tom and Kathryn talked about where they'd go on vacation this year. When the children were in bed Tom and Kathryn read for a while, then watched a show on TV. As they got ready for bed, Kathryn tried to figure out how to make her life less complicated. "Maybe I'll have more time tomorrow," she thought as she turned out the light.

Question

What time problems does Kathryn have? Give examples.

Discussion

Kathryn Lennox's job as personnel manager involves dealing with people and their problems—things that cannot always be carefully scheduled. She must be free for urgent, unexpected interruptions or for dealing with problems only she can handle effectively. That's the nature of her job and of many service-type occupations.

But Kathryn's real problem comes in deciding which of those interruptions are urgent and which are problems only she can handle. Presently, she uses so much of her time dealing with interruptions, crises, and routine tasks that she doesn't have time for planning or long-range projects that will benefit the whole organization.

People in service occupations are constantly confronted with the choice between certain long-range projects that will determine the future growth of the organization and the pressing day-by-day, minute-by-minute needs of the people they serve. It is essential to strike an appropriate balance, or the performance of both the individual and the organization will suffer.

Kathryn is now doing only part of the personnel manager's job; she is serving personnel, but she is not managing. Clearly, she works hard, even frantically, but she is not getting her job done. She is doing her secretary's job, and her assistants' jobs, and then she feels frustrated when there doesn't seem to be enough time to do her own job well. The natural tendency in a situation like that is to spend more time on the job, in an effort to catch up. But this conflicts with family life, and that leads to another kind of frustration.

It is tempting to spend time on more routine tasks. They are easier and more clearly delineated. We know how to do them well, and we like doing them. They are more pressing and require less judgment, and most often they have a definite beginning and end—a time when one can look at them and say they're finished. That is not the case with many managerial jobs.

When Kathryn spent time interviewing casual job applicants or dealing with every telephone call, she was helping her subordinates with their work rather than getting on with her own more challenging work. Needless to say, there may be times when Kathryn or any other manager will have to pitch in with the day-to-day work. But for a manager who uses time wisely and delegates well, these times will be infrequent and will not often interfere with higher-priority activities. Kathryn is actually using the office busywork as a buffer against the more difficult tasks of working on the personnel manual or the TQM program.

Kathryn was so concerned with Helen Shannon that she dropped what she was doing and saw her right away, rather than trying to set up another time. She was so solicitous of Cecil Hardy's feelings that she spent far too long listening to him talk. She was afraid of alienating the controller, so she let him monopolize time that should have belonged to her and her family. Any one of these incidents might have been necessary under the circumstances, and might not have unduly disrupted Kathryn's day. But all of them together caused Kathryn to lose control of how she spent her time. She was essentially powerless to accomplish all of her job. That feeling of helplessness and lack of control is a good sign that you're not using your time effectively.

If Kathryn were better at saying "no" or protecting herself from busywork, she would have more time available for projects that were really significant to her and the bank. She would not be working any harder; rather, she would be working smarter.

Another real challenge for Kathryn is balancing the commitments to job and family. Her relationship with Tom and the development of their children are very important to her. Yet Kathryn has a career that is fulfilling.

Working parents are particularly in need of good habits in time management. Like Kathryn, they often attend to the needs of the job from dawn to nightfall, and if they don't use their time wisely, they can feel harried, out of control, and resentful of the sacrifice of family life.

Kathryn and Tom could avoid early morning hassles with getting the children off to school if they would help the kids lay out their clothes the night before. Though modern science has not yet devised a cure for the dawdling child, children can respond very well to a sense of organization. Breakfast at the Lennox household could be a better family time, more free of crisis, if Kathryn and Tom not only planned their time but helped the children plan theirs.

There is a necessary warning about home and career combinations. If you've made the decision to climb to the top of a large corporation or make a national reputation in a particular field, you should recognize that family life may suffer. The extraordinary amounts of time and dedication required for great achievements seldom leave time for family suppers, little league games, or attending piano recitals, unless you are extraordinarily good at managing time, setting priorities, reducing routine work, and sticking to schedules.

We will deal with Kathryn's two main problems—interruptions and unwillingness to delegate—in Chapters 8 and 9.

Kathryn's Time Log

When Kathryn Lennox's husband Tom asked her how she had spent her day, she found that she couldn't really tell him. She knew only that she had been very busy and that she hadn't accomplished what she had set out to do—work on the TQM project. Kathryn had the sort of hectic, disjointed day that could best be analyzed by using a time log. She decided to keep one for a day later in the week. Following is her time log.

KATHRYN LENNOX'S TIME LOG

A.M.

6:00 Awoke, showered, dressed.

6:30 Read paper, relaxed.

6:45 Fixed breakfast.

7:00 Ate breakfast with children, Tom.

7:15 Looked for Jeannette's library book, due today. Loaded clothes washer.

7:30 Cleared table, loaded dishwasher. Found Chris's other shoe. Wrote excuse for Chris's absence. Fed dog.

7:45 Kids off to school, me to car, back to house (forgot briefcase).

8:00 Car hard to start, almost out of gas. Drove to work, got gas on way.

8:30 At work, running late. Pat waiting with urgent phone messages. Asked for instructions on report I gave her to finish yesterday.

8:45 Returned phone calls. Talked for 20 minutes to Fred Steed about job classification; couldn't get Agnes Bright; waited five minutes for her to call back; read magazine article while waiting.

9:15 Pat brought in mail. Sorted some of it. Jody asked question about someone's sick leave; our record different from their department. Looked up file; we hadn't posted for second quarter three years ago. Changed file; looked through others to see if we'd made the same mistake. All in that department were that way, but apparently no others; asked Jody to keep an eye on it; asked Pat to correct files. Stared at wall and worried about disorganization.

10:00 Started filling out forms for government CETA position; decided halfway through that Harold could do this.

10:15 Took forms to Harold, showed him how to complete them. Answered his questions about new maternity leave policy.

10:30 To coffee shop for cup of coffee. Ran into Miller Johnson, told me his daughter was getting married (she used to baby-sit for us).

10:45 Stopped in hall by Louise Hancock. She griped about her boss; said others in department felt the same way. I told her I'd talk to him. She kept talking.

11:15 Stopped by Fred Blackburn's. He asked about new employee appraisal forms. He asked what the chances were of his getting another position approved.

11:30 Back in office. Harold asked question about CETA forms; said he hadn't been able to complete them without knowing this and didn't want to do them wrong. Answered question.

11:45 Began work on personnel manual revision. Jody asked if I could talk with an applicant she had just interviewed.

P.M.

12:15 Finished talking with applicant. Called Trust Department to set up appointment with them. Went back to manual.

12:30 Rachel Murray stopped by. Persuaded me to try the new restaurant in the mall with her.

2:00 Back in office, service was slow, lines long. Just in time to get projections together for 2:30 budget meeting. Pat discovered an error in one.

2:15 Went over projections. Made list of recommendations.

2:30 Waited for Pat to finish typing list and running copies. Got to meeting at 2:35, just ahead of Ken Ward. He was called away again for a phone call.

2:45 Meeting started.

4:30 Meeting finally over. Took a lot of time to go over revisions. Got off on a lot of side issues. Back in office, gave Pat final revisions to enter into the document file. Pat said there were several phone calls on my voice mail, but she didn't know what they were about. Went through afternoon interoffice mail.

4:45 Returned two calls. One a routine question. The other from Michael Watson asking if his assistant's increase was approved. Got report from Pat, told him it had been, but not for as much as he had asked.

5:15 Finally got Watson off the phone. Responded to E-mail messages.

5:30 Straightened desk. Found another CETA form. Put it on Harold's desk.

5:45 Left office, met Ken Ward (boss) in hall. He asked when TQM seminars would start. Told him next month.

6:00 Met Tom and kids at Pizza Garden for dinner.

6:45 Took kids to miniature golf.

8:00 Home. Sorted laundry while Jeannette did homework and Chris took a bath. Started reading magazine article.

8:30 Read Chris a story and put him to bed. Called Jeannette back downstairs to clean up mess she had left in the den.

8:45 Talked with Jeannette about problems she was having with her friend down the block.

9:00 Chris in bed, Jeannette in her room reading. Read magazine article. Talked with Tom.

9:30 Sat down to watch TV. Phone rang. The volunteer grade parent for Jeannette's class about class picnic. Wanted to know what I would bring. Told her I would send something, but couldn't come, since it was at 3:30 in the afternoon. Suggested they schedule another class function some evening. Talked about that for half an hour. She also talked about the teachers, the principal, and the school bus.

10:00 Sat down for last half of TV program.

10:30 Got ready for bed, read.

11:00 Turned out light.

How Kathryn Analyzed Her Time Log

Kathryn then analyzed her time log, broken down according to the time use categories shown in Exercise 2.1. Her analysis, and the way she would have filled in column two of Exercise 2.1, follows.

ANALYSIS OF KATHRYN'S TIME LOG

Personal work		Hours
Sleep: 11 p.m. to 6 a.m.		7
Shower, dress		½
Breakfast		¼
Get ready for work/school chores		1
Get gas and drive		½
Laundry		½
Phone call from volunteer parent		½
Get ready for bed		¼
	Total	10½

On the job		
Subordinates: Secretary (15 min. a.m., 15 min. p.m.)		½
Delegation: CETA forms		¾
Routine calls/mail		2½
Interruptions: self-imposed		1
during top-priority task		½
Meeting (2 hr. + 30 min. preparation)		2½
Top priority (2 interruptions)		¼
Lunch with Rachel		1½
	Total	9½

Time with the family		
Dinner		¾
Miniature golf		1¼
Talk with children/Tom		¾
	Total	2¾

Personal growth, Leisure, Free time		
Magazine article (30 min. between interruptions)		½
TV		½
Read paper, relax		¼
	Total	1¼

Kathryn then identified several ways she could improve her time management.

1. Better planning at home could head off some of the early morning crises and make for better family relationships. This would mean organizing family chores, getting the children to carry their load better, and helping them plan for their clothes and various activities. (Note: Chapter 7 contains some guidelines on planning for homemakers.)

2. She hoped this would create a more relaxed family atmosphere and improve communications. In addition, perhaps it would give her a little more time to read for personal growth, and also some free time to relax.

3. Her lack of planning at work was a shock to Kathryn: She found she had spent no more than 15 minutes on the top-priority tasks she set out to do in the morning. Instead, she did a number of low-priority, routine tasks; it seemed to her she did this almost deliberately to avoid the more difficult tasks. She let herself get talked into a long lunch that had no real importance to her. She went up to the last minute on preparing for her meeting. (Note: Chapter 7 describes techniques for setting priorities and making daily schedules.)

4. The delegation of the CETA project to Harold was poorly done; the instructions were incomplete, to name just one error. (Note: For a discussion of basic concepts on delegation, see Chapter 9.)

5. She had to find ways of controlling interruptions when working on important projects, and avoiding the tendency to procrastinate. (Note: See Chapter 8 on controlling interruptions and Chapter 11 on procrastination.)

6. The staff meeting was very inefficient, and Kathryn wondered what could be done about it. She estimated it should have taken no more than one hour (50 percent efficient). (Note: See Chapter 10 for ideas on how to run more effective and more efficient meetings.)

After you have kept a time log for a week, the next step is to carefully analyze it. First, break it down into the time use categories by filling in column two of Exercise 2.1, as Kathryn Lennox did.

Be prepared for some surprises. People who participate in my time management seminars are invariably amazed at what their time logs show. Here are some of their comments:

"Four hours a day in meetings?!"

"Boy, I do a lot more goofing off than I thought."

"Do you know I spend almost twenty minutes on the average for a phone call? I thought I spent about five."

"I can't believe I spend an hour and a half per day in or waiting for the elevators in our building."

Then, as Kathryn did, write out some of the areas in which you would like to improve your time management. In the rest of the book, you will learn how to apply time management techniques to these areas.

TIME ROBBERS

A time robber (or time waster, as some people call them) is something that keeps us from doing things that have more value and importance to us. It is an activity at which you spend considerable time, without equivalent value or benefit. It may be an activity you must do, but it adds little to the accomplishment of your important goals. Numerous interruptions, lengthy meetings, routine tasks that could be delegated, and procrastination are some common time robbers. The objective is to control the time robber through such techniques as deferring a task when you have something more important to do, shortening the time spent on it, or eliminating portions of it.

Exercise 2.2, beginning on page 34, contains a list of 43 frequent time robbers. Go through the list and indicate which ones your time log reveals are the greatest problems for you.

As you analyze your time robbers, you will find that they fall into two general categories. The first is the external time robber—phone calls, drop-in visitors, and other interruptions. The second is the internal, or self-generated, time robber—lack of self-discipline, failure to delegate, cluttered desk, procrastination, or indecision.

Most of us tend to exaggerate the importance of external time robbers, using them as convenient excuses. Time management consultant Alec Mackenzie* writes of the experience of 40 chief executives of elec-

---

*Alec Mackenzie, *New Time Management Methods* (Chicago: Dartnell, 1975).

EXERCISE 2.2

	Big problem for me	Often a problem	Seldom a problem
Planning			
1. Not setting goals	X		
2. No daily plan	X		
3. Priorities unclear or changing	X		
4. Leaving tasks unfinished	X		
5. "Firefighting," or crisis management	X		
6. No self-imposed deadlines	X		
7. Attempting too much— unrealistic time estimates	X		
Organizing			
8. Personal disorganization/ cluttered desk	X		
9. Duplication of effort		X	
10. Confused responsibility and authority	X		
11. Multiple bosses		X	
Directing			
12. Doing it myself	X		
13. Involved in routine details	X		
14. Ineffective delegation	X		
15. Lack of motivation			X
16. Not managing conflict		X	
17. Not coping with change			X
Controlling			
18. Telephone interruptions		X	
19. Drop-in visitors	X		

	Big problem for me	Often a problem	Seldom a problem
20. Lack of self-discipline		X	
21. Too many interests	X		
22. Mistakes/ineffective performance			X
23. Inability to say "no"	X		
24. No standards, progress reports		X	
25. Incomplete information		X	
Communicating			
26. Meetings		X	
27. Under-/unclear/ over-communicating		X	
28. Failure to listen			X
29. Socializing			X
Decision making			
30. Snap decisions		X	
31. Indecision/procrastination		X	
32. Wanting all the facts			X
33. Decision by committee		X	
34. Perfectionism		X	
For homemakers only			
35. Poor planning of errands and shopping			
36. Not planning meals ahead			
37. Doing jobs other family members could do			
38. Family appointments (doctor, music lessons, etc.)			

EXERCISE 2.2 *(continued)*		Big problem for me	Often a problem	Seldom a problem
	39. Children's interruptions	_____	_____	_____
	40. Chauffeuring children	_____	_____	_____
	41. Inability to say "no" to volunteer requests	_____	_____	_____
	42. Looking for family's misplaced items	_____	_____	_____
	43. Perfectionism	_____	_____	_____
	Others			
		_____	_____	_____
		_____	_____	_____
		_____	_____	_____
		_____	_____	_____
		_____	_____	_____

trical contracting companies who participated in a time management seminar. At the beginning of the session, they were asked to list their major time wasters. Their combined list follows.

1. Incomplete information for solution
2. Employees with problems
3. Telephone
4. Routine tasks
5. Meetings
6. Drop-in visitors
7. Outside activities
8. Crisis management
9. Poor communication

Then the group watched Peter Drucker's film "Managing Time,"* in which a company president is shown wasting time in a variety of ways—

---

*Drucker narrates the film, which was produced by BNA Communications, Inc., Rockville, Md.

coming late for a meeting he had called, involving himself in the most minor details of the company's operations, and trying to accomplish an unrealistic number of tasks. After viewing the film, the chief executives were asked if the film had helped them identify any new time wasters. They developed a second list, as follows.

1. Attempting too much at once
2. Unrealistic time estimates
3. Procrastinating
4. Not listening
5. Not saying "no"
6. Doing it myself
7. Stacked desk, personal disorganization
8. Delegating responsibility without authority

What is striking, of course, is that the first list of time robbers pins the responsibility squarely on the "other guy." The chief executives imagined, as many of us do, that other people keep us from achieving our goals and eat up our valuable time.

It took the filmed image of another company president to alert this group of chief executives to an even more important group of time robbers—the internal, self-generated ones.

I hope your time log will be a similar prod for you. Look back to your own ranking of your worst time robbers (Exercise 2.2). Did you, like most people in my seminars, give undue weight to external time robbers? Was it too many routine tasks that wasted your time, or were the routine tasks an excuse to procrastinate? Was it employees with problems or your own ineffective delegation? Did too many phone calls ruin your day, or was the problem that you couldn't say "no" to any of them? Was it your secretary's inability to communicate or your inability to listen? Was the problem incomplete information, or were you trying to make too many decisions yourself?

If you seem to be your own worst problem, if you look like the biggest time robber of all, that's good. That's an area you can do something about. If your analysis of your time log shows that most of your time problems are internal and self-generated, then most of your time problems are within your power to solve.

Now that you've identified your major time robbers, you can begin doing something about them. Pick out your worst time robber and analyze it now as an exercise. Follow the Time Robber Analysis in planning your attack on it. Appendix I (pp. 233–234) contains a blank copy of the Time Robber Analysis to use for this exercise and to analyze your other time robbers. Photocopy it as needed.

SUMMARY

We have seen how a personnel manager was able to identify key time management problems—both at work and away from work—through the use of a time log. You have tried keeping and analyzing a time log of your own. And you have begun attacking your worst time robbers.

In the next chapter, we will analyze time management problems as they apply to groups of people interacting in a job setting. Other people affect our work time just as we affect theirs; we will return to Kathryn Lennox as she analyzes her team's effectiveness.

3 Analyzing the Time Problems of Your Work Team

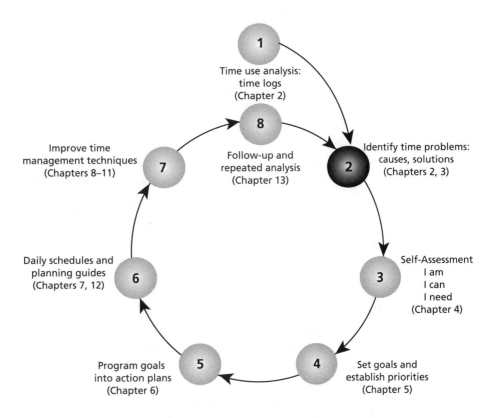

1 — Time use analysis: time logs (Chapter 2)

2 — Identify time problems: causes, solutions (Chapters 2, 3)

3 — Self-Assessment
I am
I can
I need
(Chapter 4)

4 — Set goals and establish priorities (Chapter 5)

5 — Program goals into action plans (Chapter 6)

6 — Daily schedules and planning guides (Chapters 7, 12)

7 — Improve time management techniques (Chapters 8–11)

8 — Follow-up and repeated analysis (Chapter 13)

Our time problems are very much affected by the people around us, especially at work. One person's poor time management habits will have "ripple" effects on everyone nearby. If one man likes to socialize, then other people's time will be interrupted by chit-chat about his golf game, a family problem, last night's World Series game, or the lousy working conditions. The boss who allows meetings to get off the agenda into unimportant tangents is wasting everyone's time.

Peter Drucker's film "Managing Time"* shows a busy executive whose time problems are rippling down through his entire organization. His overinvolvement in routine matters, failure to set priorities, hasty and poorly conceived meetings, and failure to listen, all cause him to allocate inadequate time to important decisions, with disastrous results. If you work for someone with sloppy time habits, you may have said, "I can't control my time; my boss controls it." True, going to the boss's morning staff meeting is part of your job. So is answering customer phone calls or following up on your subordinates. At home, dealing with Jimmy's frequent interruptions—tying his shoes or picking up his clothes after him—are part of being a parent. The fact is that whatever your job, not all of your time is your own. But how much of your time *do* you control? Let's see.

William Oncken, Jr., and Donald L. Wass, in an article entitled "Management Time: Who's Got the Monkey?,"** discuss three types of management time:

> Boss-imposed time: For accomplishing tasks that the boss requires and that cannot be ignored without swift penalty.
>
> System-imposed time: For accomplishing the responsibilities of the position and accommodating requests for active support from your peers.
>
> Self-imposed time: For doing things you originate or agree to do yourself.

The authors point out that much of what seems like self-imposed time is actually "subordinate-imposed time"—monkeys that they put on your back. Oncken and Wass recommend that the manager cut down on subordinate-imposed time by effective delegation, to free up more discretionary time.

Try looking at your own work time in these terms. You may not be able to modify boss-imposed and system-imposed requirements, but you can probably find ways of consolidating and increasing your discre-

---

*Produced by BNA Communications, Inc., Rockville, Md.

**William Oncken, Jr., and Donald L. Wass, "Management Time: Who's Got the Monkey?" *Harvard Business Review*, Vol. 52, No. 6, Nov.–Dec. 1974, pp. 75–80.

tionary time. For instance, many managers set aside a "quiet hour" each day, when they keep the door closed and don't accept phone calls.

In a seminar conducted for L'eggs, the dynamic company that revolutionized the pantyhose market, Pearline, the manager of employee benefits, related her experience with discretionary time and the quiet hour:*

> As the company grew rapidly I found less and less time to do the important planning and creative projects needed to stay on top of my job. I started working late, which I didn't like because of my family. This was okay for a while, but others were doing the same thing, and as soon as they found out I was in the office until six or later, I began to get interrupted just as during regular working hours. So I came in Saturday morning, but the same thing happened. Sunday afternoon was the only uninterrupted time I could find to do this important work.
>
> By now I was working upward of seventy hours a week, which my family really complained about. I decided I had to do something—I had to find some discretionary time during the normal workday. I decided to establish a "quiet hour" at a certain time each morning. With the help of my secretary, and our being a little tough on would-be interrupters, I'm able to stick with it most of the time. I'm now back down to a forty-six-hour workweek, which is reasonable, but I think I can still do better."

Again in the film "Managing Time," Drucker points out that most busy managers have only one or two hours a day of discretionary time to do the important tasks to further their goals. If we're sloppy with the use of our time, we can end up without any. We must understand how much time we have and when it comes in our normal workday; then we must work out ways to increase it and protect it from interruptions and firefighting.

Turn back to your time log. Choose a typical day and look at your discretionary time—that time when you could have done something to further your important goals. In Exercise 3.1, record what you actually did in this time. Then make notes on how you could have used that time better and how you might increase your discretionary time.

How much discretionary time did you find in a normal day? Remember, discretionary time is the time we need to work on important personal goals. If you don't have that hour or two to be an effective person, then how are you going to get it? Can you set up a quiet hour as

---

*Quoted here by permission of Pearline S. Jones, Compensation and Benefits Analyst, L'eggs Products, Inc., a Division of Sara Lee Corporation, Winston-Salem, N.C.

EXERCISE 3.1 | **Discretionary Time**

Time	What I did in that time	Ways in which I could have better used my time

Ideas for increasing my discretionary time

Pearline did? Have your voice mail, an answering machine, or your secretary screen out phone calls? Close the door? Find a hideaway?

As you come across ideas in later parts of this book, return to Exercise 3.1. Develop practical ways to get the discretionary time you require.

TEAM EFFECTIVENESS

As individuals in organizations, we can do much to help ourselves. But our efforts on the job will be greatly enhanced if we can better understand the common problems of our work group and make a joint effort to improve. Our aim is to increase team effectiveness.

Our team consists of people with whom we have frequent interaction. This would include superiors; peers—people who are in positions similar to our own; subordinates who report to us; and people outside the organization, such as customers, suppliers, or government officials. The team can be viewed as diagrammed below.

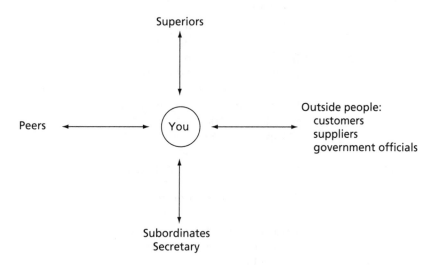

The time log you kept in Chapter 2 can help you identify how the people on your team are affecting your time, and, in turn, how you are affecting theirs. To illustrate how this works, let's go back to our case on Kathryn Lennox (see page 21). Kathryn decided team effectiveness was an important aspect of time management on which to concentrate. After reviewing her time log (see pp. 29–30), she decided to analyze her time for two more days, but concentrating just on "how I waste their time" and "how they waste my time." What she came up with is shown on the next page.

After reviewing this information, Kathryn discussed it with her two assistant directors, Jody and Harold, and her secretary, Pat. They came up with several ideas they felt would improve their team effectiveness.

First, they would have a 10-minute stand-up meeting over a cup of coffee each morning at 8:20 before the phone and other interruptions began. This would help coordinate their activities for the day, air any common problems, and establish priorities. The meeting would be limited to 10 minutes; if some important problem came up that seemed to require a longer period, a meeting would be scheduled for later.

	How I waste their time	How they waste my time
Pat	Not giving complete directions first time.	Putting too many routine calls through to me.
	Having her answer questions about benefits instead of rewriting benefits brochure.	Staying out of office a long time at the copy center, socializing; I end up dealing with visitors and calls.
	Interrupting her with a new job before he finishes the last one.	Not proofreading documents carefully.
Jody and Harold	Giving incomplete instructions, so they do only part of the project, not the whole assignment.	Asking me to make decisions they could handle. They could have referred job applicants to departments without checking with me.
	Not establishing priorities, so they sometimes spend time on small things rather than more important ones.	
Ken Ward	Getting "too busy" with details to get major projects to him on time. Delays implementation for entire bank.	Being late to meetings, having disorganized meetings.
	Often giving him more details than he wants or needs rather than concise summary.	
Department heads	Not replying quickly to requests for substitute help, new employees.	Asking me questions Pat could answer.
Employees	Not having information in written form, so they have to call to clear up misunderstanding.	Often resisting suggestions to deal more directly with others; prefer to gripe.
Applicants	Asking them same questions as Jody or Harold; appointments pile up and keep them waiting.	

Second, Kathryn, Jody, and Harold decided they needed a "quiet time," free from interruptions, to handle important employee records and other projects and to do touchy employee counseling. Since they couldn't all be "unavailable" at the same time, they decided to stagger "quiet hours" in the morning and afternoon. When one person had a quiet hour someone else would cover for him or her.

Finally, Kathryn and Pat decided they would take a few minutes when they arrived at work at eight o'clock to compare "to-do lists." Pat felt if she better understood Kathryn's needs and priorities for the day, she could be much more helpful.

The final area of real improvement Kathryn hoped for were the meetings run by her supervisor, Ken Ward. They were invariably long and often ineffective. She could see a number of improvements that could be made, but this would have to be handled carefully because Ken tended to be defensive about his leadership style. (Chapter 10 explores how to have more effective meetings.)

Now take the time log you developed in Chapter 2 and see if you can identify your team's time robbers, as Kathryn did.

If you are uncertain about some of the time robbers you have listed—such as how much time they use up or how often they occur—keep a log for a couple more days, as Kathryn did, concentrating only on team problems. Better yet, have another member of your team also keep a log for a few days and compare the results. Then go back to Exercise 3.2 and fill in the details.

Discuss these findings with other members of your team. See if together you can find some solutions. As you proceed through this book, you should be able to find additional ideas on how to increase your team's effectiveness. Later chapters focus on such team effectiveness concepts as meetings, delegation, and planning guides.

EXERCISE 3.2	**Team Time Robbers**

My team	How I waste their time	How they waste my time

SUMMARY

In Chapters 2 and 3, we have analyzed your time management problems. We will now explore your personal goals, so that you can establish meaningful priorities on the use of your time. Chapters 4 through 6 deal with self-assessment, setting goals and priorities, and developing action plans—the next three steps in our time management process.

4   **Self-Assessment**

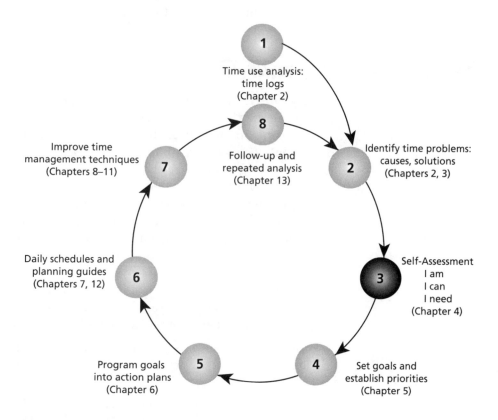

1. Time use analysis: time logs (Chapter 2)

2. Identify time problems: causes, solutions (Chapters 2, 3)

3. Self-Assessment I am I can I need (Chapter 4)

4. Set goals and establish priorities (Chapter 5)

5. Program goals into action plans (Chapter 6)

6. Daily schedules and planning guides (Chapters 7, 12)

7. Improve time management techniques (Chapters 8–11)

8. Follow-up and repeated analysis (Chapter 13)

Time management isn't simply keeping an appointment calendar or daily scheduling of events. An appointment calendar, though it is an important planning tool in our daily activities, is only one part of the total time management process.

Managing your time means managing yourself. People have needs, and we develop goals to satisfy these needs. But the higher-level needs of esteem and self-actualization, which we discussed in Chapter 1, are com-

Set Goals
Prioritize Goals

plicated. Our goals often are not clear and sometimes conflict with one another. We want a happy family life, but we also aspire to be a powerful politician. How do we go about satisfying these two very different goals?

Managing yourself means setting realistic goals, consistent with your strengths and weaknesses—goals that will satisfy your needs, including esteem and self-actualization. It is essential to concentrate on your most important goals first—to set priorities among your goals. Only then will you become an effective user of your time.

THE NEED FOR REAPPRAISAL

Have you ever heard someone referred to as being goal-oriented? If you're one of those goal-oriented people who always knows where you're going, you may want to skip this chapter. But if you're like most of us, your goals are not all that clear, your priorities are somewhat confused, or your goals may be changing.

At least two times in our lives we should probably do an exhaustive self-appraisal to set long-term goals. The first time is when we are completing our education and leaving our parents' home to set out in developing our own careers and building our own families.* Later in this chapter, we will observe a student who does a self-assessment in the course of choosing a career.

The second time is what has come to be referred to as the mid-life crisis.** The fading purpose of a career and the self-assessment that leads to a change is exemplified by the following real-life occurrence.

Jack Connors returns from a day of quelling crises at the plant to an empty house. The family is at the beach for a month, and he's commuting on

---

*A number of references can assist a person at this stage; one of the best is John P. Kotter, Victor A. Faux, and Charles C. McArthur, *Self-Assessment & Career Development* (Englewood Cliffs, N.J.: Prentice-Hall, 1978). Other worthwhile books on goals, careers, and jobs include Richard Nelson Bolles, *What Color Is Your Parachute? A Practical Manual for Job Hunters and Career Changers* (Berkeley, Calif.: Ten Speed Press, 1992); John Caple, *Finding the Hat That Fits: How to Turn Your Heart's Desire into Your Life's Work* (New York: New American Library-Dutton).

**The changing phases of adult lives, particularly mid-life changes, are discussed by Gail Sheehy in her book *Passages* (New York: Dutton, 1976).

weekends. Originally he had planned to spend two full weeks there with them, but he just couldn't get away from work with the recent expansion move.

He throws his coat down and heads for the kitchen to fix something for supper when the phone rings. It's the night supervisor; there were some power problems, and the motor on the big press burned out. They talk about how to get a replacement quickly and how to reschedule the production runs to get out some of the important orders.

Jack hangs up and opens the refrigerator, where he finds mostly leftovers, which don't look particularly appetizing. He takes out a cold beer, opens it, and takes a big gulp. The phone rings again. It's his minister, who, after a few pleasantries, reports that collections have been falling off badly. They're eating into the fund balance fast, and he thinks something ought to be done. He suggests that Jack call a crisis meeting (Jack is Senior Warden). They discuss the matter at length and finally Jack hangs up.

He goes back to the refrigerator and takes out some leftover stew, which he begins to heat up. The phone rings again. "To hell with it," he mutters, and lets it ring. In disgust, Jack turns off the stove, gets another beer, heads for the porch and flops into the hammock. Old Mr. Schwartz waves as he shuffles by. Harry Schwartz was the president of the big bank in town until he had a massive stroke three years ago. "Hope I never turn out like that," reflects Jack.

A refreshing evening breeze picks up, and Jack begins to relax and think: . . . not enjoying work much . . . just one hassle after another . . . miss being at the beach with the family . . . too busy with too many things . . . even the church work has turned into a hassle . . . what am I doing on this merry-go-round? . . . always liked teaching at the technical institute better anyway . . . hmmm . . . I wonder . . . that'd be a big change . . . think we could hack it?

Jack goes to bed early and gets up with the sun. He feels great as he heads for the beach. He stops once to get a leisurely breakfast. On the way down the highway again, he picks up the car phone and dials the plant. He gets the receptionist. "Tell my secretary I won't be in for a few days. They'll have to get along without me."

He surprises his family just as they are getting ready to head for the ocean. "Hey, gang, I've been thinking . . . what would you think if I were to . . . "

Even when we are not at a turning point in our lives, an occasional review of our goals—a periodic self-assessment and reappraisal—is important for all of us. As we and our environment change, however subtly, our goals must also change.

This chapter is too brief to provide a framework for doing an exhaustive self-assessment, but it should help you reflect on your situation, analyze your goals, and provide a basis for updating your goals and priorities.

The first section (Part A) includes worksheets and exercises that are intended to help you think about your strengths and weaknesses, your current situation, and your goals. Part B is a framework for developing a current list of goals and priorities.

PART A

The self-assessment worksheet in Appendix I (pp. 235–236) is intended to get you to take stock of yourself—to make an inventory of your strengths and weaknesses. Photocopy that worksheet to use as an exercise here. You will find a list of 35 statements. Choose the 10 (or more) that seem to best describe you and rank them in order of importance. Then check 5 or more from the remaining group that you think you could improve on.

In trying to discover what you are like, it may help to see yourself as others see you. Photocopy the self-assessment form and ask three people whom you know well—your spouse, your boss, and a close friend, for example—to use the list in evaluating you. If you do this, you may want to analyze the major differences between the rating you did on yourself and the ones other people did for you. (Space is reserved on the following rating form for this comparison.) People who have done so have often been surprised at the differences between their self-perception and that of others. Sometimes these differences are disturbing, but if approached in a constructive manner, they may help you to be realistic about yourself.

Another way of finding your strengths is to ask yourself, "Who needs me and why?" Exercise 4.1 will help you do this. First, write the names of people who need you—your spouse, children, supervisor, employees, friends, or anyone else who needs you. Then write what it is that those particular people need about you. Try to get beyond simple statements of your role in relation to these people and think of the specific traits and abilities in you that are valuable to them. Before you actually do Exercise 4.1, look at an example.

Ted, the manager of a small research and development department, wrote the name of one of his subordinates. These were some of the reasons Ted thought the employee needed him:

COMPARISON OF ASSESSMENTS

	Those that best describe me	*Characteristics I could improve*
Spouse:		
Boss:		
Friend:		

I give him feedback about his work often, which he seems to want.

I have fifteen years of experience with the company, and I can give him some of the benefit of that experience.

I keep the pressure low, and he does his best work when he doesn't feel pressured.

I am not rigid in my thinking or set in my ways, so he always feels free to develop his own creativity in my department, without fear of ridicule or rejection.

Now try your own hand at Exercise 4.1.

EXERCISE 4.1

Who needs me? Why?

Family:

Friends:

Work:

Others (community, volunteer, religious, professional organizations, etc.):

After you have your own lists, think about what is missing. What would you like to be needed for? Again, try to be specific, as in these examples.

Ken was a stonemason and worked for a commercial contractor. His wife, Joan, was a lawyer who had just made partner in her firm. Although Joan said she admired his skills as a stonemason, she had also hinted about Ken's starting his own business and expanding into areas in which his artistic abilities could be better utilized. Ken needed his wife's esteem, which would come only from a more ambitious career.

Jerome was distressed that the list he made for his son Timothy was very short. It looked as though Timothy needed him only for financial support. Jerome wished the boy needed him for what he thought a father should be—a role model, friend, and teacher.

Your own lists may point up your deficiencies similarly. Later, when you set goals for yourself, they will guide you to the areas which you want to improve in some way.

As another guide to what needs changing in your life, try Exercise 4.2. Write down the 10 things that make you most unhappy (or that you do not like or that are constraints) in your life and/or work. What does your list look like?

Fred's list looked like this:

My wife's father, who keeps insinuating that I'm not good enough for his daughter

The way I freeze and panic when I have to deliver a speech

Getting to work at eight a.m.

My beer belly

Having to face that big stack of bills at the end of the month

Feeling too lethargic to look for a better job

Yard work

Never doing anything at night but watching TV

My insomnia

When you have completed your list, fill in the two columns on the right in Exercise 4.2. Indicate with a check mark which items you could change in yourself or in your environment, and which items you are powerless to change. Later, when you are setting goals for yourself, this exercise will also point up areas in which you want to change and will help you decide if your goals are realistic.

Here's another exercise to help you get at what short-term things you would like to change in your life. Suppose that you learned today that you were going to die suddenly and painlessly in six months. Using Exercise 4.3, write what you would do in those six months. Remember, you will not die of a lingering illness. Your health will be about the same as it is now. And remember, too, that you won't inherit a million dollars. Try to keep your answer in the realm of what is possible.

EXERCISE 4.2

Write down at least 10 things that make you especially unhappy, that you don't like, or that are severe constraints on your life.

	These I can change	These I cannot change
1.	_____	_____
2.	_____	_____
3.	_____	_____
4.	_____	_____
5.	_____	_____
6.	_____	_____
7.	_____	_____
8.	_____	_____
9.	_____	_____
10.	_____	_____

Read over what you have written. Did you find that you would completely change your life, change some areas, or go on about as you are? Did something you haven't gotten around to doing suddenly become tremendously urgent? This, too, will highlight what goals are important to you.

EXERCISE 4.3

Suppose you will die in six months. Until then your health and financial condition will remain about as they are now. What would you do in those six months?

EXERCISE 4.4   What would you like to be remembered for? What if you could write your own obituary? Write your birth date and the date of death. Give yourself as long a life as your would like. Now write your obituary, including where you lived, who you were close to, your accomplishments, honors, interests, life-style, and what kind of person you were.

Birth date: _____

Date of death: _____

1. Locations lived:

2. Life-style:

3. Interests:

4. Friends:

5. Values:

6. Accomplishments:

7. Honors:

8. Remembered for:

9. Other:

Now let's think about the long haul. Not only presidents worry about posterity and immortality. Most of us occasionally think about what we would like to be remembered for—what personal qualities we want to develop and what we want to achieve before we die. What if you could write your own obituary? Try it now in Exercise 4.4.

Take a moment to reflect on what you have written. Do you aspire to be something that is a long way from what you are today? Do you have plans for achieving those goals? Are you actively moving ahead? Is what you have written realistic? Or is it wishful thinking?

If you are realistic and serious about what you have written, you must begin doing the tasks necessary for its accomplishment. You need a plan, and you should be acting on it. We will develop ways of doing this as we move along in this book.

PART B

To help you make the transition to a clear statement of goals—the subject of the next chapter—we need a framework to organize the self-assessment you did in Part A.

This framework, given in the Self-Assessment and Goals form in Appendix I (pp. 237–238), will involve making several statements about your personal characteristics in the following categories: physical/health, emotional, intellectual/education, professional/career, and spiritual/moral/ethical. Let's look at some examples.

Physical/Health

Alice awoke with a cold sore and debated whether to go to work or stay home. Her energy level was never very high, but when she was fighting an infection she often felt the best thing she could do was stay in bed. And it pained her to be around other people with the ugly blister on her lip. She was very conscious of her appearance, and she felt at a distinct disadvantage when she wasn't looking her best. But she decided she had better get dressed and go to the office. She had already missed eight days this year because of colds and other minor complaints, and her supervisor always sounded annoyed when she called in sick.

What about you? Do you have good health and a high energy level on your side or not? Do you usually feel okay about the way you look, or does self-consciousness about your appearance sometimes stand in the way of your doing what you would like to do? Is your age an asset or a liability in the things you most want for yourself?

Emotional

Gary was a physician's assistant who had recently separated from his wife. His emotions were in a turmoil—grief alternating with anger, feelings of abandonment, desires for revenge, and waves of sentimentality. But none of the patients Gary treated guessed that he had unhappiness in his personal life. His emotions didn't keep him from functioning well on his job, and he continued to be sensitive and sympathetic to his patients.

What about you? Are you on an even keel emotionally, or do your mood swings get in the way of what you want to accomplish? Do fear and anxiety sometimes cripple your efforts? Do you enjoy arguments and conflicts occasionally, or do you go out of your way to avoid conflict? Do you live with depression much of the time, or are you characteristically bouyant and optimistic?

Intellectual/Education

Carla was a copywriter in an advertising agency. She had a quick mind and was a voluminous reader. When she sat down to write a piece of copy, her word processor couldn't keep up with her abundance of ideas. She would quickly write down 15 or 20 phrases and then pick out the best. Almost everything in her life was a source of advertising ideas for Carla—billboards, television shows, newspapers, novels, conversations with friends, crossword puzzles, and things she overheard in the elevator and on the subway.

What about writing? Articulating your ideas? Have you had the kind of education that will easily permit you to get what you want out of your work, or do you lack the training or education you need?

Professional/Career

Marty recently obtained a job as an insurance salesman. He liked selling and he liked people. He also loved not being tied to a desk. But, by and large, he wasn't happy with his new work. The "product" he was selling was boring to him. He hated anything basically intangible. He often found himself selling insurance to people he felt didn't really need it or couldn't afford it. Also, he was very uncomfortable about working on straight commission. He needed the security of having a regular salary coming in.

How about you? Do you like your work structured or not? Are you happiest working by yourself or as part of a team? Do you need frequent feedback on how you are doing? Is job security very important to you? Are you happy in your work? Do you like your job? Are you satisfied with your accomplishments? Your salary? Do you want more challenging work or more money? Would you like to be an entrepreneur rather than working for someone else?

Social

Karen was a counselor of alcoholics in a mental health clinic. She was very good at her job, though she had some difficulty in her first few months overcoming her personal prejudices about people who abused alcohol. But Karen had a manner that inspired trust. Her clients felt instinctively that she was not judgmental, that she respected them as human beings, and that she did not see herself as superior.

What about you? Are you accepting of other people? Do people usually trust you? Are you good at both listening and communicating? Do you feel a need to control other people or to make them dependent on you? Do you enjoy competition or shrink from it? Are you self-confident or shy in social situations?

Spiritual/Moral/Ethical

Mort owned and operated a small automobile dealership. He was devoted to his wife and two daughters, and the family did a lot of things together. Many of their activities centered around their church, where they found many friends and rewarding experiences. Mort was a good businessman, but he got a reputation as sort of a sharp dealer. An elderly couple complained about a cracked axle in a used car they bought from Mort. A schoolteacher checked with another garage on a bill for a transmission repair and found that Mort had charged him $35 more than it would have cost at the other shop. Mort's business has not grown as much as some of the other dealers in town.

What about you? Can people rely on your honesty and integrity? Is your word your bond? Do you forgive, have compassion, give freely to people in trouble? Or do you tend to cheat a little? Forget a stroke when marking your score card? Overstate a few deductions when making out your tax form? Take a peek at the "A" student's paper during an exam? Do you brag about what you do for the church and then burn someone on a used car sale?

To show you how completing the Self-Assessment and Goals form

CASE STUDY

A Student's Self-Assessment

Nathan Snow was in the last semester of his senior year at a state university. A psychology major, he was undecided on a career, but knew he would have to begin interviewing for jobs in the next few months. His adviser had encouraged him to take the Graduate Record Examination, and his roommate was trying to persuade him to take a year off to travel in Europe. Both graduate school and travel were appealing, but Nathan had pretty much decided he would like to earn some money and to see what kinds of work were available. He expected that he would need an advanced degree eventually, but now he was impatient to be out of school for at least a couple of years.

He didn't want to spin his wheels. He had seen his older sister and a close friend in the class ahead of him take the first thing that was offered, and both had ended up quitting their jobs in less than a year. Corinne, his sister, had gotten into a management training program at a bank that was trying to recruit women. After six months, she had quit, and had ended up waiting tables while waiting to get accepted into a graduate fine arts program. Bob had been lured into a selling job he hated with an electronics company, and he still had no idea what kind of work would appeal to him.

Before writing a résumé or making appointments for job interviews, Nathan decided to take stock of himself. If he could get a fairly clear picture of himself, he thought, it would help him find a job that would contribute to the development of his strengths. Even if he worked for only a couple of years before he went back to school, he wanted his first job to be a significant step in preparing for a long-term career, a job where he could get some training and experience that wouldn't be too narrowly specialized, but would be a good match for his abilities.

(Appendix I) can help you summarize your self-assessment, let's look at a case study of how Nathan Snow, a student, went about that task.

Nathan used the exercises in this chapter as the basis for his self-assessment. Then he used what he had learned about himself to complete the Self-Assessment and Goals form (Appendix I, pp. 237–238). He made the following statements about himself.

Physical/Health

I am 22 years old, in excellent health, physically strong, energetic, and able to withstand a lot of stress.

I can play a mean game of tennis; stay up all night, if I have to, without ill effect; eat like a horse; do 50 pushups; and recover quickly from colds and other illnesses.

I need a fair amount of exercise; to be in a kind of job that isn't completely sedentary; to pay a bit more attention to eating right and getting enough sleep and exercise as I get older; regular vigorous exercise to blow off steam; some clothes other than jeans for interviews and work.

Emotional

I am sympathetic; fairly even tempered; probably too easily influenced; cheerful most of the time; and inclined to keep my troubles to myself.

I can make people feel comfortable; function pretty well even when I'm worried about something; keep a basically optimistic outlook even when things aren't going very well; work out most of my problems on my own; and accept and enjoy people with different values without getting defensive.

I need to have a lot of contact with other people; to be involved in work or other activities that have the goal of helping people; to be alone for some time every day; some training in effective ways of helping people; and to be a little more assertive and less gullible.

Intellectual/Education

I am a slightly-better-than-average student; a slow reader; a computer bug; curious; and excited about learning when it seems relevant to some problem or project I'm working on.

I can understand and communicate what I've heard or read; write clearly without using a lot of jargon; be pretty flexible in finding solutions to problems; probably get into a good graduate school if I want to; and think fast on my feet.

I need to be able to relate what I am learning and studying to something practical; to bounce my theories and ideas off other people; to be out of an academic environment for a while; a job that isn't too heavy on paperwork, forms, and reports; a job that allows me to think independently rather than just following directions.

Professional/Career

I am relatively inexperienced; a past camp counselor; a former summer recreation assistant director in an inner-city project; a failure as an encyclopedia salesman; and open to suggestions.

I can make a favorable impression in an interview; work well with teenagers; accept authority on the job; bring a lot of energy and enthusiasm to work I am interested in; and learn fairly quickly the skills and techniques needed to do work I am interested in.

I need to know more about what kinds of occupations are available; to figure out whether I would like working in a profit-making organization or should stick with the kinds of things I have done in the summers; to earn enough money to support myself; work in which I would have some fairly long-term, satisfying relationships with people; and a job that isn't the same day after day.

Social

I *am* an extrovert; a good listener; more interested in people than anything else; liked by most people who know me; and able to laugh at myself and have a good sense of humor.

I *can* get people to trust me quickly; let other people have their way once in a while; be a good friend; work well with other people; and get along well with kids.

I *need* to learn more about communication skills, if I decide to work in one of the "helping professions"; more experience in working with different kinds and ages of people; to get rid of some of the prejudices I have about people who abuse alcohol and drugs, welfare mothers, etc.; to have a lot of social involvement in my work, instead of just having the social contact in recreational stuff; and to have a job in which serving people is the main objective.

Spiritual/Moral/Ethical

I *am* moral and ethical, it seems to me.

I *can* not imagine trying to cheat anybody.

I *need* a job in an organization operated by honest, principled people. (I found that out during the encyclopedia-selling gig—I don't want to be part of any outfit that tries to con people or misrepresents the benefits of the product or service that is being provided.) This probably rules out a number of potential employers.

As Nathan worked to fill in the form, he realized that he was a lot closer to narrowing down his job choices than he had thought. The same concerns tended to surface in one category after another. It was clear to Nathan that his interests and his abilities all pointed to a social services kind of job. During spring vacation, he lined up four job interviews. He knew just what he had to offer: a college degree in psychology, some job-related summer experience; and the aptitude and interest in working with people, particularly young, disadvantaged people. He also knew what he wanted out of the job—training and experience in a helping occupation; a job in which he could use his mind to achieve some practical, visible results; exposure to different kinds of people; the opportunity to form long-term, meaningful relationships with people he was serving or working with; and enough money to live on but not necessarily to get rich.

Nathan interviewed for a job with an industry-sponsored corporation that trained high school dropouts for jobs and offered them personal counseling and tutoring to get the high school diploma; for a job as a counselor in a neighborhood delinquency-prevention project; for a job in the county mental health department's day-treatment center for adolescents and adults; and for the job of assistant coordinator of a court volunteer program that worked with juvenile offenders. He was offered two of the jobs.

Now it's your turn. When completing the Self-Assessment and Goals form, try to put at least five statements under the three self-assessment headings *I am, I can, and I need* for each of the six categories listed. What you decide to do—the goals you set for yourself—will grow out of what you are, what you can do, and what you need.

After you have finished writing these statements, look them over carefully. Do they lead to some conclusions about what you should be doing with your life? Some goal statements? Using the Self-Assessment and Goals worksheet in Appendix I, write in statements about what you want to do (desires) and must do (commitments). Make sure they are reasonably consistent with the self-assessment statements. For instance, do you really have the ability to carry out one of your "want to do" statements, such as the ability at math to become an engineer?

SUMMARY

In this chapter, we have done a form of self-inventory. We have looked at our strengths and weaknesses, the things we like about ourselves, those we don't like about ourselves, our values. We've listed things we do, like to do, don't like to do. Things we'd change.

We have attempted to identify some themes or patterns by making summary statements in categories of human ability and behavior. Finally, we have tried to draw some inferences from these self-assessment statements, which lead to logical, consistent goal statements.

In Chapter 5, you will set and analyze your important goals. Use the self-assessment and goal statements you developed to help you do this.

5 Setting Goals and Priorities

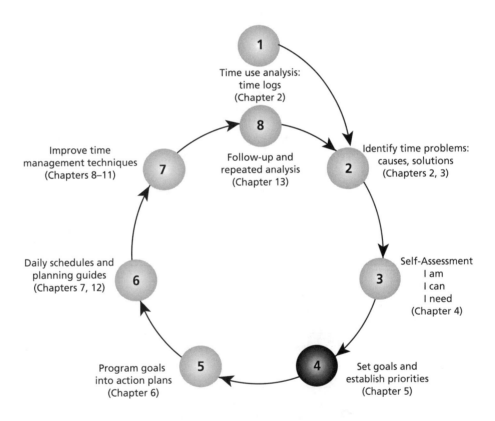

1 — Time use analysis: time logs (Chapter 2)

2 — Identify time problems: causes, solutions (Chapters 2, 3)

3 — Self-Assessment I am I can I need (Chapter 4)

4 — Set goals and establish priorities (Chapter 5)

5 — Program goals into action plans (Chapter 6)

6 — Daily schedules and planning guides (Chapters 7, 12)

7 — Improve time management techniques (Chapters 8–11)

8 — Follow-up and repeated analysis (Chapter 13)

Many of us become frustrated about our time management because we feel that we are unable to accomplish basic goals. We don't seem to be able to fulfill our expectations for ourselves. Rather, we feel we are just muddling through life.

Before you can plan what you will do in the next hour or week or year, you must decide where you want to go, what you want the results of your efforts to be, and what your goals are. The self-assessment exercises and worksheets in Chapter 4 were intended to help you get a handle on your character traits, values, interests, abilities, and accomplishments. Taking stock of personal strengths and weaknesses is an important preliminary step in setting realistic goals. Realistic goals, based on honest self-appraisal, are a must for effective time management.

In Chapters 5 and 6, we will follow through a seven-step process of establishing priority goals and building an action plan for reaching them. This process is summarized in Figure 5.1. This chapter deals with the first four steps—analyzing goals in terms of priorities and the performance tasks necessary to achieve them. Chapter 6 focuses on how to develop your action plan.

Step

1. Decide on a *goal*.	List your goal relating to work, family, community activities, and other personal goals. Set priorities and start with the A-1 priority.
2. *List key tasks* required to achieve the goal. 3. Describe *measurable results* or outcomes of each of the key tasks.	Goals are abstract; you cannot "do" a goal. Goals must be defined in terms of tasks or activities for which we can measure the outcome.
4. *Test* your goals against tasks and expected results.	If steps 2 and 3 are accomplished, can you agree that the goal established in step 1 has been achieved?
5. Place the tasks in the order or *sequence* in which they must be done.	All tasks cannot be done at once—some can be done only after others have been completed.
6. Determine what *resources* (money, people, time, etc.) are needed to carry out the task.	Resources and time are interdependent—ready availability of resources will shorten the time.
7. Put everything in a *time frame.* Indicate milestone dates for the accomplishment of the tasks and the final achievement of the goal.	

FIGURE 5.1

Goal-programming process.

GOALS—FUZZY AND ELUSIVE

A goal is a result—"the end toward which effort is directed." It tells you something about how things are going to be as a result of some action by you or someone else. When I ask people what their goals are, I usually get very general answers. Asked about their career goals, people come up with abstractions like those below.

the satisfaction of doing a good job

personal growth and development

realizing my potential

helping my employees realize their potential

be a good manager (or a good salesman, systems analyst, banker, preacher, etc.)

recognition

advancement

financial rewards

These general goals can be likened to making a profit in business. Profits are the result of specific actions, such as developing a new product, obtaining a specified share of the market, figuring out the best pricing and promotions, setting up the most efficient production line, hiring the right people, and achieving certain cost objectives. The general goals that most of us have for our life and work, although real and important, aren't very helpful because they don't tell us much about how to achieve them.

You cannot "do" a goal in the sense that you can prepare a budget at work or cook a meal. You can only do a series of tasks that, if accomplished, will denote that the goal has been achieved. For example, the tasks associated with the goal of being a good manager have to do with sales quotas, cost budgets, organization, employee training, quality control, delivery schedules, delegation, leadership, and so forth. But being sales manager involves different tasks from those of production manager or credit manager, and being sales manager of the turbine generating division of Westinghouse is different from being sales manager for a local suburban realtor. The sales manager of Carl's Used Car Lot, which trades three or four cars a week, performs tasks that are different from those performed by the sales manager of the used car division of the state's largest Ford dealer.

Let's take another example. We have a goal of being a good parent. What does that mean? We think we are good parents when we provide good homes, abundant food and clothing, moral values, honesty, education, and so on. Then, if our children take drugs, become economic bums, go with the wrong friends, or drop out of school, we feel that we have somehow failed as parents—but we don't quite know how. How do we measure the intangible quality of being a good parent?

Even more tangible goals, such as financial security, often are not very well defined. To the question, "Specifically, what do you mean by financial security?" I have often heard such answers as: "to retire comfortably," "to have enough insurance," "to educate the children properly." But the specifics of how many dollars this will take, how many insurance policies, when to retire, with how much money, and other similar qualifications, too often remain ill defined.

Robert Mager, in his book *Goal Analysis,** refers to abstract and intangible goals as "fuzzies." Mager talks about a great many fuzzy goals such as "be a good citizen," "appreciate music," "have a favorable attitude toward justice," "be a well-informed consumer," "be dedicated to one's profession." For example:

> We're all familiar with the goal, "teamwork." Have you ever had a boss who spent a staff meeting lecturing on the virtues of "team spirit" and encouraged everyone to function as a smooth running "team"? Upon leaving the meeting the sales manager, having felt the pressure of declining sales, proceeds to close an order for a machine tool that's a "little" different than standard. When the engineering manager gets the order, he finds the "little" differences require a large amount of new design. The production manager then must build a machine that has several special parts. At the next cost control meeting, he is asked why he went over budget on that job. The three managers end up in a shouting match. The president, who has goals of being a "good president" and building "teamwork," listens and ponders how to achieve these elusive goals.

Mager's approach is to define an abstract or intangible goal in terms of all the tasks that have to be performed in order to achieve the goal. He recommends sorting out these tasks and rewriting them into a logical statement of what must be done to achieve the goal. Mager then

---

*Robert F. Mager, *Goal Analysis* (Belmont, Calif.: Fearon, 1972).

suggests subjecting the statement to a final test: If I perform these tasks with the desired outcomes, will I be able to say that I have achieved the goal? Throughout this book, we will work to eliminate fuzziness by reducing intangible, abstract statements of goals to well-defined performance tasks.

Another difficulty we have is setting unrealistic goals. We all have heard or read stories about the "superperson," who has achieved fabulous success, fame, fortune, prestige, and power. Women's magazines are full of stories about glamorous models, exciting career girls, loving and sexy wives, and patient, adoring mothers. There are television programs about supermen, superwomen, and super families. Little wonder that many of us have unrealistic goals in terms of our ability, eduction, and experience. Even when we have the necessary qualifications, a different set of conditions and different timing may make it impossible to achieve the same success as the superperson we emulate.

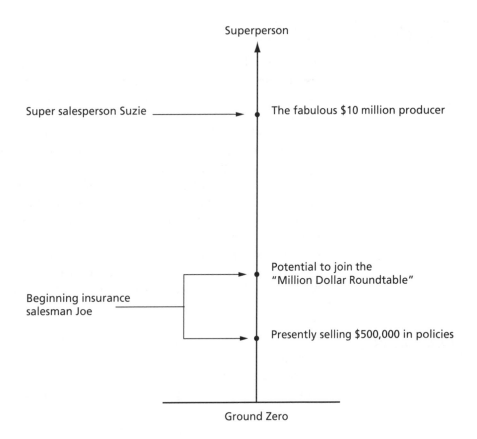

FIGURE 5.2
Sales achievement
continuum.

In addition, we often overlook the enormous sacrifices that the superperson had to make to gain success. Success does not come without its costs, and if you read the biographies of these people, you will learn how great the cost can be. A superhuman success requires a superhuman effort. If we are willing to make a medium effort, then we probably should be satisfied with medium success.

Perhaps it is worthwhile to think of our success along a line from low success to high success. Figure 5.2 illustrates how this would apply to the insurance business. The superperson is at the top; the rest of us are somewhere down the line. With more effort and organization, we have potential for greater success. A healthy objective is to peg an appropriate point, one that is consistent with your ability and willingness to sacrifice, and then work to get there. Hopefully, you will be satisfied if you do get there, even though you end up far short of the superperson.

DEFINING YOUR GOALS

In Chapter 1, you made a preliminary list of goals. Turn back to Exercise 1.4 and review your goals. Do they seem pretty abstract? Are some of them unrealistic? Let's see if we can analyze those goals more thoroughly now.

We will use the Goals worksheets in Appendix I (pp. 239–241) to begin making a complete list of goals in four categories: job/career, family, personal, and community. This exercise focuses on subdividing a general goal into subgoals or into tasks and activities, adding specifics such as how much and when. Thus, if your general goal is to be a good manager, specific goals might be "to delegate responsibility more effectively to the five people who work for me," and "to cut costs in my department 5 percent during the coming year."

As you proceed through the Goals worksheets, you might wish to refer to the discussion and instructions that follow for each goal category.

Job/Career Goals

As you start filling in your job/career goals, try not to agonize over the wording, to criticize yourself, or to worry about whether your choices would be acceptable to someone else. This list is for your eyes only. There is nothing final or binding about it. It's not carved in marble. It doesn't commit you to your goals until you are satisfied with them, and it's certainly not permanent. You change, and so will your goals.

For example, Martha Wagoner, a school principal,* came up with a list that looked like this:

General goal	Subgoals
To use my training and abilities to become an effective school principal	Keep my job
	Gain the respect and full cooperation of my teaching staff
	Have the best elementary reading program in the school system
	Make better use of my secretary
	Know each child in the school by name
	Not make any serious blunders
	Increase parents', teachers', and students' pride in the school
	Leave this school stronger academically than it was when I inherited it

Most of Martha's subgoals are still pretty fuzzy. They are end results, which together lead to the general goal of becoming an effective principal. But what does Martha mean by "increase parents', teachers', and students' pride in the school," or "leave this school stronger academically"? What action is suggested? On the other hand, "know each child by name" does suggest specific action. It's also interesting that Martha's subgoals of "keep my job" and "avoid serious blunders" reflect her insecurity in her new job. What action is suggested by those goals—play it safe and avoid risk? Playing it safe may conflict with the risk-taking associated with instituting a new, innovative reading program.

Your list, like Martha's, will probably contain statements that are both vague and specific. To test whether your statements are too vague, ask yourself, "Is this something that needs to be done now? Is there something I can do to accomplish this goal today? Next week?" If your goal is advancement or security or recognition, you'll feel bogged down as you try to answer these questions. But if the goal is defined in terms of more specific tasks such as "handle more customer inquiries than

---

*We will look at a full case study of Martha Wagoner in Chapter 11.

anyone in my department," or "know every child in the school," it will suggest a course of action.

For example, a man whose general goal was to be a better minister came up with this list of subgoals or tasks:

General goal	Tasks	Specifics: How much?
To become a better minister	To be a better preacher, by spending more time and effort writing my sermons and rehearsing them at home.	8 hours per sermon
	To help more people in my congregation, by making more visits and counseling calls this year.	20 percent more calls this year
	To develop myself, by reading several books in the next six months and attending educational seminars.	Draw up list of books
		Three seminars selected to attend

The general goal of being a better minister was far more meaningful once it was defined in very specific terms. Now fill in your own job/career goals.

Family Goals

The second part of the Goals worksheets deals with goals that relate to family. If career goals tend to be fuzzy, family goals are even more so. Most people are not accustomed to thinking of family life in terms of goal-setting. When asked to think about their family goals, they come up with abstractions such as love, happiness, security, and being a good parent, husband, or wife.

I have found it helpful to divide family goals into three categories. The first has to do with standard of living and quality of life. In setting these goals, consider what income level you aspire to, the kind and size of house you want, and the number of cars your family would like to own. Think about the life-style that seems desirable to you—whether you want to live in the city or the county or the suburbs, whether you like an active social life or a quiet family life, whether or not you wish to be fashionable and keep up with the Joneses. Think about your children's education—public or private school, college or vocational training, graduate or professional education. What about leisure time? Do you want to do more camping or fishing or concert-going? What new leisure activities would you like to explore as your children grow and your circumstances change? Along the same lines, consider travel and vacations.

The second category of family goals has to do with the attainment of that standard of living—long-term financial goals. In formulating these goals, first think about the "basics"—your house and automobile, your monthly budget, the expenses of education of any family members who will be in school, and your retirement. Consider also the luxuries that you specified as part of your life-style—vacation houses, travel, and expensive hobbies like skiing, photography, or collecting antiques. Also, think about what you want in terms of financial protection—life insurance, health and accident insurance, mortgage insurance, and savings.

You may find that the financial requirements add up to an amount that is too large for you to handle comfortably, and it may be necessary to eliminate some of the lower-priority luxuries. It's better to do this according to a plan, however, than unknowingly becoming overcommitted.

The last category is one in which most families do little in the way of deliberate goal-setting and planning. This has to do with family projects that cement family relations, promote "togetherness," communicate concern, solve mutual problems, and develop values and skills in family members. Here you might think about family times—dinner together, weekly swimming at the "Y," regular evenings out together, family vacations, and perhaps regular family conferences. You may also wish to consider "one-on-one" time. Some couples make a weekly dinner date to be alone together or set aside an hour on certain evenings for private, uninterrupted talk. Some regularly take weekend vacations away from the children. Others attend marriage enrichment seminars and retreats. Similarly, a mother may designate one hour each day to spend alone playing and talking with five-year-old John, who is jealous of the new baby and feels that he no longer gets enough attention. A father may plan to go fishing several Sunday afternoons with teenage Jeff, who is suffering the pangs of adolescence.

Almost everyone acknowledges the importance of these kinds of being together, but they rarely "just happen." As time pressures in other areas of life mount, family activities are often the first to be sacrificed. If you value close family relationships, these concerns belong on your list of family goals.

Under your family goals you may also wish to include work projects—not just the routine maintenance of house and yard, but special projects such as father and daughter building a car for entry in the soap box derby, or mother and son fixing up the basement. And you may wish to include instructional projects—sailing lessons for the whole family, husband and wife taking a parent effectiveness course, or father and daughter learning to play guitar and recorder duets, for example.

As you list your important family goals on the Goals worksheet, don't be worried about perfection. Write down everything that comes to your mind. You will sort them out in order of priorities later in the chapter.

Personal Goals

In addition to career and family goals, we all have personal goals—thus the next Goals section. We want to keep growing as individuals. Someday, we tell ourselves, I will learn French, play the piano, stop smoking, write a novel, get back the trim figure I had in college. Getting your personal goals down on paper will help you evaluate which goals are important and realistic, and which are in the realm of daydream and fantasy.

You may find it helpful to divide your personal goals into several categories. The first category might include goals relating to personal growth and self-development. Examples would be a list of books you intend to read in the next six months and courses to take in the next two years. This would also be the place to write down cultural activities you intend to pursue—a film series or membership in a book discussion club or a local theater group.

In the second category, list your goals for the use of your leisure time. This is the place to put plans for taking up a new hobby or interest—growing African violets, learning to develop photographs, or boning up on Chinese cooking. You can also set goals relating to better health—making a golf date for every Wednesday afternoon, getting on the stationary bike for half an hour after work each day instead of flopping in front of the TV, or going to the "Y" at lunchtime twice a week to run on the indoor track. Also included in this category are *social* and *spiritual* goals. You may want to develop closer relationships with friends by planning a social dinner once a week. Personal spiritual goals may involve teaching a Sunday School class, becoming a volunteer at the nursing home, or simply regularly attending church services.

Most of us don't want to wait until we retire to start doing things that give us deep satisfaction. But without a commitment and a plan for doing them, which begins with a written list of goals, these activities often elude us. Start now by writing out your personal goals.

Community Goals

The last area in which it is helpful to set goals is that of community service. Most of us feel some commitment to organizations and institutions outside of those in which we earn our living. However, we often get involved in community service because someone asks us to, not because we want to. Someone calls up and asks us to run for treasurer of the PTA, or be a den mother, or usher at church, or head up a fund-raising effort for the United Way—and we find we can't say no. We end up saddled with a bunch of worthy causes, most or many of which are all burden and no satisfaction. So you want to plan the kind of commitment that suits you.

Community work can call into play abilities and skills not used in our regular jobs. Tom, a salesman who once considered a teaching career, carries that interest and aptitude into teaching Sunday School. Beth, a housewife with young children who worked in public relations before she was married, puts out a monthly newsletter for her neighborhood association.

Many people find meaningful involvement in volunteering their time to organizations that have helped them in the past. Susan, who was hospitalized for long periods as a child, works two afternoons each week as a volunteer in a pediatrics ward. Charlie, who got into trouble with drugs in high school and was helped by a counselor, is a volunteer counselor at a drug abuse crisis center. Jane, who was able to return to her career soon after her children were born because of the availability of good day care, serves on the mayor's committee to study and upgrade day care in her community.

As you set down your community goals, it makes sense to be guided by your interests, abilities, and genuine commitment rather than by the pressure of an associate or friend, or by what will look impressive on your résumé or in your obituary. When you have a plan for how you can and want to be of service, it should be easier to say no to all those other requests. With this in mind, complete filling in your community goals.

PICKING THE PRIORITY GOALS

Now you have lists of goals in four categories—possibly three, if you don't have any community goals or family goals. It's time to set some priorities. Go over each list carefully and critically, and sort them into priorities: *A priority*, having high value and being of primary concern; *B priority*, having medium value and secondary importance; and *C prior-*

ity, being one you could do without. (You may want to start by ranking them in order.) Where two or more goals seem to be essentially the same, consolidate them. Weed out those goals that may be important sometime in the future, but that you are unable or unwilling to get started on now. Don't worry—you are not eliminating them forever, just for now.

> Joe listed as a goal having his family's dream house built this year. When he thought about his income and the expenses the family was facing— braces for Susie's teeth, installment payments on a new car and dishwasher, and a long-planned family reunion in California—he concluded that this goal was not realistic at this time, and crossed it off his list.

> Julie wrote down going to law school as a goal. But when she considered her lack of enthusiasm for studying and her undistinguished college record, she realized that she had listed law school as a goal because it seemed like the "thing to do" among her friends, not because she had any real interest in or aptitude for studying law.

Setting realistic goals does not mean setting your sights low. It means realistically assessing your circumstances, your abilities, and your commitments.

Some of your goals may present possible conflicts.

> Ike had the goal of getting transferred in the next six months to his company's headquarters in another state where the opportunities for advancement were much better. He realized that this goal might well conflict with what his immediate superior had in mind for him in the near future. He also thought this goal might conflict with his wife's wishes. The couple had been transferred only a year and a half ago, and Anne was just getting settled in this community.

When you sense potential conflicts—when your goals appear to conflict with someone else's, or with your own goals in a different category—you should try to check out your assumptions.

> Ike talked to his wife and found that she had no objection to moving. She hadn't formed a strong attachment to the community in which they were living, and she had expected that they would make several moves as Ike moved up in his career. Being settled was not one of her immediate goals.
>
> When Ike broached the subject with his boss, he learned that the company did intend to move him to the main office, though not quite as soon as Ike had hoped. Knowing that the change would be made in a reasonable length of time, Ike revised his career goal.

Paul had the goal of quitting his job to go to business school full time in September, five months off. As his salary was his family's sole source of income, and as his wife had said she would prefer to stay at home until their daughter was kindergarten age, Paul figured his goal presented a conflict.

Paul talked to Marcia and told her he was just spinning his wheels in a dead-end job and needed an MBA to do the kind of work he was really interested in. Marcia, who had been a psychiatric nurse until Melissa was born two years ago, said she couldn't consider taking a full-time job while Melissa was so young. After considering several alternatives and compromises, such as Marcia getting a part-time job and Paul going to school nights while continuing to work, they decided that Paul would postpone entering school for another year. At that time Melissa would be three, and Marcia would find a good day-care arrangement for her and go back to work on the day shift at a psychiatric hospital.

When goals conflict, compromise is often possible and may be the best solution. But sometimes you will feel that your goal is too important to compromise or delay or give up.

Felix was the managing editor of a medium-sized newspaper. His goal was to improve the quality of news reporting and writing in the paper, and to strengthen coverage of local issues—a goal that would involve hiring more experienced editors and more specialized reporters, increasing salaries to attract more qualified people, and spending more time and money for on-the-job training and planning. The publisher of the paper had the goals of keeping the newsroom budget at its present level and increasing circulation, which he intended to accomplish by playing up murders, sex scandals, gruesome accidents, and other gory stories on the front page. After several stormy confrontations with the publisher, Felix was sure that he could never accomplish his goal at that newspaper, and that he couldn't live with himself if he tried to carry out the publisher's goals. He began to look for a job with another paper.

Writing down and evaluating your goals will help you clarify what is truly important to you. Like Felix, you will have to make choices. Try to reduce your goals to those that you have the interest, desire, means, and ability to pursue right now. Don't be concerned that you may have to eliminate some important goals—you can put them back on your list when you are ready to go to work on them. For example:

Mary had two goals in the personal category. She wanted to lose 25 pounds and she wanted to stop smoking. But realistically, based on her past attempts to lose weight and quit smoking, she knew that if she tried to do both at once she would probably fail on both counts. She decided to concentrate on a diet and exercise regime, and crossed off the "no smoking" goal temporarily.

Ed found he had three goals in each category. He knew he had a tendency to take on too many projects at once and usually wound up frustrated because he didn't feel he was doing an adequate job on any of them. Ed took a hard look at his list and decided to defer the goals he had listed in the personal and community categories. At this time in his life, he decided, he wanted to concentrate his efforts on his family and his career.

Scrutinize your own goals in the same way. Eliminate those you are not ready to begin working on right now.

When you finish with your list of goals, you will undoubtedly have designated several as being A priority. Look these over again carefully, and make sure they all deserve this high ranking. Are you being realistic? Should any be deferred? A-priority goals are our prime goals in terms of their value, our ability to achieve them, and our intention to act on them immediately.

Now rank your A-priority goals in terms of urgency. Which one should you begin working on first? Where do you want to concentrate your best efforts? Designate the goals of highest value and urgency as A-1, A-2, A-3, and so on.

As an example of setting priorities on goals, let's look at the case study of David Siegel, an apparel salesman.

CASE STUDY David Siegel walked in his front door and called "hello." His wife, Rebecca, appeared with a puzzled look on her face. "I wasn't expecting you at three-thirty in the afternoon. How come you're home at this hour?"

David was already feeling guilty about ending the day so early, and Rebecca's questioning just made him feel worse. But after more than 19 years of being married to her, he knew she didn't really mean anything by it.

The week had gotten off to a bad start, and David was really frustrated. Like so many other times over the past few years, he had promised himself that this week would be different. He would plan better and then stick to the plan. He knew in his own mind that he was a good salesman, but he wasn't sure the company recognized his ability. His boss was pressuring him to get new business and bigger orders. He knew, too, that he wasn't lazy. After all, he couldn't think of another father that was involved in as many activities with his children.

David's responsibilities as scoutmaster took up at least two nights a week and one weekend a month. He couldn't give that up. Scouting was what kept him and his 12-year-old son, Jeff, so close.

Every Tuesday, he had the board of directors meeting for the baseball league, and on Saturdays he and Rebecca worked most of the day in the concession stand at the ball park. They felt they owed that much to the league. If it hadn't been for all those great people, their oldest son, Mike, wouldn't be at State on a baseball scholarship now. And 15-year-old Janice was active in the girls' league.

But those Saturday obligations were tough to meet. Since his paperwork had to be faxed to the sales manager by noon Saturday, that meant coming home by one or two o'clock on Friday to get it done. Even at that, he seldom finished before seven or eight o'clock in the evening.

He had really tried the last couple of days to do a better job. Boy, if he didn't get some new business pretty soon, he could get fired! Then what would happen to his family?

That morning David had gotten out of the house at 8:00 a.m. sharp to drive over to Harperville. He was really looking forward to the 9:30 appointment with Jim Story, the buyer for Martin's Department Store. Jim was a friendly guy and always good for at least a small order. David would have plenty of time with him because he hadn't set his next appointment until 1:30. Maybe he'd even take Jim out for lunch.

Comfortably seated in the reception room, David began to thumb through a recent copy of *Sports Illustrated*. Just as he was getting interested in an article about the World Series, Jim Story came quickly into the waiting area. This time he wasn't smiling.

"Dave, what the hell's going on? I have an ad running in two days on those sport shirts you sold me and they aren't here yet. You'd better find them—pronto!"

David was really feeling the pressure. "I dunno," he responded. "I'll call the factory right now and get the story."

After a 10-minute wait, Shipping called back to report that the shirts had gone out on time. They should have been there over a week ago. The shipping clerk offered to call the trucking

company to check, but David told him he'd do it himself.

The call to the trucking company didn't get the immediate results David had hoped for. The dispatcher who could give him the needed information was out for coffee. He'd have to place the call again in 15 minutes. What a mess! David decided that he would speak to his sales manager about this. The poor service of the truck line was making him look bad.

Finally, he reached the dispatcher and was informed that the delivery had been made to Martin's nine days ago.

David raced to the receiving dock to check. As he hurried through the stock room, he spotted the cases of shirts. Much relieved, he went back upstairs to let Jim know and to get another order. As he approached the buyers' offices, he saw Jim coming out of his office with his coat on. "Sorry, Dave, I can't see you. I've got to go to a meeting. Why don't you call me for another appointment."

"Well, Jim, I found the shirts. They've been here since a week ago Friday. I'd sure like just a few minutes to show you our new shirts."

"Glad you found 'em, but I've got to run. See ya!"

David was upset. Making the call and not showing the new line would sure look bad on his call report. Oh, well, it was Martin's fault anyway. The receiving dock should have let Jim Story know that the order was in.

Nevertheless, he had to get something on the report for the day that would look good.

Back out in the car he scanned the list of targeted new accounts that the sales manager had sent. From the printout, he selected a name that showed four chain stores and a main store. David decided that the account looked like a strong possibility. Feeling a little better, he headed across town toward The Emporium.

As soon as he was inside he asked a salesperson in the Men's Department where he could find the buyer and was the buyer in. He was. David could sense that his adrenalin was pumping a little faster. This call could save the day. He'd have an order, and his sales manager would not lean on him so hard because he'd have a new account.

In the buyer's reception area he greeted the secretary and asked to see Mr. Lefkowitz.

"Do you have an appointment?" she asked.

"Well, no, I didn't know that I needed one," he answered.

"Are you a salesman?" she continued.

"Yes. You see, I represent Leisure Time Sportswear and I'd like to show the line to Mr. Lefkowitz."

"I'm very sorry but Mr. Lefkowitz sees sales representatives only on Fridays between one and five. If you'll come back on Friday, I know he'll be glad to talk with you then."

David felt a wave of disappointment. "Oh, I see. Well, thanks." As he walked back to the car he tried to sort out how he could get this account and still do his paperwork on Friday. There just had to be a way. Feeling pretty rejected, he drove over to a nearby restaurant for some lunch.

At 1:30 he walked into Carson's to see Frank Joyce. After a rather short sales call, Frank explained that his money for next season was already spent. Maybe he could look at the line the following season.

As David walked to his car he thought of his philosophy of "an order a day." Then the idea to call on Peters in Bainbridge hit him. Mr. Peters always bought a few shirts.

At the store, though, David found out that Mr. Peters was on vacation. David felt like kicking himself! Sure, he knew that! Why didn't he remember?

"Well," he thought, "this has been a wasted day. I'll just go on home. I'm in such a lousy mood now that I probably couldn't sell anything anyway. Besides, if I get home early, I can *really* plan for tomorrow!"

David was frustrated in his attempt to do an effective job as a salesman. In addition, his sales work and family goals were in conflict. David decided to list his goals and try to establish priorities. He used the Goals worksheet. How they looked after he had worked on them for a little over an hour one evening is shown on the next three pages. (Note: A blank copy of this worksheet for your use is provided in Appendix I, pp. 239–241.)

Suppose David asked you to comment on his list of goals, particularly the A-priority goals. Do they still seem pretty abstract? Fuzzy? How would you go about accomplishing those goals? Would you know when they were achieved? Do they seem realistic? David has made a pretty good start at analyzing his goals, although there are still some fuzzy areas.

Now look again at your own list of goals. Ask those same questions. Do you need to rearrange your priorities? What can you do right now, or soon, to advance your A-1 goals? Add details to make the goals more specific and action-oriented, less fuzzy.

GOALS
Job/Career Goals

Priority	General Goal	Subgoals	Specifics: How much? When?	Specific tasks and activities required to perform the goal
A-1	**Short-term job goals** Keep my job	Meet my sales quota Open new accounts	This quarter One or two a week	Make more calls Get better organized Make a list of new prospects Find ways to do it before Saturday
B	Get paperwork done before Saturday			
C	See if I can get one of the new company cars			
A	**Long-term job goals** Regularly exceed my quota, and do it earlier		By 10% By 2nd month of quarter	
B	Become sales manager		In 5 years	Take sales management courses Be a top salesman
B	**Personal career growth** Do some reading on selling techniques, regularly		*Sales and Marketing Management*— trade magazine Seminar—Amer. Mgmt. Association Books on salesmanship	
B	Take a close look at the sales management courses at the community college			Get company to pay for it Go to library, put together list
A	**Long-term career goals** Be recognized as a good salesperson—like Leonard Oakley	Do good job as salesman (first step) Get in line for assistant sales manager job		Visit admissions office and get details

Family Goals

Priority	General Goal	Subgoals	Specifics: How much? When?	Specific tasks and activities required to perform the goal
	Standard of living or lifestyle			
B	Some extra money to travel and vacation with family		A couple thousand dollars a year	
A	A good education for the children	College—maybe grad. school	College like State, or better	
B	To live well but not extravagantly		$4,000/mo. take-home pay	
	Financial			
	Short-term			
B	$1,800 of overdue bills to pay			Talk to bank about a loan
B	$2,000 to take the family to Yellowstone Park		Could be put off but we keep doing that	Take from savings
A-1	$600 for a new refrigerator			Sears charge account
	Long-term			
A-1	Finish Mike's education		About $9,000	
A	Janice and Jeff's education		Who knows? maybe $25,000	
B	More disability insurance		Should have $2,500/mo (only $1,200 now)	
C	Cottage at the lake		When children through college —would prefer it now	
B	Comfortable retirement		$4,000 after taxes, $750,000 net worth	
	Family projects			
B	Scout meetings—Mondays and Wednesdays, usually (could miss one or two)		See schedule	
B	Baseball—to games with Jeff and Janice		Same	
A-1	Championship game (could miss some but not championship)			
B	Buy Rebecca the new dress she wants		Next week	
B	Take her out to dinner			
A-2	Need to talk about some things			
A-1	Need to talk to Janice about ground rules—dating, staying out late, spending money			Set a time next week
C	Build workshed (could do without)			Design and get materials

Personal Goals

Priority	General Goal	Subgoals	Specifics: How much? When?	Specific tasks and activities required to perform the goal
B	**Personal growth/education** To learn more about scouting		Read books Go to workshops	
	Leisure-time activities			
A	Travel to national parks and wildlife preserves			A way to pay for it
B	A place at the lake to relax with Rebecca			Not sure when we'll be able to afford it
	Health			
A	Get in shape by jogging		Three times a week for at least 20 minutes	Stop by high school on way to practice
	Social The children are our social lives			
	Spiritual			
B	Need to get the kids involved in church			

Community Goals

Priority	General Goal	Subgoals	Specifics: How much? When?	Specific tasks and activities required to perform the goal
	Little league baseball			
A-1	Board of Directors meeting Tuesdays	Must get program budget approved	See schedule	
B	Concession stand Saturday			
A	Leadership role in scouting (important, but long-term)	Don't know	Need to think more about this one and discuss with a couple of higher-ups	

THE GOAL-ANALYSIS PROCESS

Once we have outlined our goals, we need to express them in terms of tasks or performances. We must list all the activities that lead to the accomplishment of the goal. Then we must define outcomes or results and ways to measure them. Using these measures or standards, we will be able to judge whether or not we've accomplished the tasks and, in turn, the goal. Let's look at an example:

Priscilla, a CPA, is shy and retiring. When she's at a social gathering she is quiet and very seldom says anything unless asked a direct question or the topic is accounting, which, of course, it seldom is.

Her personal goal is to become a better conversationalist. She decides to attempt two activities: first, to read a broad range of periodicals and books, and second, to attend the Dale Carnegie course.

For her first activity, she identifies these tasks and measurable outcomes: (1) she'll read the local newspaper, the Sunday *New York Times, Cosmopolitan, Newsweek, Sports Illustrated,* and *Business Week,* plus one book from the best-seller list every two weeks; (2) she will note one interesting article from each of the periodicals on a three-by-five card so she can remember it; (3) she will carry around at least ten cards on current articles in her pocketbook at all times for easy reference; and (4) she will introduce one new topic into the conversation each time she's in a social group.

If she completes these tasks, according to these measurable outcomes, can we agree that Priscilla has accomplished her goal of being a better conversationalist? The answer is yes. She still may not be a good conversationalist, but introducing one topic is better than zero. She can always elevate her goal later.

Let's return to the case study of David Siegel. How is David going to become a more effective salesman? How is he going to make that elusive sales quota? Open new accounts? How will he keep from losing his job?

David also has some high-priority activities when it comes to his family. Job and family time allocations must be balanced carefully. If he becomes a more effective salesman, he will not only relieve the job security pressure, but perhaps free up more time for his high-priority family activities.

Let's see how David better defined a minimum goal of meeting his sales quota.

David first wrote down what he thought were the "key tasks" in meeting his quota. His list looked like this:

1. Make more calls.
2. Sell more to existing customers.
3. Open new accounts.

He looked at his list critically. It was exactly what he had been telling himself for months, and he still wasn't meeting his quota. The list was just too vague to be useful. Of course, he would have to make more calls and sell more and open new accounts, but how could he plan to make those things happen? He tried a second list. It looked like this:

1. Schedule six calls a day.
2. Show the line to four existing customers and get sample orders from three each week.
3. Get two new accounts each week.

That looked better—a little more specific, anyway. But it bothered David, because that list, too, represented the kind of approach he had tried in the past, and it hadn't always worked. He knew full well that making six calls a day was no guarantee of any sales. He could do all the things on the list and still not meet his quota.

Now David really had to think about what kinds of tasks got results. His next list took him much longer to compile. He thought about techniques that had worked well for him when he had used them, about advice the sales manager had given him, about what he knew successful salespeople did, and about some things he remembered from conventions and workshops he had attended. His last list turned out to be much longer and more detailed than his first attempts. He organized the key tasks according to an article he had read in a trade magazine that said salespeople should plan, organize, and control their selling efforts.[*]

Plan

1. Prepare a written plan each day.
2. Lay out economical routes to save on travel time (e.g., avoid 40 miles out of the way to Bainbridge).
3. Concentrate the most effort on high-volume accounts, ones that might buy more than 100 dozen at a time.

---

[*]The application of the management process to time management and the development of 10 principles was explicitly presented in an article, "Time, One More Time," by Robert L. Adcock and John W. Lee, *California Management Review,* Vol. 14, Winter 1971.

4. Have alternate calls noted on calendar in case an appointment is canceled.
5. Set a specific objective for each call.
6. Increase sales to existing customers by 20 percent.
7. Try to sell 10 percent of the quarterly quota each week, instead of taking it easy for the first few weeks of each quarter.

Organize

8. Phone ahead for appointments or note any limited buying schedules (e.g., Friday, one to five).
9. Schedule appointments tighter. Instead of 9:30 and 1:30, try 8:00, 9:30, 11:00, 1:15, 2:45, and 4:15.
10. Make appointments to take buyers to lunch at least three times a week.
11. Do paperwork for an hour or two each evening or over lunch or early each morning, instead of doing it all on Friday afternoon.
12. Instead of reading *Sports Illustrated,* do paperwork.

Control

13. Plan a weekly phone call to verify that your customer's shipments have been delivered (check all of them with one call).
14. Let the shipping clerk track down orders so you can spend the time selling.
15. Note vacation dates and days off of customers.
16. Notify customers of late deliveries.
17. Develop a record-keeping system that can be carried around in the car—look into the laptop computers.

David may have to strike some of these items from his list if he finds they don't pay off, or he may add some tasks that more effectively get the desired results, but this list is a very good beginning. All of the tasks are well within his means to do and are aimed at (1) providing the best service to his customers so that they will be inclined to keep buying his products and increase their orders, and (2) giving him time to show his line to potential customers.

What measures of success will David apply to the results? In this case it's a very explicit number—his sales quota.

Describing measurable results is sometimes difficult. Many tasks and, in turn, goals, cannot be measured in terms of explicit outputs such as gallons of beer produced this month, dollars in the paycheck, or a sales quota. Instead, the result can be measured only in terms of an intrinsic feeling of achievement, a sense of well-being, a satisfying reward.

For example, Gus spends a Saturday afternoon helping his son fix the brakes on his old jalopy. Gus never brings up the subject of the boy's poor grades and other problems of adjusting to a new school. Nonetheless, at the end of the afternoon, Gus "feels" a sense of accomplishment. Their relationship is closer and more open. The next day, Gus decides to have a heart-to-heart talk with the boy, feeling more confident now that the relationship has been strengthened.

Sometimes we can use surrogate or substitute measures. For example, we measure the inputs rather than outputs and then assume that if the specified inputs are made, we will get the expected outputs. In education, we measure the quality of the incoming students via test scores and grade point averages, along with the number of faculty who hold doctorates, the volumes in the library, and the dollars in the budget. If all these inputs are up to standard, then our assumption is that we will achieve our goal of quality education. Of course, it's desirable to test this assumption. Will it produce an intrinsic sense of accomplishment? Should we attempt to verify it by questioning students, parents, and employers? Can we test outgoing students? Should we contract an outside team of evaluators?

What's important is not whether we can measure the results of our actions in a precise number, or must rely only on an intrinsic feeling. What is important is the discipline—the thought process—of subjecting our intended result to a standard of measurement.

Since goal analysis is so crucial to time management, let's look at the whole process in another case study. Sally Petrillo is a homemaker who is experiencing time management problems that relate to goals she has set for herself and conflicts that have developed. As you read about Sally, see how specifically you can analyze her time management problems.

CASE STUDY

Sally Petrillo

Just before he turned off the lamp on the bedside table, Robert turned to Sally and said, "We never seem to talk anymore. You're always too busy or too tired."

Sally resented that remark, but she knew it was true. She should have more time now than she had had for years. Scott, their three-year-old, was in nursery school three mornings a week now, and Robbie and Melissa were in school until three every afternoon. Since Robert's promotion two years ago they had been able to afford a housekeeper one day a week, and Sally no longer had to worry about the heavy cleaning.

Basically, this was just the life she had envisioned for herself: three children well spaced in ages, a happy, stable marriage, and the freedom to use her education and abilities and extend her interests in worthwhile community activities.

Sally had a degree in music and had taught school before Robbie was born. She kept up those interests in her volunteer work. This year she was president of the Symphony Guild, chairman of the education committee of the Junior League, a leader of Melissa's Girl Scout troop, a junior high Sunday School teacher, usher at the Children's Theater, and a member of a garden club. And just last week Robbie's teacher had asked her to take over as the volunteer parent for the class because the original parent had moved away.

Maybe she shouldn't have accepted, but she thought it would be fun to get back into the school again, and it would probably be good for Robbie to have her more involved in his school life.

But as Robert drifted off to sleep, Sally lay awake and felt guilty. Somehow it had gotten to be a merry-go-round, and she wasn't really doing any of her projects as well as she thought she could.

She got out of bed quietly and set the alarm for 6 a.m. She would get up a half hour earlier and give herself a little quiet time for planning before the daily round of activities got under way.

When the alarm rang, she remembered her resolution and hopped right out of bed. She went down to the kitchen and put on the coffee, then brought the newspaper in off the porch. She took the paper to the patio and glanced through it while the coffee brewed. Why hadn't she done this before? This was the quietest part of the day.

She went in and poured a cup of coffee and mentally got down to business. The most pressing project seemed to be to start on some fund-raising plans for the symphony, maybe a bazaar in the spring and a benefit dance before Labor Day. Both of these would need to be organized right away, and she began to think about where to hold the dance, the expenses involved, publicity schemes, committees, and key people to line up.

Her mind moved to her other projects as she went upstairs to wake the children. She really should prepare Sunday School lessons for the next three weeks. They would be taking a trip to the mountains, and she would have to find a substitute teacher and have some lesson plans ready for her.

And she musn't forget the Girl Scouts. Maybe there would be a few minutes today to look through some craft magazines and pick some projects and get up a list of materials she would have to buy for them.

Also, the bridge club was coming for dinner and a bridge evening Saturday. That would mean scouting up another card table, getting out to the store for some tallies and prizes, and planning a menu. Sally liked entertaining, but this week was beginning to look too hectic. Maybe just a buffet supper this time, and skip the first course.

Sally started down the stairs to get breakfast ready. But just then Melissa appeared at the top of the stairs, crying. "Robbie won't let me into the bathroom and I have to blow dry my hair," she complained.

Sally straightened out the argument and started to dress Scott, but she was interrupted by Robbie, who couldn't find his favorite jeans. Sally remembered that they were still in the dryer and went down to the utility room to retrieve them.

Scott wandered in, still in his pajamas. She asked Melissa to dress him while she finished up the breakfast and lunches. She had to get him dressed because this was her day for the school carpool and he would have to ride along. "Why do I always have to do it?" Melissa complained. "Why can't Robbie do it?" Robert ordered Melissa to dress her brother, grabbed his briefcase and was out the door.

Finally everyone was fed, the books and lunches were rounded up, and Robbie and Melissa delivered to school. When Sally headed back home with Scott at 8:30 a.m., she felt that she had already lived through about half a day, and she would have liked a quiet half hour with the newspaper and a second cup of coffee.

But she knew she couldn't afford a break today, so she got out Scott's blocks and started poking around for a paper and pencil and her telephone lists. She moved her papers to the dining room table and started to write down the numbers of people to call for the symphony bazaar.

The doorbell rang. It was Peg, a neighbor, stopping by to return a punch bowl. Sally offered her a cup of coffee and they went into the living room, where Peg launched into the latest chapter of her marital problems.

The phone rang and Sally noticed with surprise that it was almost ten. The caller was Maureen, one of the other parents in the ballet carpool. She had developed a mysterious muscle cramp in her back and could barely sit up, and she wondered if Sally would take the carpool this afternoon.

As soon as Sally hung up the phone rang again. This time it was Melissa's school. Melissa had vomited and had a slight fever, and they thought she should go home.

Sally explained to Peg, Peg left, and Sally went upstairs to get Scott and put his shoes and socks back on. She drove to the school to pick up Melissa.

She put Melissa in the television room and got some clay out for Scott, and then decided she really couldn't get going on her paperwork and phone calls with the housework hanging over her head. She gathered up a load of laundry and stuck it in the washer, then got out the vacuum cleaner. Then she remembered about the ballet carpool and realized she couldn't do it today because Melissa wouldn't be going to class. She called three of the other mothers before she finally found one at home.

By then it was 11:30, and Scott was hungry. She heated some soup for him and put the breakfast dishes in the dishwasher while he was eating. Then she put Scott down for his nap and went back into the dining room with her Sunday School books.

She had one lesson plan outlined when Robbie burst in from school, hungry as usual. She fixed him a snack and spent a few minutes talking with him in the kitchen.

When Scott woke up he wanted to play outside, so she got out his wagon and pail and shovel and took him to the backyard. As soon as he seemed happily absorbed, she went back in and rummaged around for her list of the education committee members. It would really help if she had a desk somewhere to keep all this stuff, she thought. She called all the members and asked them to come to a meeting at her house the next morning. She hated organizing a meeting on such short notice, and it didn't work very well because three of the women had other conflicts, but she felt guilty because they should have begun planning for the year at least two weeks ago.

It was 4:30 and she would have to get the pot roast in. She wished there were something quick to fix for dinner, but the meat was thawed and had to be cooked today. Scott wouldn't be able to wait until seven when the meat would be done and Melissa still felt queasy and wanted something light, so Sally made soup and grilled cheese sandwiches for them.

Robert called to say he would be home at 6:30, and the house still looked chaotic. She cleared her papers off the dining room table and set it for dinner. She remembered the clothes in the washer and moved them to the dryer. She had just finished making the beds when Robert drove into the driveway.

After dinner she washed the dishes, got Robbie settled at the kitchen table with his homework, gave Scott his bath, and read him a story. By nine, all three children were in bed and Robert was watching television. The house was quiet, and she got out her Sunday School books again, but as she tried to read them she found she was too exhausted to concentrate.

Her mind wandered to the next day. Scott would be at nursery school, the Junior League meeting in the morning, soccer carpool, and an evening meeting of the garden club. Somewhere, she would have to find time to get to the bank, the cleaners, and the grocery. The symphony, Girl Scouts, and Sunday School lessons would all have to wait at least another day.

Sally went up to take a bath and think over the day. In spite of her determination and her early morning planning, she didn't feel that she'd accomplished any of the things she really wanted to do. She needed that mountain vacation, but she knew that a week away would only leave her further behind in everything. All she could think of now was sleep. Robert was right; she was too busy and too tired.

Question

By now, you have gained some skills in analyzing time problems. What are Sally's time problems? Be as specific as you can.

Discussion

Sally suffers from three common time management problems. First, she has no grasp of where her time is going, how long things take, or what her limitations are. Second, her goals are not defined in terms of specific tasks with measurable results. Third, she has not established priorities in order to distinguish between important activities and less important ones. As a result, she has drifted into more activities than she can handle effectively.

In Sally, we see many of the time problems of homemakers. People who must cope with both a paying job and the job of homemaker usually recognize the need to make choices, set priorities, and plan for the effective use of their time. But those who do not work outside the home, like Sally, often do not recognize the need for management. And unlike the working woman, Sally does not have the daily example of business life that would help her learn to organize herself and to schedule her activities.

But Sally *is* a manager, and she needs to take a more businesslike approach to her work. She could start by setting up an "office," or at least a desk, for herself in a quiet place in her house. She needs to have her Sunday School materials, membership lists, phone lists, files, and a telephone together in one place that isn't used for other purposes.

Feeling that she has the luxury of a lot of time, Sally has never stopped to think about how long things take. She fails to consider how long it takes to set up a meeting, how much time she spends driving her children around, or how much time she spends doing housework and preparing meals.

Keeping a time log would put Sally in a better position to know how much volunteer work she can reasonably handle. Presently, she accepts almost any community work that is offered to her—far more than she can handle. To do a good job on any project, Sally would have to give up some of the others. She might well select the two or three that give her the most satisfaction and that she is most qualified to do.

When Sally comes to see her time as the precious commodity it is, she can begin to think of ways to use her time more efficiently. She may find that she spends too much time driving around, for example, when she might consolidate all her shopping and errands in one or two trips a week. She may decide that early morning and early evening, when all the family is at home and the house is hectic, are not times to be trying to do her volunteer projects. She can devote her full attention to her husband and children then, and use the morning hours when her children are in school for the community jobs that need her full concentration.

Homemakers need to think seriously about their priorities. Sally wants to have good relationships with her husband and children, and to pursue her own interests outside the house. These two major goals seem reasonable and need not present her with constant conflicts, as they do now. But if she wants to achieve these two goals, she probably cannot afford to devote so much time to household chores, elaborate entertaining, and gossiping with the neighbors. With her important goals firmly in mind, Sally could easily find ways to streamline her housekeeping—making one trip to the grocery store each week, cooking several meals at one time and freezing some for future use, doing all the laundry during one afternoon each week—at a time of day when she knows she is not at her peak of mental energy or when she is likely to be interrupted by other demands, such as those of the children.

Finally, Sally must recognize that interruptions and household crises are the essential nature of the tasks of a homemaker and parent. Children will fight with each other, lose their lunch money, and wake up with a fever. The vacuum cleaner and the washing machine will break down, and the housekeeper will fail to show up occasionally. Buttons will fall off, the potatoes will burn, and the alarm clock won't go off in time. With good planning, though, these events don't have to be crises. Many of Sally's time problems would be alleviated if she didn't wait until the last minute to do what is necessary, and if she developed some contingency plans for the inevitable times when things go wrong.

Analyzing Sally's Goal of Community Involvement

Let's see how Sally planned for her goal of community involvement, which seems to be the crux of her problem. First, she kept a time log for one week, analyzed her problems, and began to consider ways to overcome them. After carefully reviewing her commitments, she reaffirmed that she wanted to spend most of her time as a wife and mother while her children were young. She decided that she could allocate only 15 hours a week to community activities, which meant that most of her volunteer projects would have to go. But it was difficult to know where to begin cutting back.

She asked herself, "What do I want out of my general goal of community work?" Her answer took the form of a list of three subgoals:

Having the satisfaction of being a good teacher

Social contacts with adults other than the neighbors and Robert's business associates

Using my mind and my education

Sally looked at her list of volunteer commitments: usher at Children's Theater, Girl Scout leader, Sunday School teacher, garden club,

Junior League education committee, Symphony Guild president, and grade mother. At least half of these activities weren't contributing to her three subgoals. The garden club was pleasant enough, but it really was just getting together with neighbors, and the monthly club meetings at her house meant extra work all around, so Sally decided to cross it off. Being a grade mother and a Scout leader were things she was doing not for herself, but for Robbie and Melissa. Neither job used her special abilities, and both activities involved getting a baby-sitter for Scott, throwing the household routine out of kilter. Since they didn't further any of her three subgoals, she crossed them off. And being an usher was an activity she could justify even less, although the time involved had seemed insignificant when she had been talked into it.

That left the Symphony Guild, the Sunday School class, and the Junior League committee. All of these were satisfying, contributed to at least two of her subgoals, and would fit into the 15 hours a week she had available.

Sally's next step was to begin turning her goals into action plans. All of the community activities required some time on her own at home and some meeting time with others. The meetings were obviously "key tasks" in achieving her three subgoals, but Sally was hard-pressed to think of other key tasks and measureable results in relation to her volunteer work.

Certainly community goals are more difficult to analyze than, say, career goals. However, you will almost certainly be a much more effective volunteer worker if you do analyze what results would affirm that you have achieved your goals in community work.

On page 92 you'll see how Sally analyzed one of her subgoals, using the Goal Analysis worksheet. (Note: a blank copy of this worksheet for your use is provided in Appendix I, p. 242.) I think you will agree that Sally is much more likely to achieve her goal of being a good teacher if she goes through this process, instead of panicking each Saturday afternoon and thinking, "I've got to think of something to do with that bunch of kids tomorrow."

ANALYZING YOUR A-1 PRIORITY GOAL

Now it's your turn. From the Goals worksheets in Appendix I select your number one goal—the A-1 priority. Then turn to the Goal Analysis worksheet (in Appendix I, p. 242) and do the following.

GOAL ANALYSIS

A-Priority Goal:

　　To have the satisfaction of being a good teacher.

General approach:

　　To teach the junior high Sunday School class at St. Andrew's.

Key tasks:

Thoroughly prepare for each class.

Write an outline of units to be covered in each block of the church school year.

List reading to be done in preparation for each unit.

Plan for special projects such as dramatizations and field trips, and buy any necessary materials.

In each week's lesson plan, write down questions and topics for discussion.

Build a review of previous lesson into each week's lesson plan.

Check community calendar and television listings each week for related programs, lectures, and other events to suggest to students. Clip news stories, cartoons, and magazine articles that reinforce or can be related to lessons, and suggest that students do same.

Measurable results:

75 percent or better attendance each week.

Demonstrated interest in the material presented, e.g., students raising questions, bringing in ideas or clippings for class discussion, carrying out home assignments.

Mastery of material covered, demonstrated by questions raised, the relating of personal experiences to the lesson material, and answers given to teacher's questions.

Participation of all class members in discussions and other class activities.

Test: If the key tasks are completed with the indicated results, would most people agree that the goal has been achieved?

Yes ___✓___　　　　　　No _____

Are you sure?　　　　　　Why not? What's the problem?

I think so

Write down the A-priority goal you have chosen as A-1.

Decide on a general approach or strategy to achieving the goal.

List the key tasks or activities that must be done to achieve the goal.

Describe measurable results that, if achieved, would indicate that the tasks had been successfully completed.

Answer this question: If the key tasks are completed with the indicated results, would most people agree that the goal has been achieved?

If your answer is affirmative, you are ready to go on to the next chapter and put the goal in action. If not, rework your key tasks and measurable results until you can answer yes. Then go on to Chapter 6.

SUMMARY

In this chapter, you have set priority goals and have determined key tasks and measurable results that are required to achieve them. Appendix III contains additional resource materials on goal setting. In the next chapter you will program these tasks into an action plan following three steps: sequencing the tasks, considering resource needs, and putting your plan into a time frame.

6 The Action Plan

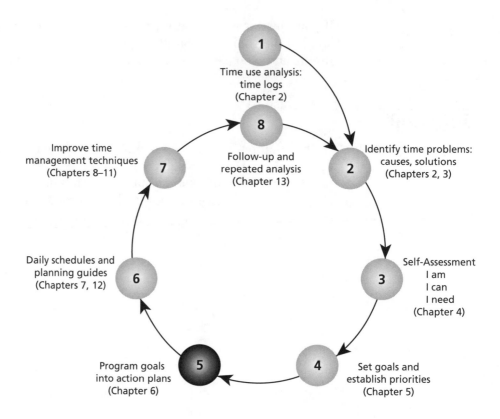

1 Time use analysis:
time logs
(Chapter 2)

2 Identify time problems:
causes, solutions
(Chapters 2, 3)

3 Self-Assessment
I am
I can
I need
(Chapter 4)

4 Set goals and
establish priorities
(Chapter 5)

5 Program goals
into action plans
(Chapter 6)

6 Daily schedules and
planning guides
(Chapters 7, 12)

7 Improve time
management techniques
(Chapters 8–11)

8 Follow-up and
repeated analysis
(Chapter 13)

In Chapter 5, we discussed the first four steps in the seven-step process of goal programming.

1. Decide on a high-priority goal.
2. Identify performance tasks necessary to accomplish that goal.
3. Establish measurable results to assess the successful completion of the tasks.

4. Test to assure that if the tasks are completed with the desired outcomes, the goal will have been achieved.

In this chapter, we will proceed through the last three steps.

5. Arrange the tasks in a logical sequence.
6. Consider any resources needed to carry out the tasks.
7. Develop a time frame for the completion of each task and achievement of the goal.

We will look at brief examples of each of these three steps. Then we will expand upon the case study of plant manager Chet Craig and see how he programs two important goals in the categories of work and family. Finally, you will complete these three steps for two of your own high-priority goals.

SEQUENCING TASKS

Sometimes we can do tasks leading to a goal in any order, but often ordering is important. To do A before B may be more efficient—it may even be necessary if B cannot be started until A is complete. As an example, consider the following situation.

Mel has a goal to completely redecorate the living room in his condominium. He jots down some activities to accomplish this:

Buy the materials (carpeting, wallpaper, furniture, paint, fixtures, etc.)

Hire someone to do the work

Consult with an interior decorator

Make up a budget

Mel sees an ad in the paper on discounts on some close-out carpeting. When he gets to the store, he discovers an orange plaid that he really likes, and he buys it. "Good buy," he says.

Obviously, Mel has not sequenced the activities correctly. By buying an orange plaid carpet before planning and coordinating all the things that must go into the room, he greatly limits his decorating options. Even if he got a good buy on the carpet, he may now have budget problems with other items. Certainly, planning the decor with the decorator and checking out the budget before committing to any purchases would be a preferable sequence.

Betty is the owner/manager of a firm that provides office, secretarial, book-keeping, and other clerical services to local businesses on an as-needed, contract basis. She has a goal of expanding her business by opening another office in a city 50 miles away. She knows the key steps will include the following:

a. Renting an office
b. Hiring a manager
c. Running ads and lining up part-time personnel
d. Spending two days a week with the new manager until the business is rolling
e. Researching the market to find out what services are needed
f. Getting a loan from the bank for $30,000 to get the business started
g. Preparing a budget

We would all recognize that some of these activities should precede others. What order would you put them in? Indicate by letter which task you would do first, second, and so on. Any that could be done simultaneously?

Sequence	Task (a, b, c, etc.)
1	
2	
3	
4	
5	
6	
7	

What order did you come up with? Probably something like e, g, f, b and a (simultaneously), c, d.

Betty decided to research the market before making any commitment on the new office. She was not at all certain whether the new market for her firm's services was really large enough to make a reasonable return on her investment.

Once she found a substantial need, she prepared a detailed budget to see exactly how much money was necessary to start the business and when she would be able to repay the loan.

The budget indicated that she would need only about $27,000 from the bank and could repay it within 18 months. To leave a little safety margin, she applied for $30,000 to be repaid in 18 months, and the loan was approved.

She then began to look for a manager and an office to rent. She waited to do any other hiring so that she and the manager would both participate in employee selection.

Obviously, Betty would not spend two days a week in the new office until all the other tasks were complete.

Betty's sequence of tasks was logical and financially sound. For example, it kept her from committing to personnel or a lease on an office until she was convinced of the need for her services.

RESOURCE NEEDS

In most cases, the pursuit of a goal cannot be done without using some resources. Some goals do not require resources. For example, if your goal is to lose weight by cutting down on lunches, then having a carton of yogurt, a piece of fruit, and a diet cola in your office may actually economize on the time and expense of going out to your favorite restaurant halfway across town.

But most goals are not achievable in that way. Most require at least some time. For instance, recall David Siegel from Chapter 5. The time he was spending on family activities conflicted with the time he needed for effective selling. Many busy executives have a goal of being a better parent, as David Siegel appears to be, but they are often unwilling to take time away from business to spend with their family. The essential resource—time—is limited.

Sometimes the necessary resource is money. Mel cannot redecorate his living room without some expenditure of money. If he has a lot of money, he can do everything he would like and do it immediately. If he has limited funds, he may have to do it over a period of time and take some shortcuts.

Sometimes a variety of resources are needed. Take the case of Jerry, an independent salesman who sells the products of several manufacturers on a commission basis.

Jerry has the goal of doubling his sales and commissions during the next two years. His plan for accomplishing this requires these resources: (a) a training program to increase his selling skills; (b) computer and software to help with correspondence, reports, call schedules, and other routine paperwork; (c) a direct-mail promotional budget so that potential customers have a continous flow of information about the products he has to offer; and (d) $20,000 to get a junior salesperson started to handle the more routine calls while he is working with the large customers and making missionary sales calls to open up new accounts.

Jerry will, of course, have to evaluate whether or not his goal is worth this substantial amount of resources.

THE TIME FRAME

To be most effective, a plan should include a time frame. We should set a target date for achieving our goal, and, if the plan involves several steps, milestone dates along the way for the completion of each key task. For example, Betty set dates for the opening of her new office as follows.

Complete market study	By 3rd month
Prepare a budget and secure loan	By 4th month
Hire manager and rent office	By 5th month
Solicit business and hire personnel	By 6th and 7th months
Work with new manager	By months 6–12
Office becomes profitable	By 15th month
Repay loan	By months 18–24

Without a time frame, plans are usually useless. Without a time frame, we may take action prematurely or put off action, procrastinating because we don't have a deadline to meet. As an example:

Gloria and Glen work in the same accounting office. Both are heavy smokers and would like to quit. Gloria tends to act impetuously, and she decides to quit "right now." Right now, however, is just before the April 15 tax-crunch time. After a particularly trying week, she's out with a few friends and succumbs to a couple of cigarettes to "relieve the strain of all those tax reports." Soon, Gloria's smoking her two packs a day again.

Glen, on the other hand, tends to procrastinate. He logically decides to wait until after the tax crunch. But then there's the budget to get together, then the report for the auditors, and next the year-end closing. His quit-smoking goal never even gets off the ground.

Not setting a realistic time frame for achieving their goals was, at least in part, the reason for Gloria and Glen's lack of success.

A realistic time frame often depends upon the availability of resources. The resource needs must be analyzed carefully before the time frame is worked out. In effect, they are like hand and glove.

> Susan is the recently appointed new products manager for Zippy Communications, and her job goal is to be a "good new products manager."
>
> The president, after prompting by the sales manager, decides that the new product the company really needs is a miniature CD player. Susan's department is understaffed, and she has neither the technical people nor the equipment necessary to develop the product. She is asked to come back with a detailed program for the project and an estimate of how fast she can get the president his miniature CD player. (He wants it in a year or less.)
>
> Susan works hard putting together the project plan, showing the product specs; the personnel, equipment, and facilities needed; the implementation steps; and the control and evaluation procedures.
>
> Susan reports back that the miniature CD player can be developed in less than a year, but the cost will be approximately $375,000. The president says the company can afford only $200,000 at this time.
>
> Susan would very much like to undertake the project and figures out ways to use some of her existing staff. But no matter how she estimates it, the project will take almost two years with the resources available.
>
> Finally, the project is scrapped. The president believes that the technology is changing too rapidly to wait two years for the new product, and the company simply does not have more than $200,000 to put into the project.

As in Susan's case, goals sometimes are unattainable because the timing is not consistent with the constraint of resources. How much better that we should know that before we start rather than learn it after we have spent a great deal of time and money. Other times we can work out a compromise between the resources and the time available.

THE COMPLETE GOAL-PROGRAMMING PROCESS

We have now described all seven steps of the goal-programming process. Let's take a look at two people who applied the process to important goals in their lives.

CASE STUDY Jane attended one of my time management seminars. She was about thirty years old, divorced, with two children. She worked for a small company that sold and distributed industrial products. The owner performed mainly as a sales manager; there were several salespeople, a warehouse manager, a couple of truck drivers, a bookkeeper, and an inventory clerk. Jane's job was to enter and process customer invoices and do certain other clerical tasks. She worked from the salespeople's orders, on which the warehouse clerk had noted what had been shipped, back-ordered, and so forth. She processed about 40 or 50 such invoices a day, which had a total dollar value of about $8,500.

When she came to the seminar, Jane had been on the job a little over a year and apparently was doing a good job. She'd become dissatisfied with this position, however, in terms of job satisfaction, challenge, and pay. She also felt that much of the selling effort was disorganized and that several things could be done to increase the efficiency of the selling staff in order to achieve more sales and profits. She specified several items—such as better follow-up of customer inquiries; organization of brochures, product information, and specifications; more effective follow-up on back-order items and returns; periodic analysis of sales by customer and salesperson; and a formal procedure for recording customer complaints.

In our discussions, Jane and I agreed that an appropriate goal for her would be to develop into a sales administrator, the type of person who would perform the duties just described. This function would have value to the company and would easily justify a better salary. Although Jane seemed to have the interest, personality, and intelligence to handle such a job, she did some self-assessment and took a couple of standardized tests in order to validate this. She obviously needed training, however, and, although it was impossible for her to return to school full-time, she could take courses at the local community college in the evenings.

The next question was strategically how to pursue the goal, Jane could, of course, talk to her boss to gain his support. Alternatively, she decided that her approach would include taking courses in the evening in business math, statistics, marketing, and sales management. She would then begin doing some of the tasks noted earlier on her own initiative; for example, analyzing sales by customer and salesperson, and incorporating these into a report for the owner. She felt that these efforts would demonstrate her willingness, initiative, and competence. Thus, she would approach the boss on the new position in mid-stream.

From the resource point of view, she knew that an additional clerk would be required to do the invoicing work once she assumed a new position. She also needed funds to pay for the educational programs and the baby-sitting while she attended classes. This was not easy for her to handle, but she finally managed to borrow the necessary money.

All this was developed into the details of an action plan. The time frame was set at just under two years. Jane progressed with the plan; when she talked to her boss, he agreed to her suggestions but would not add the additional clerk immediately. After several months, it became obvious that he was doing little more than giving lip service to his commitment to Jane. He still looked on her as someone to enter and process invoices and handle other routine clerical work. In fact, he made more demands for this type of work, which kept her from doing new projects. It wasn't clear why; perhaps he felt threatened. This frustrated Jane, but she decided to continue with her courses and initiate what new procedures she could. Even if the boss did not eventually make good on his commitment, she felt she would then be in a good position to look elsewhere for a better job.

This is, in fact, what happened. The boss never

considered her in any sort of managerial capacity, even though she had the potential and the credentials to take on much more responsibility. Eventually, she was able to demonstrate her capabilities to a larger firm in the area, where she became assistant sales manager at almost twice the salary. She not only had the satisfaction of doing a more challenging job, but she also substantially increased her compensation. It took her about six months longer than she had planned.

Take a moment to review the goal-programming process in Figure 5.1. Now let's see how Jane applied these seven steps to her important goal.

Jane set a high-priority goal of personal growth and job promotion. She assessed her ability and interest in pursuing that goal. She defined tasks for achieving the goal. She set dates for taking training programs and producing the first statistical report for her boss, with an overall two-year completion date for the goal. The resource needs that Jane could control were met, but the extra clerical help, which her boss controlled, was not met, and this caused a problem in the plan.

The measurable outcomes were the completion of training programs, producing statistical reports, taking over various administrative functions, the ability to handle sales administrative work, and the ultimate promotion.

Jane's boss frustrated part of the plan and it had to be modified. The promotion had to come from outside the company where she worked, which delayed the final completion date by six months.

With hard work and commitment, Jane eventually achieved her goal through the systematic process of goal programming.

Now let's look at another example. Bill set about to achieve a personal goal that related to his church and religious beliefs. As you read, assess how well he applied the goal-programming process.

CASE STUDY Bill decided that an important personal goal is service to people; he would like to achieve this goal through work in his church. Also, from a personal point of view, he would like to get closer to God—to learn more about the teachings of the church and participate more in the religious events.

Bill talked to his minister about his goals. Since Bill is a businessman with some management skills, they agreed that the most valuable service that he could provide was to take a leadership role in the church. The minister suggested that Bill consider two committee assignments, Outreach programs and the Finance Committee. This would prepare Bill to later serve on the governing board and perhaps eventually become the chairman.

Regarding his second goal—getting closer to God—the minister suggested some source books for independent study. He also mentioned certain courses at a nearby university and retreat-type seminars sponsored by the national church. He suggested that Bill might like to become a "lay reader."

Bill talked to his family and others in the church, as well as friends who were engaged in similar church work, and investigated educational opportunities available.

Finally, on a warm spring Saturday morning, Bill rose early as usual. He made himself a cup of coffee, got the paper, and walked out to the porch. But instead of reading the paper in his usual leisurely way, he decided, "This is the day I'm going to plan out my church-related goals."

He picked up a pen and pad and began to write out the various committee tasks and educational programs he thought made sense. He estimated the resources needed. A little money was needed for the educational programs, but the toughest resource was time. He was busy with the family and business, and he needed a couple of evenings and some quiet time to study.

Bill decided to analyze his time use. This way he could identify activities to cut down freeing the time needed to do the church work. He found that he was already involved in a number of community service activities that were consuming surprisingly large chunks of time. He decided to cut out several that took time while providing little usefulness and satisfaction. He also decided that he could delegate a number of tasks at work.

Thus, Bill made available the time he needed to accomplish his goal. He was then able to schedule his church work: become a member of the Outreach Committee in the fall and the Finance Committee the next year; follow a reading schedule for the next six months; register in a course in religious history and a bible study retreat. Overall, Bill's plan encompassed a total of five years.

Bill concluded with, "If I do this, I'm going to feel a lot better about myself."

How well did Bill apply the seven steps of goal programming? (Refer to Figure 5.1.) To help you answer this question, fill in Exercise 6.1.

As you analyzed the facts in Bill's case, you probably saw that Bill applied all the basic elements of the goal-programming process.

1. Bill's goal was greater service to people. He wanted to focus on two elements of this, which became subgoals. First, he wanted to serve people through the programs of his church; second, he wanted to learn more about the teachings of the church and the worship of God.

2. The activities he chose to accomplish these goals had two thrusts: planning and administering the programs of the church, and spiritual enrichment. Specifically, Bill accepted two committee assignments—Finance and Outreach programs. He developed a religion study program and participated in worship activities. In deciding on these activities, he consulted with his minister, friends, and family. Their experience undoubtedly helped Bill design a workable plan of action.

3. For measurable results, Bill relied at first simply on the "doing"—that is, the actions of taking on committee assignments and engaging

EXERCISE 6.1   **Bill's Goal Programming**

What important personal goals did Bill have?

What key activities or tasks did he decide to undertake in order to achieve the goals you identi-fied above? He got some help on defining these tasks. From whom?

Key tasks/Activities   *Who advised him?*

Have the tasks been defined so that the outcomes are reasonably measurable? How?

Key tasks   *Measurable results*

Did he apply the test? Is this what he meant by the statement at the end of the case study?

Bill's test

What resource needs was he concerned about? How did he go about getting the important resources he needed?

Resource needs	How Bill secured them

What was the sequence and timing of some of the key tasks? What was the overall time frame of Bill's plan?

Sequence of tasks	Timing	Completion date

in educational activities. Later, however, he worked to better define results. For example, he made a detailed list of things he wanted to know more about, and checked these off to measure his learning progress as he read and attended retreats and workshops. He also kept a log of his religious experiences and the development of beliefs from which he could assess his progress in that direction. Finally, he set specific objectives for each committee assignment against which he could later evaluate his performance and contributions.

4. His test was, "If I do these activities, I'm going to feel a lot better about myself." It was expressed as an intrinsic feeling of accomplishment, a sense of well-being.

5. Bill's main resource need was time, which he had to free up from a busy schedule of business and community activities. He did this by keeping a time log and identifying some low-priority community activities that he could cut back, and tasks at work he could delegate. He took the steps necessary to acquire the key resource. A

small amount of money was also needed to undertake the educational program.

6. These activities had a logical sequence: initial committee assignments (Outreach Committee in the fall, Finance Committee next year) and educational programs (scheduled for the next six months) that would lead to a responsible position on the governing board and lay reader. His plans involved a total of five years.

ACTION PLANS

To help you develop action plans for your important goals, use an Action Plan worksheet. (See Appendix I, p. 243.) On the next page is the worksheet as Betty filled it in when she developed her action plan for opening a new office.

After you have looked at Betty's worksheet, turn again to the Goal Analysis worksheet in Appendix I (p. 242) and review the goal you analyzed and the key tasks you decided were required to achieve that goal. Then fill out your own Action Plan worksheet (Appendix I, p. 243) for that goal, following these guidelines:

1. Write the goal at the top of the worksheet.
2. Arrange the tasks in sequence leading to that goal down the left side.
3. Note any resources you will need—such as time, money, training, and other people—in the middle column.
4. Indicate realistic times for completing each of the tasks on the right side. Then determine a final completion date for the goal (bottom right corner). Think about the tasks involved and about some of the problems that might get in your way. Give yourself a little slack on that final completion date so that when something goes wrong, you have a little safety margin in which to make adjustments.

This goal-programming process and the Action Plan worksheet have been effective for many people. They helped Betty to be successful at her goal. They can help you break almost any large, tough task into manageable steps.

Use the Goal Analysis and Action Plan worksheets to program another goal. If these worksheets help you with the process of programming important goals, then photocopy them and use them often. If you

A-Priority Goal:

1. Open a new office in Johnson
2. Provide a needed service in that city
3. Earn a satisfactory return on my investment—20 percent or better before taxes

ACTION PLAN

Key performance tasks or activities (must be done to achieve the goal)	*Resources needed* (money, people, time, etc.)	*Time frame:* Date I expect to begin: ________
		Completion dates:
1. Market study: Obtain a list of businesses, design survey, conduct survey, analyze results	List from Chamber of Commerce Survey cost: $1,200	3 months
2. Prepare a cash-flow budget: Determine cash needs, set repayment schedule		4th month
3. Secure loan from bank: Determine size of loan and collateral needed	$27,000 estimated need	4th month
4. Hire manager: Talk to agencies, run ads		5th month
5. Rent an office: Study alternative locations	May need 3 months advance rent	5th month
6. Solicit initial business: Organize direct mail, advertising, personal calls	Initial budget $3,600	6th and 7th months
7. Hire temporary personnel: Contact agencies, run ads	Initial salaries $6,400	6th and 7th months
8. Work with manager to develop business	2 days per week	Months 6–12
9. Office shows a profit		By 15th month
10. Repay loan		Months 18–24
11.	Total $ needs about $27,000, but borrow $30,000	
12.		
Date I expect to achieve my goal: ________		18–24 months

Time Line

feel some modification would work better, then design one of your own and make duplicate copies.

I personally like to keep these worksheets in a looseleaf notebook along with my time logs, list of goals, and daily planning guides. I keep this notebook in a handy place on my desk where I can refer to it often.

Now let's examine a detailed case study to get a good overall view of the goal-programming process. We meet Chet Craig again, a plant manager of a large printing operation, who is concerned about his goal of being a more effective plant manager. Following the case description, we will analyze Chet's time problems and explore how he might best reach this goal.

CASE STUDY

Chet Craig, Plant Manager of the Norris Printing Company

Chet Craig was in good spirits as he swung his car out of the townhouse complex parking lot at 7:30 on a Monday morning. The drive to the Norris plant, just outside Midvale city limits, took about 20 minutes, and Chet liked to use his driving time to think about plant problems without interruptions.

Chet was satisfied with the course his career was taking. He had joined the Norris Printing Company right out of Ohio State, as an expediter. The company owned and operated three quality printing plants and enjoyed a nationwide commercial business, specializing in color work. Chet had started out at the Newark plant, the smallest of the three. After three years, he had been promoted to production supervisor, and two years later he became assistant manager at the Newark plant.

A year and a half ago, he had moved to the central plant, where the company had its main offices, to fill in for the plant manager who had been seriously injured in an auto accident. Six months later, he had taken over as plant manager because the other man was unable to resume his duties. (The organization chart for Chet's company is shown on page 108.)

Neither of Chet's parents had graduated from high school. His father still worked on an assembly line, as he had for 35 years. Chet had decided early that he wanted a better life for himself and that education and hard work was the way to get it. He was nicknamed "Grind" in high school, but the grinding had paid off—he earned a full scholarship to college. His nickname stuck during college. He didn't go in for sports or dating or much recreation of any kind. Work was still the consuming interest of Chet's life, though now he was married and he and Cheryl had a daughter and a son.

Chet figured that there would be time enough later to travel and read books and get involved with the life of the community, but for now he just wanted to stay on top of his job.

"This is going to be the day to really get things done," he thought to himself as he pulled onto the Interstate. He began to run through the day's work, trying to establish priorities. After a couple of minutes he decided that the just-in-time scheduling was probably the most important. On Friday, his boss, the Manufacturing vice president, had casually asked him if he had given the project any thought, and Chet had admitted that he hadn't. He had been meaning to get to work on this idea for four months, but something else always seemed to crop up.

Norris Printing Company
Organization Chart

President

- Vice Pres. Human Resources
- Vice Pres. Engineering: Janet
- Vice Pres. Manufacturing
- Vice Pres. Sales
- Controller-Treasurer

Vice Pres. Manufacturing

- Central Plant Mgr.: Chet Craig
- Memphis Plant Manager

Newark Plant Mgr.: James Quince

- Office Manager (Marilyn)
- Routing Supervisor
- Composing Room Supervisor
- Stereotyping Supervisor
- Layout Supervisor
- Folding Room Supervisor
- Stockroom Supervisor (Al Noren)
- Shipping Room Supervisor
- Receiving Room Supervisor
- Press Group I Supervisor
- Press Group II Supervisor
- Press Group III Supervisor
- Press Group IV Supervisor
- Press Group V Supervisor
- Press Group VI Supervisor

4 to 6 press operators in each group
2 to 3 press helpers in each group

Central Plant Mgr.: Chet Craig

- Folding Room Supervisor
- Layout Supervisor
- Press Group I Supervisor
- Press Group II Supervisor
- Press Group III Supervisor
- Press Group IV Supervisor
- Press Group V Supervisor
- Press Group VI Supervisor

4 to 6 press operators in each group
2 to 3 press helpers in each group

Night Supervisor

"I really haven't had time to sit down and work it out," he said to himself. "I'd better get going and hit this one today for sure." With that, he began to break down the objectives, procedures, and installation steps of the project, and roughly calculated the anticipated savings and improved customer service that would result.

Chet had first conceived of the idea just before leaving the Newark plant. His boss had agreed it was worth looking into, but the project had been temporarily shelved when Chet moved to the central plant. And the just-in-time scheduling was not the only project he had not had time to get started on. He started to think through a procedure for simpler transport and handling of dyes to and from the Newark plant. Visualizing the notes on his desk, he thought about the inventory analysis needed to identify and eliminate some of the slow-moving stock items; the packing controls, which needed revision; and the need to design a new special order form. He decided that this was the day to settle on a job printer to do the simple outside printing of office forms. Several quality control matters also needed attention. "Some of the procedures are too loose. Maybe we should consider Total Quality Management," Chet reflected. There were a few other projects he couldn't recall offhand, but he could tend to them after lunch, if not before. "Yes, sir," he said to himself, "this is the day to really get rolling."

As Chet walked into the plant, the first person he encountered was Al Noren, the stockroom supervisor. "Great day, Al," he said cheerfully.

"Not so good, Chet," Al growled back at him. "My new man isn't in this morning."

"Have you heard from him?" Chet asked.

"Not a word," said Al.

"These stock handlers seem to think that if they're not here we'll know they're not here and they don't have to call in," Chet said. "Better ask Human Resources to call him."

Al hesitated. "Okay, Chet, but can you find me someone? I have two cars to unload today."

"Let me call you in half an hour and let you know," said Chet.

Making a mental note to get back to Al, Chet headed for his office. He greeted the group of workers gathered around Marilyn, the office manager, who was discussing the day's schedule with them. As the group broke up, Marilyn picked up a few samples from a clipboard and asked Chet if they could be shipped that way or if it would be necessary to inspect them.

Before Chet could answer, Marilyn went on to ask if he could suggest another clerical operator for the sealing machine to replace the regular operator who was out sick. She also told him that Janet, the Engineering vice president, had called and was waiting to hear from Chet.

After telling Marilyn to go ahead and ship the samples, Chet made a note to get a substitute sealer operator and then called Janet. He agreed to stop by Janet's office before lunch and started on his morning tour of the plant.

He asked each supervisor the types and volumes of orders they were running, the number of people present, and how the schedules were coming along; helped the folding room supervisor find temporary storage space for consolidating a carload shipment; discussed quality control with a press operator who had been running poor work; arranged to transfer four people temporarily to different departments; and talked to the shipping supervisor about pickups and special orders to be delivered that day. As he continued through the plant, he saw to it that reserve stock was moved out of the forward stock area; talked to another press operator about his request for a change of vacation; had a heart-to-heart talk with an expediter who seemed to need frequent reassurance; and approved two type orders and one color order.

Returning to his office, Chet reviewed the production reports on the larger orders against his initial projections and found that the plant was running behind schedule. He called in the folding room supervisor, and together they went over the lineup of machines and made several changes.

During this discussion the composing room supervisor stopped in to cover several type changes, the routing supervisor telephoned for approval of a revised printing schedule, and a sales rep in Indiana called to ask for a price quote. Chet made a note to attend to this as soon as the folding room supervisor left, but the phone rang again and the stockroom supervisor told him that two standard, fast-moving stock items were dangerously low. He called back five minutes later to advise Chet that the paper stock for the urgent Dillon job had finally arrived. Chet made several calls to notify other people of these developments.

He then put delivery dates on important and difficult inquiries received from customers and salespeople. (Marilyn handled the routine inquiries.) He was interrupted twice—once by a sales correspondent from the West Coast asking for a better delivery date than had been scheduled, and once by the training director asking him to set a time for a training and induction interview with a new employee.

When he had finished dating inquiries, Chet walked down the hall for his mid-morning conference in the executive offices. At this meeting, he answered the sales manager's questions on "hot orders," complaints, the status of large, volume orders, and potential new orders. Chet remembered that he hadn't gotten back to the salesperson in Indiana yet.

He then met with his boss to discuss a few ticklish policy matters and to answer his questions on several specific production and personnel problems. Before leaving the executive suite, he stopped at the office of the controller-treasurer to inquire about a delivery of cartons, paper, and boxes, and to place new orders for paper.

On the way back to his own office, Chet stopped to confer with Janet on two current engineering projects which had called about earlier. When he reached his desk, he looked at his watch. It was ten minutes before lunch—just time to make a few notes of details he needed to check to answer the sales manager's questions.

After a quick lunch at a drive-in across the street from the plant, Chet started again. He began by checking the previous day's production reports; did some rescheduling to get out urgent orders; placed appropriate delivery dates on new orders and inquiries received that morning; consulted with a supervisor on a personal problem; and spent 20 minutes at the Fax machine going over some mutual problems with the Newark plant manager.

By mid-afternoon Chet had made another tour of the plant, stopping again to check with several supervisors and press operators. Most of these people had been at the plant for years and were very dependable, but Chet liked to keep tabs on every detail. He was ultimately responsible for their work, and he wasn't going to have any slipups if he could possibly prevent them. After his tour, Chet met with the Human Resources manager to review a personal problem raised by one of the clerical workers, the vacation schedules submitted by the supervisor, and the pending job evaluation program. Then he hurried back to his office to complete the special statistical report for the Universal Waxing Co., one of Norris' best customers.

The report reminded him of the price request from the salesperson in Indiana. He looked at the clock; it was almost six, probably too late to reach the person. Chet dialed the number and got to talk only with the answering machine. He was furious with himself. He had quite possibly lost a big order. Now his stomach started to punish him. He felt the sharp pain that signaled another gastritis attack. His doctor had told him six weeks ago that death and taxes were no more certain than ulcers for Chet if

The Action Plan   **111**

he didn't stop pushing himself so hard, but Chet figured, "What does she know about industry?"

As he turned out his office light and went down the hall, Chet noticed that he was the last person in the office. On the way out of the building, he was stopped by the night supervisor for approval of type and layout changes. When Chet finally got to his car, he realized that he had not remembered to get a stock handler for Al Noren. He was tired and his stomach hurt and he was disappointed with himself.

He thought back over the day and tried to figure out why there hadn't been a minute to get started on the projects he had planned so optimistically in the morning. He knew he hadn't wasted any time. Everything he had done that day was something that had to be done. And today had been a typical day. There was no reason to think that there would be any more time available for what he considered real executive work tomorrow.

"Executive work! Am I an executive? I'm paid like one, respected like one, and have a responsible assignment with the necessary authority to carry it out. Yet, the greatest value a company derives from an executive is his creative thinking and accomplishments. What have I done about it? An executive needs some time for thinking."

Chet continued, "Night work? Yes, occasionally. That's understood. But I've been doing too much of it lately. I owe my family some time, too. When you come down to it, they are the people I'm really working for. And what about volunteer work—and my stomach? When do I get time to do something about these things? Maybe I need an assistant, but as tight as our budget is, we can't afford one."

"There must be a solution, but I don't know what it is," Chet thought, as he took one hand off the wheel to reach in his pocket for an antacid tablet.

Questions

First, let's analyze Chet's time management problems. We have discussed time logs and time robbers. Test your skills by answering the following questions.

1. What were the plans that Chet made as he rode to work?

2. Were these plans important?

3. Could they realistically be accomplished in a day?

4. What kinds of interruptions during the day kept Chet from accomplishing his plans?

5. What has been Chet's career path through the Norris Company? Trace it.

6. Apparently he did a good job to have been promoted so rapidly. Is he doing a good job now? Is he promotable? What has changed?

7. What time management problem areas does Chet need to concentrate on?

8. What do you see as a general approach for Chet to work out of his problems and become more effective as a plant manager and executive?

Discussion

1. Chet started the day planning a series of creative projects: just-in-time scheduling, dye transport system, inventory analysis, packing controls, design of new order form, deciding on a job printer, and quality control.
2. Yes, they are important. Some, such as the just-in-time scheduling, are more important than others. Some, such as the inventory analysis, could be delegated. All are the types of projects that can contribute to the long-term growth and prosperity of the business. Every job has some high-value projects such as these. The good manager is one who can visualize what they are and get them done.

3. These projects could not possibly be accomplished in a day. Many hours of work are involved: priorities need to be set, and plans and schedules should be worked out for their accomplishment.

4. The projects were not accomplished because day-to-day problems, interruptions, crises, and routine tasks claimed Chet's attention: phone interruptions, people interruptions, self-imposed interruptions, and too much involvement in routine tasks.

5. Chet has advanced rapidly in the company, being recently appointed plant manager after serving as an expediter, production supervisor, and assistant plant manager.

6. In his previous positions Chet was concerned with short-term delivery problems and day-to-day operations, jobs he apparently did well. But for the chief operating manager different tasks become increasingly important: development of the organization and people; new ideas, concepts, and systems, such as the just-in-time scheduling system; and allocating sufficient time for making large equipment acquisitions.

   Chet has not recognized the changed nature of his new assignment. As management responsibilities increase, the nature of the work changes. The "doing" skills—such as bookkeeping, writing, computer programming, and selling—become less important. The management skills of working through people (delegation, communication, motivation), conceiving of new products, and instituting new control systems become increasingly more important.

   The result? Chet is performing ineffectively as a plant manager. In some respects, he is an example of the Peter Principle*: he has been promoted to his level of incompetence.

7. Chet ends up with more than he can do and not enough time in which to do it—a time management problem, or specifically, several of them.

   He has too many people reporting to him; that is, his organization is too flat.

   He is not delegating effectively. He may or may not have people who are presently properly trained to carry out delegated tasks—we can't tell from the description.

---

*A concept developed by Laurence J. Peter and Raymond Hull in their book *The Peter Principle* (New York: Morrow, 1969).

He is too involved in routine tasks, and is too accessible to others (e.g., two plant tours a day).

He needs to formalize plans in writing, with time schedules and deadlines.

He has little sense of relative priorities among decisions and tasks.

8. Chet Craig is a line manager with considerable responsibility—a plant full of expensive printing equipment and 350 employees. Effective management of these resources requires many tough decisions involving costs, quality, schedules, personnel, and equipment acquisition. You can't do it alone, but must work through others. This, in turn, requires effective organization, delegation, communication, training, planning, priority setting, and follow-up. These are the general skills Chet must develop if he is to become an effective manager.

Analyzing Chet's Goals

Chet is frustrated by his inability to be a more effective manager. We have examined his problems, their causes, and some general approaches to a solution.

Let's see how we might assist Chet in analyzing his goals and developing an action plan that will help him achieve them.

Suppose Chet goes home, has his usual vodka tonic and his favorite dinner (fried chicken, a big salad, and strawberry pie), helps his son with his homework, and then, while his wife is putting the children to bed, sits down to watch Monday night football. It's still 20 minutes before kickoff. He sits back and thinks once more about his time problems. He reaches for the phone and calls you for advice and help. You decide that what Chet needs is some "goal programming."

Phase 1: Chet's Goals

The first step is to write down his important goals. What are Chet's goals? What facts in the case support your views? (Write your answers in the space provided in Exercise 6.2 before continuing to the discussion that follows).

Chet talks quite specifically about job goals. He says clearly that he thinks a good manager (an executive) must accomplish creative projects and not just keep up the daily routine. Presumably, these projects would enhance his plant's efficiency, productivity, cost savings, growth, and

EXERCISE 6.2   **Chet's Goals**

Job

Family

Community

Personal

ultimately profits. The organization chart shows a president and several vice presidents. Chet is a plant manager and, along with the other plant managers, reports to the vice president of Manufacturing. If Chet achieves his goal of being an executive, a logical result would be an eventual promotion to vice president of Manufacturing, supervising all three plants. This, therefore, would be a reasonable long-term objective depending on when that position might open up.

Chet also has some family objectives. He says, "Night work? Yes, occasionally. That's understood. But I've been doing too much of it lately. I owe my wife and kids some time, too. When you come down to it, they are the people I'm really working for."

Chet expresses concern for his family and a desire to spend more time with them. This goal is in conflict with the time demands he feels for his job. Most busy managers experience this conflict. In Chet's case, the family appears to come off second best. If Chet can learn to manage his work time better, then he will have more time to allocate to this family. Of course, family goals involve more than just spending time. Chet will need to develop more specific objectives for his family life.

Chet also mentions volunteer work, a community-type goal. He is frustrated by job demands that infringe on that activity.

Finally, Chet expresses concern for his aching stomach—his health. He needs to set a personal goal of physical fitness. Getting his job under control can help this in two ways. Becoming better organized and more effective at work will undoubtedly relieve some of the tension that's aggravating his stomach. It will also free up time to eat properly, get enough relaxed sleep, and some exercise.

Phase 2: How Should Chet Accomplish His Job Goal?

Using the Goal Analysis worksheet in Appendix I, describe the general method or strategy you would recommend for accomplishing his goal. Assume that Chet filled in the first section. His A-priority goal is: "To be an effective manager. To reach executive status eventually and supervise several printing operations. To achieve promotion to vice president of Manufacturing." What are the most important long-range activities? Do this before proceeding to the discussion that follows.

Chet's most critical problems relate to poor organization; if he focuses on that area, the other tasks may fall into place. A reorganization has two elements: (1) restructuring assignments and responsibilities, and (2) developing personnel and their capabilities. Since Chet's budget won't allow adding expenses, he should follow the strategy of developing people from within the organization rather than bringing them in from the outside, which might be faster but more costly. Therefore, a two-phase plan seems in order: an initial restructuring of key assignments, and then a gradual expansion to restructure the entire organization. Particularly important is the development of an assistant, if Chet is to free himself from so many day-to-day details and to spend large blocks of time on creative projects—and to get himself into position for a promotion to vice president of Manufacturing.

As Chet delegates more of the daily routine, however, he will need good follow-up and control. Follow-up is an important step in the delegation process, as we will see in Chapter 9. Therefore, Chet must develop a system to help his subordinates plan the tasks he delegates and a regular follow-up procedure to assure that the implementation is going according to the objectives and plans.

Phase 3: Tasks Involved in Accomplishing Chet's Job Goals

In the Goal Analysis worksheet, write down the key tasks Chet must accomplish to get to his job goal, giving reasons for their importance. Then go on to the discussion that follows.

These are some key tasks that should appear on Chet's worksheet. Your action plan for Chet may differ somewhat in detail.

1. *Restructure the organization.* Even though Chet has no budget for additional people at this time, he can restructure his staff to provide another layer of management on the day shift, such as a general supervisor of the press operations and an administrative support person to take over some of the tasks in human resources, scheduling, production, quality control, and purchasing that Chet is now performing himself. In the longer term, he may want to add an assistant plant manager or empower the existing people in their present positions.
2. *Management development.* Since most of the supervisors were probably originally operators, and few of them seem to be capable of decision making without consultation, Chet will have to carefully select and develop people who have supervisory potential.
3. *Develop job assignments and procedures.* All of the procedures emanate from one source, Chet Craig. If the plant is to operate without total reliance on him, then job assignments and procedures

must be formalized in a manual and delegated to the managers he has selected. (See Chapter 9 on delegation.)

4. *Initiate staff meetings.* Rather than handling every problem one at a time, a number of plant problems could be covered with all the appropriate personnel at one time through periodic staff meetings, such as a 15-minute meeting over coffee each morning. (See Chapter 10 on conducting effective meetings.)

5. *Delegate routine tasks.* Chet should decide what routine tasks he can assign and empower other people to do. Some tasks he can assign now; others will have to wait until he develops personnel able to handle them. (See Chapter 9 for more on delegation.)

6. *Develop a habit of daily planning.* Although Chet does some planning on the way to work in the morning, it remains in his head. He needs to commit to a plan in writing each day on a regular basis. (See Chapter 7 for a description of daily planning techniques and planning guides.)

7. *Develop operational controls.* As Chet proceeds with the delegation process, he will increasingly require controls and feedback to know when problems arise.

8. *Establish short- and medium-range planning.* Once the organization begins to function without Chet's minute-by-minute involvement, he should have the time to plan general operations better to avoid some of the crises and to plan special or "creative" projects, such as the just-in-time scheduling and Total Quality Management (TQM) programs.

9. *Perfect the delegation process.* By (1) assigning day-to-day operating responsibility to an assistant, and (2) an MBO (management by objectives) system for all managers and supervisors.

10. *Concentrate on long-range planning and creative project work.*

Phase 4: Measurable Results

In the Goal Analysis worksheet, indicate what measurable results we might look for to evaluate whether the key tasks have been successfully performed. Then apply the test: If the key tasks are performed with the desired results, will we be able to say that the goal has been accomplished?

GOAL ANALYSIS

A-priority goal: To be an effective manager of a printing plant. To reach executive status eventually and be able to supervise several printing organizations. Promotion to vice president of Manufacturing

General approach: Concentrate priorities on reorganization; do it in two phases—restructuring then expansion; must involve evaluation of personnel, job descriptions, and manpower development programs. Longer-range priorities on planning and control systems.

Key tasks:	Measurable results:
1. Restructure organization	1. Boss's approval of restructuring plan
2. Management development programs	2. Boss's approval of management development plan
3. Develop job assignments and procedures	3. A formal written manual
4. Initiate staff meetings	4. Reduce interruptions and crises—evaluate _____% efficiency and _____% effectiveness of meetings
5. Delegate routine tasks	5. Measure against my checklist of key steps in the delegation process
6. Develop habit of daily planning	6. Once a week review of time management problems/progress
7. Develop operational controls	7. Daily, weekly, and monthly control reports successfully initiated
8. Establish short- and medium-range planning	8. Weekly, monthly, and annual planning procedures and reports initiated
9. Perfect delegation process	9. MBO (management by objectives) evaluations
10. Concentrate on long-range planning and creative projects.	10. Develop a specific plan—deadline 6 months.

Test: If the key tasks are completed with the indicated results, would most people agree that the goal has been achieved?

Yes ___✓___   No _____

Are you sure?   Why not? What's the problem?

My own MBO will contain targets on productivity, growth, profits, quality, etc.—objectives that relate to being a good plant manager. To accomplish those objectives will require a good organization and time to plan and initiate creative projects. Thus, I believe the tasks lead to the desired goal.

After you fill in the measurable results, compare your completed worksheet with the model on the next page.

Phase 5: Action Plan

Using the Action Plan worksheet in Appendix I (p. 243), put the tasks that we have described into an appropriate sequence. Add details or break large tasks into subtasks as necessary. What resources will Chet require? Approximate any dollar amounts. Estimate the amount of time Chet is likely to require to accomplish the various tasks. How long before Chet becomes an "executive"? This is an action plan, so it needs to be as realistic and as detailed as possible.

Complete this exercise and then read on for the discussion of Chet's completed Action Plan.

Chet's approach to the resource needs was to phase them so that the benefits did not lag too far behind the expenditures. Usually, when budgets are under pressure and there are a lot of things to do, the only practical course of action is to spend a little on step 1, get some results, go on to step 2, get more results, and so forth. The programs must be phased in one step at a time rather than several being attempted at once. Obviously, this takes longer, but often it's the only way. Sometimes as we demonstrate positive results, people's confidence builds up, and approvals for larger expenditures may be forthcoming.

Chet felt that to achieve this plan would require a minimum of three years. Both optimistic and pessimistic time schedules are often helpful to provide some latitude. Because of the overall length of the total plan, however, it is vital to establish a number of milestone dates along the way.

Chet's Action Plan is shown on the next page.

A Final Practice Run

You must develop good habits if you are serious about achieving important personal goals, but it takes practice. While your action planning skills are fresh from working with Chet Craig's example, try developing an action plan for one of your A-priority goals. From your list of goals on the Goals worksheet, pick out another A-priority goal, and follow through the seven-step goal-programming process. Make copies of the worksheets in Appendix I if you need them.

Good luck!

A-Priority Goal:
To be an effective manager of a printing plant. To reach executive status eventually and be able to supervise several printing operations. Promotion to vice president of Manufacturing

ACTION PLAN

Key performance tasks or activities (must be done to achieve the goal)	*Resources needed* (money, people, time, etc.)	*Time frame:* Date I expect to begin: Now
		Completion dates:
1. Restructure the organization; plan how to fill spots; get approval from boss	3 days of my time	By end of 1st month
2. Initiate staff meetings: short one in early a.m.; general meeting once a week		By end of 1st month
3. Evaluate personnel; select potential supervisors; delegate expanded responsibilities	10 days, help from Marilyn and Human Resources	By end of 2nd month
4. Develop job assignments and procedures	More time, assistance from Human Resources and Engineering	Month 3
5. Begin management development program for potential supervisors	$12,500—squeeze from current budget	By end of 3rd month
6. Develop better time management techniques: daily schedules; develop team effectiveness—attend seminar	$240 for seminar	Time Line: By end of 6 months
7. Develop operational controls; get feedback on problems; evaluate new supervisors and delegation process	Help from Human Resources and Engineering	Months 6–14
8. Establish short- and medium-range planning: better operational planning; special projects (A-priority)		Months 6–12
9. Select most promising potential supervisors: undertake expanded management development program; delegate expanded responsibilities	Request $36,000 in next year's budget	Months 12–24
10. Select assistant; begin transferring day-to-day responsibilities	Need to add this position, need justification	By end of 24th month
11. Perfect delegation process: MBO system for managers; management control system	Retain a consultant—$1,800/mo.	Months 24–36
12. Concentrate on long-range planning and creative projects. Take a vacation!		Months 24–36
Date I expect to achieve my goal: ________		3–4 years

SUMMARY

Once you have finished your goal programming, you will be ready for the nuts and bolts of time management. You have identified the key tasks that need to be accomplished and set milestone dates. These then become the high or A priorities in your daily schedule, and you can set specific deadlines. Although you will confront other lower-priority tasks, many of which have to be done as part of your job, you can return promptly to the A-priority tasks whenever you have discretionary time. These daily planning steps will be discussed in more detail in later chapters.

7 Planning Guides and Daily Schedules

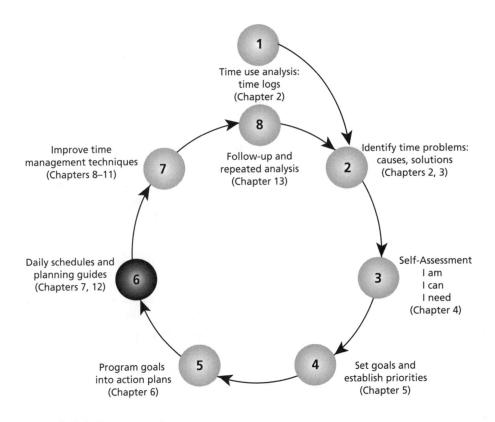

1 — Time use analysis: time logs (Chapter 2)

2 — Identify time problems: causes, solutions (Chapters 2, 3)

3 — Self-Assessment I am I can I need (Chapter 4)

4 — Set goals and establish priorities (Chapter 5)

5 — Program goals into action plans (Chapter 6)

6 — Daily schedules and planning guides (Chapters 7, 12)

7 — Improve time management techniques (Chapters 8–11)

8 — Follow-up and repeated analysis (Chapter 13)

So far in the book, you have analyzed your time management problems using a time log and have identified your important goals. In Chapter 6, you programmed an A-priority goal: You described the key tasks, arranged them in an orderly sequence, estimated resource needs, and set milestone dates for accomplishing these tasks.

In this chapter, we will develop a process of daily planning that will assist you in completing (1) tasks to achieve your top-priority goals, and (2) day-to-day tasks to fulfill your job, home, family, and other personal obligations. Daily scheduling is essential for accomplishing both kinds of tasks. A haphazard approach to daily activities usually results in overemphasis on the daily maintenance tasks because they have greater urgency: We must talk to the customers, go to the staff meetings, and take Jimmy to band rehearsal. Tasks toward top-priority goals, however, are all too easy to put off, because they tend to be longer-range and less urgent. Take Floyd, for example.

> Floyd decided that he wanted to find a better job in the next eight months. He figured that he would have to put together a list of companies he might want to work for, get the names of people to contact in those companies, revise his résumé, and so on. Each of the tasks that would move him toward his goal was relatively simple and not distasteful. But week after week went by, and Floyd took none of those steps. A month after he had written down his goal, he was no closer to its accomplishment.
>
> Before he drifted off to sleep at night, or in the car on the way to work, Floyd would tell himself, "Today I must dig my résumé out of the files and look it over," or "I'd better get hold of the annual report of the XYZ Company tomorrow and read it." But each day his working hours would fill up with seemingly more pressing things to do, and Floyd never got around to his job-hunting activities.

Trying to fit a new and important project into his already busy schedule, Floyd needed to have his job-hunting tasks literally staring him in the face each day. That's why you need to develop a system of short-range planning and daily scheduling, in written form for instant review so you do not miss tasks. Such planning guides should be used regularly, becoming a daily habit.

The short-term planning and scheduling process involves two important steps:

First, you take what one person described as an "airplane view" of where you want to go during the next several days or weeks.

Second, you use some form of daily planning guide to get down to the hour-to-hour scheduling we all need to be effective time managers.

Planning guides can take a variety of forms. The most common include:

Appointment calendars

To-do lists

Weekly planning guides

Salesperson's planning guides

Homemaker's planning guides

Trip plans

Whatever planning guides you adopt should match your particular situation—the requirements of your job, your family situation, your behavior patterns. The planning guide I use to schedule my time during the fall semester at the business school is obviously inappropriate for a salesperson, homemaker, or manager of a large manufacturing plant.

Various planning guides are described and illustrated in this chapter. Whatever you use, however, the critical point is to *get one that works for you, and use it regularly.* We are familiar, of course, with the various printed forms of calendars, such as "Day Timers," as well as the electronic calculator and computer-based ones. There is much computer software available to assist us. Some of us like to have little appointment books on a computer monitor, others prefer a homemade form. But I repeat, what you use is not crucial, as long as you are comfortable with it and use it regularly. Appendix III contains information on calendar and computer software that are available to aid in scheduling time.

PRIORITIES MAY BE THE MOST IMPORTANT ASPECT OF TIME MANAGEMENT

We can classify things to do into two categories:

• Urgent

• Important

	A Priority IMPORTANT (to us)	
	Highly important	Of little importance
Of crisis proportions	*AX Priorities* (Important and urgent)	*X Priorities* (Urgent, but not so important)

Little urgency	*A Priorities*
	
	(Very important but
	  can be deferred)
		C Priorities
		
		(Avoid doing
		  neither important
		  nor urgent)

X Priority
URGENT

Without planning and control, the *urgent* will drown out the *important*. Consider the above matrix, which relates the urgent to the important in a system of priorities.

The Matter of Priorities

If there is one message I would like to convey to my readers, it is the crucial nature of priorities in becoming effective managers of time. There is not time to do everything. We should spend our time doing the things that are important to us. Therefore, it is essential that we commit to a system of priorities. The system illustrated in the matrix just given is the one I suggest. It separates tasks according to their importance and their urgency. It is a system of A's, X's, and C's.

- A priorities are things that are important to us. They relate to our important goals.

- X priorities are things that are urgent. They are required by our work, something our boss demands, or other people's A's.

- C priorities are neither urgent nor important and should be avoided, if possible.

This priority system is a little different from the usual ABC. (Note: Some people like to retain the use of B priorities as denoting something of medium importance.) To me, an A priority is something that has importance to me. You should plan adequate time to do it, and do it right. In my priority system, an X priority signifies an urgent task—the X stands for crisis.

Thus, a task that falls in the upper left quadrant of the matrix is an AX priority because it is both urgent and important. For example:

> The annual planning meetings of the Premier Office Machinery company are coming up in six weeks. Rae has been asked to present a proposal for expanding the company's line of copy machines. Rae is currently a project manager in the new products section and aspires to taking over the department when the vice president retires in two years. Six weeks is barely enough time in which to put together a sound proposal. Rae clears away other things to do and designates the copier proposal as AX.

AX priorities are things most of us have little trouble getting done. They are important and they are urgent—like Rae's proposal for an expanded line of copiers. Serious procrastinators may find excuses to delay, with disastrous results. These tasks are often tough, unstructured problems that require creative juices, and they can be tough to get started doing. For most people the urgency forces us into action.

The A priorities frequently pose the real problems. They are important but not urgent. They are easy to put off. These are the objects of our procrastination. Take the following example:

> Kimberly is an assistant professor at State University. She knows she must have several articles accepted for publication in top journals in her field if she is to be granted tenture. But three years have passed with little progress made toward her publication goals. Kimberly fills her days with students, class preparations, and committee work.

X priorities, of course, tend to get done:

> The key supplier calls and says he won't ship the materials Jim needs to keep the production line operating unless he has a written purchase order. Jim drops everything to Fax a handwritten purchase order to the supplier.

The important thing to remember about X priorities is that they may be urgent, but they often don't add much value. Therefore, don't spend much time on them. When it comes to X priorities, resist being a perfectionist. Do them quickly, get them out of the way, and get on with an A priority.

Finally come the C priorities, things that are neither important nor urgent. Try to avoid doing them at all. Give them a waiting period. Put them in a C drawer. After a few days, throw them away. Do them only if they become urgent or important. Remember Pareto's Law: 80 percent of the things in life have low value; the other 20 percent have 80 percent of the value.

Most people spend too much time doing X's and C's. They are easy, quick, something that can be checked off our to-do list, and they give us a *temporary* feeling of accomplishment. And we can justify doing an X because it is demanding.

Eighty percent of everything in life is an X or a C. But neither has much value, so it doesn't follow that you should spend 80 percent of your time on them. Rather, the opposite should be true—spend only as much time as they deserve. Do X's quickly—avoid C's. Use the freed-up time to work on your A's.

Apply the system of priorities given in the matrix on page 126. It is easy to accomplish and will have big payoffs. Resolve something else: try never to work overtime on X's and C's. Surely, you have something better to do! Finally, you cannot eliminate all of your X's. They are an important part of your job, of maintaining your families and homes. You have to allocate sufficient time to do them, flexible time. But you can shorten them and organize them better. Set an objective for yourself. Reduce the time spent on X's and C's by one hour a day. Use that hour to work on an A priority. For most of us, this is a very doable objective. And think what you could do with an extra 365 hours this year to work on A's!

As you fill in your daily calendar, allow time for your X's—those urgent conferences, memos, letters, and phone calls that are a big part of your job. Having kept and analyzed your time log, you know, for instance, that the weekly staff meeting usually runs about an hour and a half; that returning six phone calls takes more than half an hour; that in the course of a day you usually have two hours of crises and expediting to do with getting rush orders out and rearranging shipping schedules.

Don't overschedule and thereby frustrate yourself, as so many people do. Leave yourself plenty of flexible time—unscheduled blocks of time during which you are free to take care of crises and respond to interruptions, phone calls, and questions from subordinates. If you have a break in this kind of activity, have an A-priority task handy that you can turn to.

Most people cannot schedule more than half of their time. The rest must be used for the day-to-day crises and interruptions. In some jobs, you probably cannot schedule more than an hour or two a day. Once you recognize how little time you actually can schedule and control, you place real importance on what happens in that small block.

QUALITY TIME: SCHEDULING AND THE INFLUENCE OF BIOCYCLES

We all have times when we are highly productive and other times when we can accomplish little. Some people work best in the morning, whereas others perk up in the afternoon. On certain days, such as the Monday morning after a weekend at the beach or the day after the Christmas party, it is impossible to get going.

The concept of biocycles, also called biorhythms, has been much discussed. These long-term cycles begin, presumably, the day we are born and continue throughout our lives. Research suggests a physical cycle of 23 days, an emotional cycle of 28 days, an intellectual cycle of 33 days, and an intuitive cycle of 40 days. Many people feel that plotting where you are on each of the cycles can help you predict your ability to do certain kinds of tasks on a given day. For example, coaches and odds-makers have attempted to do this with football players, with mixed results. The Japanese have worked extensively with biorhythms and believe strongly in their influence.

Although we may question some of these theories, we certainly have ample evidence of our own individual "ups and downs." In scheduling our time we should take into account our cycles and other factors that may affect our ability to perform long or difficult tasks. If your most productive time is first thing in the morning, try to schedule your A-priority tasks then. If you require a warm-up period before really getting into things at, say, 10 a.m., then schedule routine, pleasant tasks early, and the A-priority tasks at ten o'clock. If Monday mornings are a drag, schedule productive, but simple and pleasant tasks then, and wait until afternoon to attempt the difficult ones.

If you have a series of difficult tasks coming up next week, such as the annual forecast and budget plan, make sure you are physically and emotionally ready. Forget about the late evening of bridge and cocktails with friends. Get plenty of rest, regular meals, and some exercise. Cancel out on a meeting you're not much involved in anyway—or get someone else to go—to give yourself some breathing room.

If you're the kind of person who can go like crazy for awhile but then fades, don't schedule a tough renegotiation of a bank loan back to back with the evaluation of a problem employee. Give yourself a break in between—like lunch with a favorite customer. And please spend some quality time with your family. Don't just come home every night, tired and grumpy, and fall asleep in front of the TV. Your family needs quality time to take care of important relationships and family matters.

Many people become frustrated in carrying out their schedules because they have attempted to do the wrong things at the wrong times. There is no percentage in trying to beat your own biocycles!

TYPES OF PLANNING GUIDES

Calendars

Most of us have a calendar in some form—pinned to the wall or on our desk—in which we can schedule business meetings, doctors' appointments, exam dates, holidays, and the like. Many homemakers need only a calendar that shows the days of the month with enough room to write in Suzy's dental appointment, the first day of school, or the family's birth dates. Other people with heavy daily commitments require a day-calendar broken into 10- or 15-minute increments.

All of us need some form of calendar to keep track of important dates and meeting times and to get an "airplane view" of our time ahead. I personally need a day calendar to keep track of specific times and details, as well as an annual calendar by month to get the longer view.

Using the perforated 12-month calendar in Appendix I (pp. 261–266), fill in the important commitments you face over the next several months. In my own case as an educator, these include:

1. Key dates in the university calendar, such as school opening and closing, holidays, exam schedules, faculty meetings, meeting dates of committees I'm serving on
2. My class schedule for the coming semester
3. Outside seminars I'm committed to
4. Professional meetings I plan to attend such as the Case Research Association and the International Council for Small Business annual meeting
5. Commitments to community activities, such as the meeting dates of the City/County Utility Commission
6. Important birthdays to remember

7. A long weekend of golf
8. A block of several mornings to work on an information survey to present at one of the professional meetings
9. Two other blocks of time to do case research on valuation of a small electronics firm for acquisition purposes, and write an article on predictors of failure in the screen print industry
10. A block of time to develop a new course in management control involving field trips

To-Do Lists

Almost everyone realizes the value of to-do lists, and probably most people have used this type of list when faced with an unusual or complex project. For instance, a woman planning her daughter's wedding will rely on written reminders to arrange for a photographer, reserve the church, send out invitations, schedule fittings, order flowers, meet with the caterer, and so on.

Anyone who has used such a list knows that it works. You see what you have to do, and you cross off each item as it is accomplished. When you have a lot of things to do, you can save yourself time and energy by writing them down rather than relying on your memory. You will make better use of your time if you make a to-do list, not just for your extraordinarily busy days, but for every day.

Time management expert Alan Lakein* says that most people in business "know about" to-do lists, but lower-level employees and less successful managers tend not to use them, whereas very successful people invariably rely on them.

You can make your to-do list in the evening, or early in the morning, or at both times. One effective approach is to make your list at night and then add to it in the morning after you have looked at your in-basket and as some of the events of the day unfold. Be sure to indicate the priority (A, X, C) of items on your list. Do the A's first and carefully question the necessity of the C's.

Weekly Planning Guides

A weekly plan is an extremely valuable tool in time management, yet very few people use it systematically. Many of us will glance at our calendars for the week ahead and jot down a few notes, when we can benefit from a more thorough approach.

---

*See Lakein, *How to Get Control of Your Time and Your Life* (New York: Peter H. Wyden, 1973).

A weekly planning guide should contain the following elements.

Key activities such as A- and X-priority phone calls, meetings, luncheons, written reports, correspondence, and other important tasks. Don't bother putting down the C's—they'll take care of themselves.

Key projects: A-priority projects of a medium- and long-term nature. This will provide a basis for assessing how the project is progressing, what changes need to be made, and the key tasks that are coming up in the week ahead.

Key persons: In Chapter 3, we discussed our "team" (subordinates, secretary, boss, others). At the beginning of each week, we should look at the important assignments the team is working on and reevaluate the priorities of each. This makes a good subject for a Monday morning staff meeting with our boss or assistants.

The great advantage of the weekly planning guide is that you can combine all of your planning and scheduling for a whole week on one piece of paper. Space can be provided for updating key projects and key person assignments. Daily to-do lists and day calendars can be included for the whole week, providing a means for sorting out and scheduling key activities and appointments.

Formats for the weekly planning guide are shown in Appendix I (pp. 245–259). There are four different types that meet different needs:

Manager's weekly planning guide

Salesperson's weekly planning guide

Homemaker's weekly planning guide

Trip plan

I encourage you to photocopy the planning guide that applies to you, and to try it out. After experimentation, you may decide you need something a little different.

Weekly planning guides are flexible in design and use, and can be adapted to the varying needs of people. The guides can be relatively simple or modified to meet special needs, with additional headings, columns, and spaces. You can also include an analysis sheet for reviewing the week, identifying time problems, and measuring improvement. An analysis sheet is included with the planning guides provided in the Appendix I.

If need be, design your own planning guide, or look at what's available in the office supply stores. Refer to Appendix III for others that are available. But get one that works for you, and use it.

Let's look at some examples. On page 134, we will see how a manager's planning guide worked for Kathryn Lennox, whom we met in Chapter 2, on pages 21 to 26.

Kathryn requires a fair amount of flexibility in her schedule, since part of her job is responding to crises. Still, she needs blocks of time to plan and execute long-range projects. Kathryn decided that her most creative time was the morning, when she felt fresh, and when most people at the bank were too busy to bring her their problems. She needed afternoons for meetings, troubleshooting, interviews, and dealing with routine matters.

She scheduled the time from 9 to 11 on four days of the week for getting started on the employee manual and the TQM program. She left Thursday morning open to handle problems from the other days and to catch up on paperwork. She carefully planned this time so the morning wouldn't degenerate into just another firefighting marathon full of calls and interruptions.

Kathryn discussed these plans with Pat, Harold, and Jody, and they agreed to protect her from interruptions. Jody and Harold were so taken with the plan that they scheduled quiet hours for themselves twice a week to work on important projects and tasks. Kathryn agreed to cover for them at that time, if necessary.

Planning was a large part of Kathryn's job. If she took time to do that properly, she could organize work to be delegated to Jody, Harold, or Pat, and thereby "leverage" her time into even more productivity for Webber Bank. When she took time to plan the benefits manual, for example, she could then delegate to her assistants the actual writing of the first draft. She then planned to edit their work, and the manual would be ready for suggestions from others by the first of the next week. That is something that Kathryn could never have accomplished if she had tried to do all the work herself.

Kathryn took a few minutes on Sunday evening to make a first cut at her Planning Guide for the coming week, shown on the next page.

Weekly planning guides for salespeople can have enormous payoffs. Salespeople have a lot of flexibility in using their time, but unplanned time can turn out to be very unproductive. Recall, for example, the case study of David Siegel, pages 76 to 81. His weekly planning guide, including his sales plan for the first two days of the week, is shown on page 135.

MANAGER'S WEEKLY PLANNING GUIDE

Kathryn Lennox

To-Do List (indicate priorities)

WEEK OF: _____May 22, 19_____

Key activities

Key People	Key Projects	A-Priority Tasks	Writing	Meetings	Phone
Boss: Ken Ward / Get approval on TQM schedule	TQM program: develop plans and timetable	1. Outline employee manual 2. Assign tasks	Vacation memo		Donna / Dentist / Sylvia
Secretary: Pat / Budget materials	Employee manual: benefit section	Meeting with controller	Assign benefits sections to Jody and Harold	Jody / Harold / Controller	
Jody / Delegate part of benefits manual description	Benefits brochure	Schedule TQM			
Harold / 1. Schedule of costs and benefits 2. Analysis of exit interviews	Budget: Get approval on increase	Cover TQM with Ken Ward	1. Suggestions for Salvation Army 2. Personnel manual revision	1. Salvation ····Army board 2. Ken Ward	
Controller / Key meeting to discuss budget have proposals ready		Evening with Tom and kids			
Spouse: Tom 1. Schedule for week 2. New carpet for living room		Exercise tennis			

Schedule

Date	Morning	Afternoon	Evening
Mon. 22	7 Plan day assign tasks 8 9 Plan benefits brochure 10 11 Return calls	12 1 2 3 4	5 6 7 8 Work on benefits brochure 9
Tues. 23	7 8 Meet with Jody and Harold on benefits 9 manual rewrite 10 11	12 1 2 Meeting with controller 3 4	5 6 7 8 Symphony concert 9
Wed. 24	7 8 Plan TQM timetable 9 10 11 Return calls	12 Lunch with John Flagler 1 2 Dentist appointment 3 4	5 6 7 8 9
Thurs. 25	7 8 9 10 11 Return calls	12 Lunch meeting with Ken Ward discuss TQH timetable 1 2 3 Board Meeting Salvation Army 4	5 6 7 Dinner at Williams s 8 9
Fri. 26	7 8 9 Edit benefits revisions 10 from Jody and Harold 11 Return calls	12 Lunch with Sylvia Gray 1 2 3 4 Plan next week	5 6 Tom and kids dinner and movie 7 8 9
Sat. 27			Neighborhood covered dish supper
Sun. 28		Tennis Donna	

SALES PLANNING GUIDE

Call Plan   Schedule

David Siegel   WEEK OF: _June 19, 19____

Call Plan

Customer	Objective of Call	Priority	Route	Alternative	Expenses
1. Anchor Store	Get initial order	A*	45 mi.		Travel: 125 mi. @ $.25 = $31.25
2. Athletic Discount	Show line	B	15 mi.	Fines	Lodging: Great Northern—$68
3. Sam's Sportswear	Try for sample order	B	5 mi.		Meals: lunch $12.50
4. High Style	Due for a reorder	A	close	Herman's Clothing	dinner $26.75
5. Just Pants	Small order	B	10 mi.		Other: drinks $16.00
1. Country Store	Show line	C	close		Travel: 118 mi. @ $.25 = $29.50
2. Jeans Ltd.	Small order	C	close	Ragpicker	Meals: Breakfast $8.60
3. Casual Shops	Repeat order	B	15 mi.		Lunch $12.50
4. Shirt Shop	Should get huge order	A	10 mi.	Father-Son	Dinner $21.75
5. Robins	Show line	C	close		
6. Showroom	Small order	B	close		

Schedule

Date	Morning	Afternoon	Evening
Mon. 19	7 / 8 8:30 Anchor / 9 / 10 10:30 Athletic Discount / 11	12 12:15 lunch with Sam / 1 / 2 High Style / 3 / 4 4:30 Just Pants—Max	5 Have a drink with Max / 6 Drive to Mocksville—dinner on way / 7 / 8 Reservation at Great / 9 Northern—late arrival
Tues. 20	7 / 8 8:30 Country Store / 9 9:30 Jeans Ltd. / 10 / 11 Casual Shop	12 12:45 lunch—Shirt Shop / 1 / 2 / 3 Robins / 4 Showroom	5 Return home—dinner on way / 6 / 7 / 8 / 9
Wed. 21	7 / 8 / 9 / 10 / 11	12 / 1 / 2 / 3 / 4	5 / 6 / 7 / 8 / 9
Thurs. 22	7 / 8 / 9 / 10 / 11	12 / 1 / 2 / 3 / 4	5 / 6 / 7 / 8 / 9
Fri. 23	7 / 8 / 9 / 10 / 11	12 / 1 / 2 / 3 / 4	5 / 6 / 7 / 8 / 9
Sat. 24			
Sun. 25			

*Note: David liked to classify sales calls by the ABC system—A calls are of high sales value, B calls of medium value, and C calls of low value.

135

HOMEMAKER S PLANNING GUIDE

WEEK OF: January 10, 19____   **Schedule**

Sally Petrillo

Spouse/Children	Just for Me	Household Chores	Shopping	Driving	Day/Date	Morning	Afternoon	Evening
		Laundry in a.m.			Mon. 10	7 8 9 10 11	12 1 2 3 4	5 6 7 8 9
	Get Sunday School lesson plans together in afternoon		Shop for the week see grocery list	Nursery school, Bank, Post office, Shopping	Tues. 11	7 / 8 8:15 Nursery School carpool / 9 10 11	12 1 2 3 / 4 Basketball practice	5 6 7 8 9
Pizza Garden with Robert and kids		Sewing finish dress for party			Wed. 12	7 8 9 10 11	12 1 / 2 Symphony Guild meeting / 3 4	5 6 7 8 9
		Clean house		Pick Robbie up from practice	Thurs. 13	7 8 9 10 11	12 1 2 3 / 4 Basketball practice	5 6 7 8 9
Talk to Melissa about school after shopping	Tennis lesson		Clothes shopping with Melissa get my father a birthday present	Tennis lesson, Melissa school, Dentist, Shopping mall	Fri. 14	7 8 9 10 11	12 / 1 Tennis lesson / 2 3 / 4 3:30 dentist appointment	5 6 7 8 9
					Sat. 15		2:00 Robbie s basketball game	7:30 Dinner at Harris s
Talk to Robert about his working so hard					Sun. 16	9:30 Family service		

136

TRIP PLAN

Chet Craig   Business to be Transacted   WEEK OF: October 8, 19____   Schedule

Who to See	Purpose	Information Needs	Expenses	Date	Morning	Afternoon	Evening
			Travel: plane tickets $423.00 Lodging: Meals: Other:	Mon. 8	7 8 9 10 11	12 1 2 3 4	5 6 7 8 9
Newark Plant: Chuck Weaver	Quality problems	1. Quality report from J. P. Henning 2. Sample of off-quality work	Travel: drive to airport—18 mi. @.25 = $4.50 Lodging: Quality Motel—$82.30 Meals: snacks $3.60 Other: tips $12.00	Tues. 9	7 8 9 10 11	12 12:25 flight—United 318 1 Afternoon in Newark 2 plant: quality problems 3 4	5 Dinner with Chuck Weaver (Newark plant mgr.) and J.P. Henning (quality control mgr.) 6 7 8 9
(1) Bond Company (2) Niagara Corp.	Get order Go over color, tone and quality Go over pricing Explain late shipments Go over new schedule	Bond Co. file: quotation and sample on new job Niagara Corp. file: new shipment schedule	Travel: rental car $68.75 Drive home $4.50 Lodging: Meals: 3 total $53.70 Drinks-tips: $25.50	Wed. 10	7 8 8:12 flight to Rochester—US Air 597 9 10 Meeting and lunch with Bill Reid, Bond Co. 11	12 1 Rent a car and drive to Buffalo 2 3 4 Meeting and drink with Sam Parks, Niagara Corp.	5 6 7 7:55 flight home—American 818 8 9
				Thurs. 11	7 8 9 10 11	12 1 2 3 4	5 6 7 8 9
				Fri. 12	7 8 9 10 11	12 1 2 3 4	5 6 7 8 9
				Sat.			
				Sun.			

Like salespeople, homemakers often have considerable flexibility in their schedules, and all too often they fail to commit themselves to a specific plan. They tend to jump from task to task as impulse and crises dictate. Family crises are inevitable, but tangible benefits can be derived from some basic planning. An example of a homemaker's plan for Sally Petrillo (from pp. 86–92) is shown on page 136. Sally has entered some items for the current week.

Business people often lament the time they spend traveling to meetings, conferences, negotiations, sales calls, and so on. On occasion a business person might travel all day for a 1-hour meeting—a great expenditure of time, energy, and travel dollars.

To make the most of your travel time, plan your trip time even more carefully than your time in the office. On page 137 is a trip plan that Chet Craig made the day he went to the eastern plant to help out with some quality control problems. On the way, he also made two calls on key customers.

Working with the weekly planning guide of your choice for a few minutes on Sunday afternoon or early Monday morning will help you get your whole week organized. The half hour of planning at the beginning of each week may be the most valuable time you spend all week. You will be able to schedule your A-priority tasks in high-energy time, when you will have a good chance of protecting yourself from interruptions. Go over the plan with your family or staff early in the week—it's a simple and effective means of communication.

As the week progresses, update your planning guide to reorder priorities, add tasks, and reschedule key activities. Working with your basic plan will tend to keep you on track.

Your Own Custom-Designed Time Management System

You have studied and learned how to use the following key worksheets in the time management process.

The time log

Goals worksheet

Goal Analysis worksheet

Action Plan worksheet

A 12-month calendar

Planning guides

To-do lists

Experiment with the ones that apply to your situation. If you find a form that works for you, photocopy it and use it regularly. If a form needs modification, design and print it yourself.

Once you've found the right forms for you, make photocopies of them and put them in a small looseleaf binder. Keep the notebook in a handy place at home or work, wherever you would use it most frequently. If you keep the notebook at work, but would like to plan the coming week at home Sunday evening, the looseleaf form allows you to remove the planning guides for the coming week and take them home over the weekend. If you prefer, a similar system can be developed for your personal computer.

Similarly, keeping priorities and schedules visible can be important. The looseleaf form lets you remove your to-do list and daily calendar so that you can put them on your bulletin board. Then, when the phone suddenly stops ringing and you have some discretionary time, you can refer immediately to an A-priority task instead of neatening your desk or taking a coffee break.

THE IMPORTANCE OF HABIT

Unlike keeping a time log, which is an occasional thing, daily planning should become as much a habit as brushing your teeth. Develop a system that works for you, and use it every day. The purpose of daily planning is to unclutter your desk and your mind, to allow you to see what you have done and what remains to be done, and to ensure that you get the most important things done without forgetting smaller but important tasks. Daily planning is one of your strongest allies in getting control over your time rather than letting events and people and crises control you. Daily planning is the bridge between what you want to do and the time you have to do it.

SUMMARY

In this chapter, you have learned some of the techniques of daily scheduling. In the next four chapters, we will focus on the main time robbers we all must contend with, to find ways to minimize these time robbers in order to maximize the amount of time we have under our control.

8 Controlling Interruptions, Crises, and Routine Paperwork

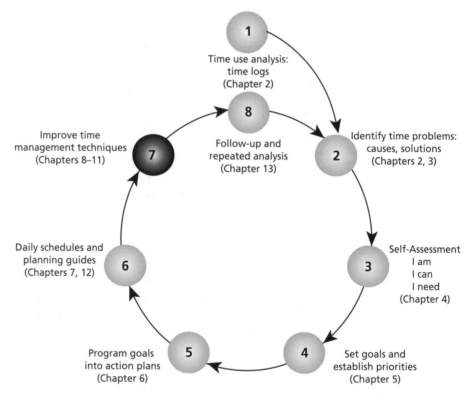

1. Time use analysis: time logs (Chapter 2)
2. Identify time problems: causes, solutions (Chapters 2, 3)
3. Self-Assessment I am I can I need (Chapter 4)
4. Set goals and establish priorities (Chapter 5)
5. Program goals into action plans (Chapter 6)
6. Daily schedules and planning guides (Chapters 7, 12)
7. Improve time management techniques (Chapters 8–11)
8. Follow-up and repeated analysis (Chapter 13)

There are two extremely useful questions that can help you manage your time:

What is the best use of my time right now?*

---

*From the videotape "Time of Your Life," written by Alan Lakien and produced by Cally Curtis Co., Hollywood, Calif.

Is there something I'm not doing that I will eventually say . . . "I wish I had?"*

Time robbers keep you from doing the "wish I had's."

High on almost everyone's list of time robbers are interruptions. Phone calls, drop-in visitors, unscheduled meetings, crises, mail, noise, and self-imposed interruptions can eat up hours every day. When you're solving a difficult problem or making progress on an important project, you resent these intrusions, even though you realize they can't be totally eliminated.

Although the telephone might be such a nuisance that you sometimes want to rip it out of the wall, it is also a tremendous timesaver. Imagine what it would be like to have to write a letter or drive across town or fly across the country each time you needed to communicate with someone. Whether you are a homemaker or a company president, you undoubtedly rely heavily on the phone for giving and getting information. The Fax machine is another source of interruptions, because we tend to view Fax messages with some urgency. On the other hand, if you want to send or receive information immediately without the delay, the Fax is an invaluable tool.

Nor would you want to cut out all drop-in visits. You need to be accessible to your boss, subordinates, and colleagues. You can't afford to be isolated from the people you need to work with.

So your goal is not to eliminate all interruptions but to control them. Again, a system of priorities can help you accomplish this. A-priority interruptions have high value, are urgent, and cannot (or should not) be deferred. For example, you've been waiting two days for your best customer to call back about a very large order; he finally calls during your weekly staff meeting. Should you take that interruption? Probably. Or the school calls to report that your daughter has broken her leg in a gymnastics workout. Obviously, you will put aside whatever you are doing to handle that emergency.

But few interruptions are of the "I *must* handle it now" type. Whatever their importance to the interrupter, most interruptions are medium- (X) or low- (C) value, at least to you. Most can be deferred, at least temporarily; some can be delegated to someone else. Some, like much of the routine paperwork that comes across our desks, needs no handling at all.

---

*From the videotape "Taking Control of Your Work Day," by Dick Lohr.

The key to controlling interruptions lies in handling the medium- and low-value ones.

Shorten the time spent on X and C priorities, keeping the time spent in balance with their value.

Defer them temporarily to make room for a "quiet hour"—time you have blocked out to handle an A-priority project.

Eliminate some X- and C-priority interruptions by handling them more efficiently, by delegating them, or by deferring them indefinitely.

For example, if the phone call involves a routine question, get to the point and end it in a couple of minutes. Accumulate routine calls or reports and handle them all at one time. Don't spend more time on them than they deserve. Don't be a perfectionist in handling routine, low-priority items. Answer a memo from the sales department asking about a routine shipment with a note in the margin—not a perfectly worded letter that ties up you and your secretary for a full hour. In this chapter, we'll explore various ways to control interruptions.

THE NEED FOR ANALYSIS

As we discussed in Chapter 2, people tend to blame external factors—other people and things—for wasted time, until they accurately analyze their time use. Analysis usually shows that many of those external causes are really our own fault.

For example, we sometimes *look* for interruptions because we are procrastinating about doing a tough or unpleasant job, as Kathryn Lennox did (in Chapter 2). Kathryn took a full hour for a coffee break and talked to three people about personal trivia, office gripes, and chances of promotion. These interruptions were self-imposed and nonessential—and they took up an hour that Kathryn could have used to work on an A-priority project such as the TQM system.

If interruptions, crises, and routine paperwork are a major problem for you, the first step toward controlling them is to find out more about them. Make a log of your phone calls and drop-in visitors. Keep a record of whom you talked with, the purpose and what was accomplished, and how long it took. Then put a priority on the interruptions in terms of the value. The maldistribution rule says that only 20 percent of the interruptions will be high-value; the other 80 percent will be low- or medium-value.*

In Appendix I (pp. 267–271) are five worksheets titled "Analyzing Interruptions," to be used for the following types of interruptions.

Phone calls

Drop-in visitors

Unscheduled meetings

Other causes (crises, noise, visual distractions, and self-imposed interruptions)

Routine paperwork

These worksheets will help you analyze your own interruptions. Make copies of the worksheets and keep them with you. Make a log of interruptions for a day to start with. Later, you may find you need more data and you can keep the log for a longer period.

Before you begin to analyze ways to shorten or eliminate your interruptions, let's look at how Kathryn Lennox set about analyzing hers.

Kathryn knew Friday was always a busy day for phone calls and drop-in visitor interruptions. Everyone seemed to want to get the end-of-the-week business cleaned up. She logged the interruptions for a typical Friday.

Kathryn took her log home over the weekend. Saturday afternoon was rainy, so, while Tom took the kids to a movie, she analyzed the log. She found some interesting things:

I had 20 phone call and drop-in visitor interruptions, for a total elapsed time of 247 minutes—over four hours, about twelve minutes each! No wonder I didn't get to work on any big projects. Along with the meetings, the interviews, and the paperwork, my day's time is gone.

---

*Usually credited to the nineteenth-century Italian economist Vilfredo Pareto. The Pareto principle states that the significant or important items in a group usually comprise a relatively small number of the total items.

ANALYZING INTERRUPTIONS

Phone Calls and Drop-in Visitors

Priority	Who	Purpose/Accomplishment	Elapsed time	Ways to shorten or eliminate
X	Ken Ward	Question about budget	10 min.	
X	Joyce Hicks	Question about maternity benefits	8 min.	
C	Ross Perry	Perry Employment Agency, recommending employee	14 min.	
X	Harold	Question about benefits manual	15 min.	
C	Pat	Wants to leave early for dental appointment	3 min.	
X	Ken Ward	Asked about cost of the employee benefits brochure	10 min.	
C	Ross Perry	Another employee—wanted to discuss over lunch—NO!	7 min.	
C	Ken Ward	Asked about distribution of employee benefits brochure	11 min.	
A	Sam Cox	Long discussion on TQM—he's an expert—lots of good advice	28 min.	
X	Jody	Forgot to ask at meeting earlier. Can we go to top of pay scale for new systems analyst—tough decision	9 min.	
X	Controller	Bugging me again about answer to his memo on my budget variances	15 min.	
X	Ken Ward	Discussed poor performance of several salespeople	22 min.	
A	Vice Pres., Production	Wants to meet to plan employee needs for expansion move	5 min.	
C	Cecil Hardy	Dropped in again to pass time of day—real time-waster!	15 min.	
X	Penny Morgan	Husband gave her list of questions about the life insurance	20 min.	
C	Melissa	Wants me to pick up a notebook, chatted about her school day	10 min.	
X	Rhoda F.	Insurance question—how much extra for private room	4 min.	
C	Ken Ward	Wanted to know the maximum pay scale for his secretary	7 min.	
C	Tom	What time will I be home for dinner, talked about problems he is having at work	18 min.	
C	Controller	Asked about one of my budget variances	16 min.	
		Total Time	247 minutes	

Only two of the twenty interruptions were A-priority. Of the many medium-value ones, only a few were really urgent and couldn't be put off for a while. Nine were low-value C priorities.

Ways to shorten or eliminate:

1. Five calls from Ken Ward. Try to find a time to meet with him once a day to exchange questions and information.
2. Three calls on employee benefits. Refer to Harold and Jody, since I've already delegated most of the writing of the manual to them.
3. Ross Perry and Cecil Hardy. Be tougher on getting rid of them, at least on busy days.
4. A- and C-priority calls just take too long. Keep a clock visible and see if I can't hold them to five minutes in most cases.
5. Stop procrastinating about analyzing the budget variances. It cost me thirty-one minutes getting bugged by the controller.

Run a log on myself again in thirty days to see what progress I've made.

You'll find many ways to shorten or eliminate interruptions, crises, and paperwork. Remember, they won't go away; they're part of everyone's job to a greater or lesser extent.* But we can control them. Start by analyzing your own interruptions. The discussion that follows should provide you with additional ideas for handling the specific varieties of interruptions.

Controlling Phone Interruptions

You will spend less time on the phone if you plan to make all your important calls at one time. Get all the phone numbers together, note the subjects you need to discuss, and have on your desk any files or correspondence or background information that you are likely to need. Dial the numbers yourself—having your secretary place all your calls is often a waste of time for both of you and doesn't impress anyone. After you hang up, note what you discussed and decided during the call, and include the date. Keep these records and reminders handy for as long as they are needed, perhaps as a permanent part of your files. If a memo or written confirmation is needed, write or dictate it immediately while the call is fresh in your mind.

---

*For an interesting training film on control of interruptions and crises, look at the film *A Perfectly Normal Day,* written by Alan Lakein and produced by Cally Curtis Co., Hollywood, Calif.

For some people, the length of phone calls is as much a problem as the number of calls. In the next few days, check to see if you are spending too much time in small talk. Tape-recording your end of the phone call can be a good way of checking on this—on how you sound. Your job and the nature of your relationship with the people you talk with on the phone may dictate a certain amount of chit-chat. But if you find you have spent five or ten minutes rehashing the Monday night football game with six different customers, you're wasting time.

If the problem seems to be not you but the gabby guy on the other end of the line, supply yourself with a set of phrases that will get the conversation back on the track. Here are a few ways to get to the point:

"Here's what I called about."

"Can we do that?"

"I've got a long distance call coming in that I've been waiting for, but can we agree quickly to do thus and so?"

"I've got an appointment in a few minutes, and I'm going to have to run."

You can make the most of the time blocked out for A-priority tasks if you have your phone calls intercepted during this period. While you steam ahead on an important task, your secretary or receptionist or the company switchboard operator can take your calls. If possible, the person taking the calls should take a message and find out when the caller will be in to accept your return call. That person should be alerted to your priorities if you are expecting any important calls for which you would want to be interrupted; and, of course, you would have to rely on that person's judgment about what constitutes an emergency call situation.

If you work alone, without a secretary, then voice mail, an answering service, or an answering machine with a recorded message can serve this function. These arrangements are also useful for times when you are with clients or away from the office. If you use voice mail or an answering machine, you can word the recorded message to ask for the caller's name and number and other pertinent information so that you can return the call. If you are on the road a lot, a cellular phone will enable you to keep in touch and make callbacks and other important phone calls.

Many executives establish a definite period during each day when they don't accept phone calls and a definite period for making and receiving calls. This system has distinct advantages. If your secretary always says, "Mr. Q. will be available between eleven and twelve," people who frequently call you will get the idea that it's pointless to keep calling at 9:30. During the period you have established as your phone time, you would make all your callbacks and answer your own phone when it rings. It may take some time, but regular callers will learn that they can get through to you quickly and directly if they call between 11 and 12.

Controlling Interruptions from Drop-in Visitors

Controlling interruptions from drop-in visitors is often a matter of making some changes in your physical environment. If you have a private office, the first step would be not taking the phrase "open door policy" too literally.

Although you may want to be accessible to the people who work for you and with you, you don't want them to interrupt you every time they pass your office. Close your door when you need to concentrate. To most people, a closed door means "Do Not Disturb." Here again, there is value in having a regular period each day when you choose not to be interrupted. Your regular drop-ins will get the idea that dropping by at that time is not acceptable. Remember, by closing your door sometimes you are not cutting off your availability, you are simply limiting it.

A desk facing the door is an open invitation to be interrupted. A handy side chair is an invitation to sit down and chat. Rearranging the desk so that your back or side is toward the door will help you avoid eye contact, which will in turn reduce interruptions. A briefcase in the chair discourages squatters, unless you remove it and invite someone to sit down. If you must meet with a long-winded person, don't invite him or her to your office—go see them. That way you can go about your business and leave.

If you find that you are constantly interrupted by subordinates with questions on minor details and decisions, your problem may go deeper than interruptions. This kind of pattern suggests poor delegation, which we will discuss in Chapter 9.

If you work in a room with several people and have no door to close, the interruptions may come not so much from drop-in visitors as from "socializing" with fellow workers. In this "open landscape" situation, people need to have even greater respect for one another's privacy and time. In some such offices and departments a "quiet hour" is established, during which time employees agree not to interrupt one another or disturb others by talking. You could try pushing for that policy where you work. You might also be able to modify your physical environment by using partitions, by placing shelves or file cabinets or other dividers in front of or beside your desk, or by turning your chair to face the wall instead of facing someone else. When you really need a quiet time for concentrated effort, you may need to find a hideaway. This could be the library or an unused office or conference room. The objective of all these tactics is the same—to limit your availability.

If people have become accustomed to barging in during your working time, it will take some firmness on your part to change the situation. You may have allowed interruptions to get out of hand for a variety of reasons (e.g., you don't like offending people, you love to be involved in everything that goes on in the office, it makes you feel important to be consulted often, you aren't very good at terminating visits, you have required your employees to check everything with you, or you just like talking). If your time log shows that you are killing time with a lot of little visits, you must make it clear that you no longer welcome interruptions. Develop several comments to alert your drop-ins to the new state of affairs, such as:

> "I'm up against a deadline now. Can we discuss this at coffee break?"

> "I'm right in the middle of a report now. This sounds like something you can handle, but if you run into some trouble, I will be available after lunch."

> "I'm working on a presentation for a meeting this morning. Why don't you jot down your thoughts on that and bring it up at the staff conference on Wednesday."

> "I'd like to hear more about that, but I can't spare the time now. Let's have lunch together Friday."

There are times when we must say "no." You don't have to say it nastily. Say no gracefully. Give the person an option, but later.

If you have a secretary to screen visitors as well as phone calls, be sure to clarify what your priorities are, which people you would be willing to see at almost any time, and how you want unwelcome drop-ins handled. If possible, have your secretary find out when you can call the visitor or return the visit.

Your secretary can also help out when a visitor has stayed too long—for example, by prearrangement coming in after 10 minutes and saying, "Your meeting begins in five minutes," or "Your three o'clock appointment is waiting," or something that will tactfully let your visitor know that his or her time is up.

Controlling Interruptions at Home

Interruptions are often a problem for people who are trying to get work done at home and have friends and neighbors with time to spare. The homemaker who needs to get all the housework done in the morning in order to go to accounting class in the afternoon, the freelance writer, the woodworker with a shop in the garage—all need to communicate their seriousness about their work to friends and neighbors who are prone to long phone calls and leisurely visits. Too few people have cultivated the courteous habit of calling before coming over or of beginning their telephone conversations with, "Is this a convenient time for you?" If you don't want to be at the mercy of unwelcome callers, you have to tell them:

> "Mondays are a bad time for me, Joan. I need to spend all morning cleaning because I volunteer at the hospital every Monday afternoon."

> "Could I call you back this afternoon, Cathy? Mornings are when I always work on my book."

> "I'd love to ask you to come in, John, but I'm studying for an exam now. Evenings and weekends are really better times for me now that I'm back in school."

Some people take the phone off the hook or just let the phone and doorbell ring. But, because there are emergencies and legitimate reasons for which you would want to be interrupted, you probably don't want to be that unavailable. An answering machine can be a good answer.

If you feel that you are a victim of every long-winded, lonely, or bored soul you know, it helps to recognize that you have played a part in your victimization. These folks don't bother people whom they perceive to be too busy to interrupt, so interruptions are not so "external" as they first appear to be. To control such interruptions, let people know that you value your time—let them know when you are available and when you are not. There are many ways to control interruptions, if you are willing to work at it, view a videotape,* read an article, or talk ideas over with others in similar situations. But don't just make excuses like "My job is different; I can't control my interruptions."

CRISIS MANAGEMENT

"If anything can go wrong, it will." Do you find yourself invoking that Murphy's Law very often? If so, you probably listed crisis management or "firefighting" as one of your major time robbers.

Like interruptions, crises can't be entirely eliminated, but they can be controlled. Think about the crises you have been dealing with lately, and see if you can classify them. Do they seem to revolve around a particular person or people? Do they have to do with one particular project or task? Is equipment failure or deadline pressure the villain?

When you know where the problem is, you can anticipate break-downs and failures and take some preventive action. Look at the following example.

> Jeff was the editor of the in-house newsletter of a large company. It seemed to him that the few days each month before the newsletter was printed were always chaotic, with one crisis after another. Invariably, a few last-minute important stories had to be put in, and Jeff and his two assistants often worked until midnight the night before they took the paper to the printer.
>
> When Jeff analyzed his problem, however, he realized that these last-minute items could be anticipated. So he planned to use the first three weeks of the month more effectively—laying out certain pages, making sure all of the features and promotion announcements and so forth were written and measured well in advance of the deadline. That took most of the pressure off the last few days of the month, and he and his two assistants were able to do a thorough, more relaxed job on the late stories.

Expect the unexpected—expect that the computer will be down occasionally, the report will contain some errors, or that Marie will be

---

*A recently published videotape is "Controlling Interruptions," written by Verne Harnish.

out sick some days—and think about what you will do in those events. Don't overschedule yourself; leave some time for the inevitable crises. Plan better to prevent crises and develop some contingency plans. Remember, some problems turn into crises because we keep putting them off. If you know that preparing the budget is going to be more difficult this year because of new tax legislation, don't wait until the last minute to start working on it. If you know your new assistant is moving along slowly on a project because he is just learning the job, follow a timetable of reviewing and evaluating his performance to avoid a zero-hour disaster.

CONTROLLING PAPERWORK AND THE MESSY DESK

This one is very personal. Some people function very effectively in the midst of chaos—we all know someone whose desk looks like a disaster area but who somehow knows exactly where everything is. At the other extreme, some people are too organized and spend huge chunks of time color-coding, alphabetizing, and cross-filing every memo that comes their way. If shuffling paper and hunting for things is one of your time robbers, you probably don't need new skills as much as new habits.

A good beginning is to handle each piece of paper only once after it has been sorted (by you or your secretary). You can write an answer on the bottom of a letter, or quickly dictate a reply, or pick up the phone and handle it that way. Throw away as much as you can, and, if you can't bear to throw it away, do as Alan Lakein* says: Stick it in a special drawer called the "C" drawer, for low-priority items that will probably disappear if you don't do anything about them. Keep the paper moving. Don't let it pile up so that you have to wade through a whole stack to find what you need for that day. Rather than keeping reports and memos and reminders on top of your desk, use your weekly and daily plan sheet to record things you need to remember.

Develop a procedure for organizing your desk and processing paperwork that fits your needs, and stick to it. As an example of handling paperwork, let's return to Martha Wagoner, our school principal. (We'll look at a full case study of Martha's time management problems in

---

*Another film by Lakein—"The Time of Your Life," produced by Cally Curtis Co., Hollywood, Calif.

Chapter 11.)

Being in a large educational system, Martha seemed to be constantly flooded with all sorts of paperwork—E-mail from the schoolwide network, letters from parents, reports and memos, direct mail promotions, and reference materials.

Martha logged the paperwork that came across her desk for a couple of days. Her list of ways to shorten or eliminate paperwork handling was as follows.

Train my secretary to sort my mail into three categories:

1. E-mail, letters, and memos that are high-value and urgent. I will allocate one hour to this "A-priority" folder each morning—10 to 11 a.m.
2. "Need to know" memos and reports—not urgent but should review. Hold for my attention late in the day or one evening in front of TV.
3. "Junk mail"—to be skimmed and most discarded by my secretary.

Background reading—articles on new educational methods, books, etc. Ask the librarian to screen journals, magazines, and book lists and forward interesting-looking material. Spend a couple of late afternoons or dinner times skimming.

Have my secretary set up a tickler file to collect parent letters, interdepartmental memos, and any other materials that need to be followed up on key dates, e.g., parent visitation days, teacher/administrator work days.

Treat paperwork with the same hard-nosed priority system you apply to other time robbers.

READING SPEED

Slow reading speed is a problem for some people, especially those who have to read very technical material—the slow reading speed required for such material often becomes the speed at which they read everything from the newspaper to the cereal box. If this is the case for you, or you are becoming bogged down in your paperwork and required reading because your speed is slow, the best bet might be a speed reading course.

Many people can get control of this time waster, however, by being more discriminating about what they read. For example, you may decide that you need to read a newspaper or news magazine for general information, business or professional journals to keep abreast of developments in your field, and a number of reference books related to your work. But you don't need to read them all the same way. You can scan the headlines of the newspaper for 15 minutes each morning, reading very few articles in full, or you may decide to skip the daily paper and spend a leisurely hour or two catching up on the week's news in the Sunday paper or a news magazine. You can look through the table of contents of your professional journal and choose one or two articles. Look at the subheadings and summaries and decide whether you want to read the whole article. The maldistribution principle applies here, too—most of the printed material that passes before your eyes is not going to be of great value to you. So be selective.

SUMMARY

Once, in a seminar with a group of administrators from a federal agency, the subject of controlling interruptions came up. One member announced, "None of that will work in this agency—we're different." Needless to say, a lively argument ensued and other group members came up with a number of ways in which interruptions really *could* be controlled—even in that agency.

Don't be defeated by a self-fulfilling prophecy that your interruptions can't be controlled. To control interruptions, you must analyze and reanalyze the causes—and then apply some common sense and a positive attitude. Appendix III contains additional helpful resources on controlling interruptions.

In the next chapter, we will take a look at another major time robber—ineffective delegation.

9 **Effective Delegation**

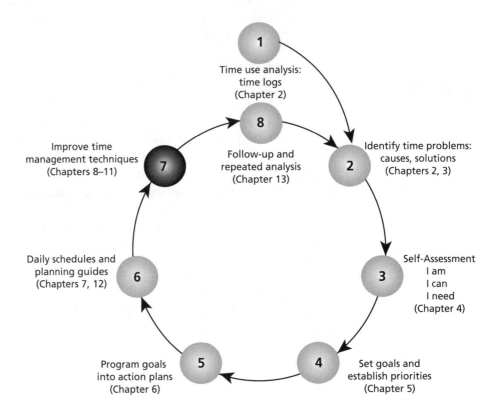

1 — Time use analysis: time logs (Chapter 2)

2 — Identify time problems: causes, solutions (Chapters 2, 3)

3 — Self-Assessment I am I can I need (Chapter 4)

4 — Set goals and establish priorities (Chapter 5)

5 — Program goals into action plans (Chapter 6)

6 — Daily schedules and planning guides (Chapters 7, 12)

7 — Improve time management techniques (Chapters 8–11)

8 — Follow-up and repeated analysis (Chapter 13)

Remember Chet Craig, the overworked plant manager who wondered whether he was really an executive? As you recall, Chet started out as an expediter and moved up to assistant plant manager. When he was promoted to plant manager, he took his old responsibilities upstairs with him, failing to delegate any authority to his subordinates. As a result,

Chet was botching up not only the management of the plant, but also his chances for the promotion he wanted, because no one was being trained to move into his job.

In this book, we are treating delegation as a time management technique, but failure to delegate can have more serious consequences than wasted time, as Chet's case shows.

Many managers balk at the idea that delegating is a solution to some of their problems, quite often because they don't understand what delegation means. Delegation is implicit in the most commonly accepted definition of management: getting things done through people. Delegation doesn't mean abdicating one's responsibility, or assigning detailed tasks, or parceling out work while retaining authority. In a more formal sense, to delegate is *to achieve specified results by empowering and motivating others to accomplish some of the results for which you are ultimately accountable.*

Some managers say their jobs don't permit delegation. If you're tempted to say that, ask yourself these questions about particular tasks in your job.

	Yes	No
1. Is there someone who can do the task better than I can? Am I really taking advantage of the expertise and experience of my people?	____	____
2. Is there someone who can do the task instead of me, even though it may take him or her longer to get it done?	____	____
3. Is there someone who can do the task with less expense than I can?	____	____
4. Is there someone who can do the task with better timing than I can, like right now?	____	____
5. Is this task one that could contribute to the training and development of one of my people?	____	____

You can probably answer an honest "yes" to some of these questions. That means some of the work you are doing yourself could be done by others.

The real reasons for failing to delegate are often psychological. Consider the following examples. They may illustrate a reason for your inability to delegate.

Andy has recently been hired as executive director of the county arts council, after getting a master's degree in arts administration. He is 24 years old and overwhelmed with his new responsibility. His three key subordinates are all older than he and have several years experience with the organization. Andy is afraid they will find out that he doesn't know as much about their jobs as they do, so he doesn't ask for their suggestions or pass on work to them. Instead, he immerses himself in details, isolates himself from his staff, and loses the perspective that he was hired to provide.

Miranda, an extremely sharp copyeditor for a book publisher, was promoted to the position of supervisor. Miranda is a perfectionist, a good quality in a copyeditor. As a supervisor, though, she feels she cannot trust any of her subordinates to be as accurate as she is. She spends all her time hovering over them, criticizing them, and double-checking their work.

Gene runs a large customer service department. He is proud to have 22 people reporting to him and wants to make sure he gets credit for everything that is done in his department. He insists on signing every letter that goes out to customers, although this practice causes daily bottlenecks and leads to serious morale problems. His subordinates, knowing they can never get credit for a job well done, are not motivated to do the job well.

Barry is the city editor of a newspaper. His new assistant, Claudia, is bright and competent. At first, Barry was relieved, but as he saw how quickly Claudia learned, he became anxious. If he is on the phone or away from his desk and one of the reporters asks Claudia for a decision, he becomes jealous and usually finds a way to criticize her decisions or to undermine them by giving orders counter to what Claudia authorized.

PRINCIPLES OF DELEGATION

Many managers want to delegate but don't know how. It helps to think of delegation, not as a one-way street, but as a contract in which two parties come to an agreement. When responsibility is delegated, the manager and the subordinate should agree on the following:

> The scope of the job
> Specific results to be achieved
> A time schedule
> The authority needed to carry out the job
> A way of measuring performance

Although organization charts and job descriptions are often described as aids to delegation, in practice, they are often useless. They don't refer to the *results* expected of an employee, nor do they take into account changing priorities in the work. And, worst of all, they don't address the unique qualities the individual brings to a task.

Following is a list* of the principles of delegation that may help you improve your delegating skill.

1. Select the right person. Choose someone who is capable of doing the task, and give that person the accountability and authority to do it.
2. Delegate the good and the bad. If you just give others your dirty work and tiresome chores, you will block their motivation, commitment, and development. Delegate interesting, rewarding, and challenging projects, too.
3. Take your time. Your subordinate will need time, maybe a year or more, to acquire the training and expertise to handle all that you might want.
4. Delegate gradually. If you have been underdelegating, don't try to transfer all responsibility overnight. If your subordinate is new to the job, don't expect him or her immediately to assume the same amount of responsibility as others on the same level who have been with you longer.
5. Delegate in advance. Try not to wait for a problem to develop before delegating a task.
6. Delegate the whole. When it is possible, delegate a complete project or action to one person rather than giving away just one piece of the action. This will give your subordinate control and coordination, and cut down on confusion and errors.
7. Delegate for specific results. Instead of describing to your subordinate the scope of the job, describe the specific results you expect.
8. Avoid gaps and overlaps. A gap is a job for which no one has been assigned responsibility. An overlap is when two or more people have responsibility for the same job.
9. Consult before you delegate. Delegation flows both ways. Let your subordinates participate in determining what is delegated to them.
10. Leave the subordinate alone. Once the delegation has been made, let George do it. From now on, George makes the day-to-day decisions, he gets the headaches, and he has free rein to use his own resourcefulness. Don't pester him.

*Reprinted, by permission of the publisher, from *No-Nonsense Delegation,* by Dale McConkey, pp. 80–89. © 1974 by AMACOM, a division of American Management Associations. All rights reserved.

Although we tend to think of delegation in terms of business, it is equally applicable to homemakers, volunteer workers, and anyone who has responsibility for a job or project that involves more than one person.

CASE STUDY Ben, a lawyer, was widowed in his late 30s. The responsibility for keeping house became solely his when his wife died. Ben hired someone to come in to clean one day a week, which helped some, but he found that most of his evenings and weekends were taken up with marketing, laundry, cooking, running errands, and washing dishes. Lisa, his 15-year-old daughter, had been used to setting the table and helping with the dishes, and Ted, his 13-year-old son, took care of feeding the dog and mowing the lawn. Both children were supposed to keep their rooms straightened up. Ben quickly realized that he couldn't and shouldn't assume the burden of all the other housework. Both children were willing to help more, but had little experience in doing housework.

With their agreement, Ben decided gradually to delegate grocery shopping and meal preparation to Lisa, and laundry and kitchen clean-up to Ted. In making these decisions, Ben considered his children's ages, their schedules, their limitations—such as being too young to drive. It was a simple matter to teach Ted to operate the washing machine and dryer, but the boy tended to leave things until the last minute, and Ben sometimes thought it would be simpler to do the whole job himself. But he didn't, and he knew that, in the long run, learning responsibility would be valuable for Ted. Also, delegating some of the work would give Ben the time he needed for relaxation and recreation and for doing some pleasant things with the children. Lisa was more mature and reliable, but needed help in learning to cook and shop. Ben arranged for a neighbor to help Lisa with meal planning and preparation, and was good-natured about her occasional burnt offerings and uncoordinated dinners, just as he had been when his wife was learning to cook. He praised his children when they did their work well and was patient when they made mistakes.

Let's see how Ben rates as a delegator.

1. Is his planning realistic?

   Yes. Ben knows it will take some time before his children learn to do their jobs as well or as quickly as he can perform these tasks. And when he decided which tasks to delegate, *he took into consideration each child's capability and limitations.*

2. Does he control his children too much?

   No. Ben made it clear to Lisa and Ted that the responsibility for certain household matters was now theirs. He doesn't remind Ted to clear the table and wash the dishes each night, and he doesn't ask Lisa every morning if she has remembered to pack the school lunches. Knowing that the children understand what they are responsible for, and have the means of carrying out their jobs, Ben doesn't have to keep checking on them. *He trusts them.*

3. Does he ignore his role as supervisor by undercontrol?
   No. Ben doesn't just drop all responsibility in his children's laps. He makes sure they get the training they need to carry out their jobs. If he opens his drawer one morning to find no clean socks, he lets Ted know what he expects in the way of clean laundry, without telling him that he must do the washing at a particular hour on a particular day. He tells Lisa how much she can spend for the week's groceries. *He sets boundaries on their authority.*

4. Does Ben give frequent, detailed orders to Lisa and Ted?
   No. Lisa knows she is expected to have dinner ready by seven each night, but when she cooks and what she cooks is up to her. Ted knows he must keep the family in clean clothes, but it's up to him whether he does it all on Saturday or spreads the job out over the week. *Ben lets the children know very clearly what he expects in terms of results, but he leaves the details of managing the tasks up to Lisa and Ted.*

5. Is Ben too critical of Lisa and Ted?
   No. *He praises their good results, and is patient with their blunders and lapses.*

6. Does Ben make too many decisions for Lisa and Ted?
   No. Ben understands something about motivation. He knows that Lisa and Ted would be deprived of pride and satisfaction in their work if they were simply following his orders. *He knows that the only way the children will grow in competence and responsibility is to let them make their own decisions and their own mistakes.*

It's clear that Ben is delegating effectively. He has avoided the common pitfalls. Although at first he thinks it would be less trouble to do all the work himself than to train Lisa and Ted, and suffer through their long learning process, he wisely takes the long-term view, which is in the best interests of all the family members. He is clear about what he expects from both children, and he makes sure they have the time, training, and money to carry out their jobs. He delegates gradually, so that the children won't be overwhelmed by more responsibility than they can handle all at once. He doesn't expect perfection, because he knows that all people make mistakes. He knows that positive reinforcement motivates better than punishment. He knows there is no one right way to accomplish a task, and he lets Lisa and Ted figure out their own methods. And Ben knows that learning new tasks and assuming new responsibilities can be their own rewards. He doesn't deprive Lisa and Ted of those rewards by issuing detailed orders and frequent reminders.

If your own delegation up to now has not been effective, the problems probably boil down to either overcontrol or undercontrol. If you are afraid of failure, if you feel more comfortable "doing" than "managing," if you constantly involve yourself in the details of everyone's job, if you are envious of your subordinate's ability, or if you have been delegating the responsibility without the authority, you are probably controlling too much. Try to loosen up, take yourself a little less seriously, be a little less of a perfectionist, and develop some trust in your people. If you have been giving unclear or insufficient instructions, if things never get done on time, if some things aren't getting done at all, you aren't controlling enough. You need to make your expectations clear through explicit instructions and regular reviews.

Now let's see how these principles of delegation work in a business setting. Following are two incidents that illustrate both good and bad practices of delegation. Read the experiences of Jim Mitchell and Sheila Burke, and then answer the questions that follow.

CASE STUDY

How Not to Delegate

Jim Mitchell had been on the go all day, and time was running out. He had to catch a plane for California in two and a half hours. Jim was assistant service manager for a medium-sized industrial air conditioning manufacturer in Kansas City. The customer service center in Sacramento was having problems, and the manager had asked Jim to come out for a couple of days and get them straightened out.

It was Monday. Last Friday, Jim's boss had issued him an ultimatum to get the budgets in on the district service centers. Jim had started to work on the budget Friday afternoon and had taken the work home over the weekend, but personal commitments kept him from getting much done.

Besides, he needed information from the field to do the job. He had come in early this morning, but he had several urgent matters to take care of before leaving for California.

He sat in his office, pondering what to do. He had promised his boss the budgets would be in by Friday noon. He realized he couldn't possibly have them in good shape with the trip cutting into his week. At best, he'd get back late Wednesday night, and there would be catching up to do on Thursday.

What to do? Just then, Otto Stone passed by Jim's door. Otto had been with the company for years in various service expediting jobs and knew most of the company people. But he was kind of an abrasive guy; he had his own ideas about how things should be done, and had been passed over several times for promotions. Jim found him difficult to work with, but still considered him pretty competent.

Jim thought, "Maybe old Otto's the answer to my budget problem." He ran to his door and yelled to Otto that he had a job for him. Otto came in and Jim explained briefly about his problem with the budget and his trip to Sacramento. He dug out last year's budget and the worksheets and scribblings he had been working on. His instructions to Otto were, "I want you to piece this budget together so I can look it over when I get back and make any needed changes in time to get it upstairs Friday."

Otto grumbled, "I have all my end-of-the-month reports to get together. How do you expect me to do this at the same time?"

Jim's secretary interrupted with an urgent phone call from an important customer in Toledo who was having problems with some equipment. The call took the better part of twenty minutes.

Otto sat fidgeting with last year's budget. When Jim got off the phone, he began making a list of things he had discussed with the Toledo man that he would have to remember. His assistant in charge of field personnel walked into the office. "Jim, you know the policy change on expense reimbursements for the field people? Well, we're running into some problems on that." He began describing the complaints he had received.

Finally Jim told his assistant, "Look, I'm kind of rushed right now. Let me get back to you on that in a couple of days."

His secretary came back in to tell him that it was time to leave for the airport. Jim turned to Otto. "I've got to leave now," he said. "Any questions? You should be able to handle it okay. Give me a call if you get hung up on something."

Jim grabbed his briefcase and coat and headed for his car. "Whew, that takes care of that one," he told himself.

Questions

1. Budgets are two thirds human behavior and one third the mechanics and process of budgeting. Did Jim select the right person to delegate the budget to? Why?

2. Does Otto have the ability? The experience? The training?

3. Were Jim's instructions clear? Did he specify the time frame? The results expected?

4. What is Otto's attitude? Is he motivated?

5. What outcomes would you expect?

Discussion

1. Otto may be an old hand in the organization, but he is not well liked. He will find it hard to get cooperation, or good information, or the participation and commitment from people he will need to work with on the budget. Otto was a poor choice for this project.

2. No, no, and no! Nor does Otto have the authority. Jim did not define the limits of authority, and Jim failed to notify field managers and others whom Otto would need to consult. Otto will come as a surprise to them, and they may be unwilling to cooperate with him.

3. Jim's instructions were given on the run. They were so incomplete and inadequate that Otto may have a completely different idea than Jim has of what is expected.

4. Otto's attitude is negative. He resents having a last-minute job dumped on him, and Jim did nothing to motivate him to want to do it well or do it at all.

5. There are several possible outcomes:

a. Otto may do a slipshod job, a simple rehash of last year's budget, and offer the excuse that he didn't have enough time to do anything more.

b. Otto may alienate other people in the organization, and do himself and Jim irreparable harm.

c. Otto may not do the job at all.

d. Otto may try hard but may find that he simply doesn't have the training and experience to do the job right.

e. Or, by some miracle, Otto may do a very good job.

I would predict that the first and second possible outcomes would result from this delegation.

Also note that near the end of the case study of Jim Mitchell, we have an incident that is sometimes referred to as "reverse delegation." Jim's assistant in charge of field personnel comes in with a problem on expense reimbursement. Jim is rushed and doesn't have the time to solve the problems for his assistant. So he says, "let me get back to you on that in a couple of days"—reverse delegation.

Avoid this whenever you can by a four-step process:

1. Make sure your subordinate gives you a clear—not fuzzy—statement of the problem. Asking for it in writing often stops reverse delegation immediately, because it's trouble to write it, and when reduced to writing it sounds silly.
2. Ask your subordinate, "What are possible alternatives/options for solutions?"
3. Ask your subordinate, "What are your recommendations, and why?"

By this time, subordinates can usually solve the problem themselves. Reverse delegation does not occur. The subordinate becomes a better manager. The subordinate goes to the manager with real problems.

In reality, this is a way of weaning subordinates from the umbilical cord of the manager. This brings up the fourth step:

4. Reward subordinates for taking care of the routine problems that belong to them, but also encourage them to give you feedback on any big, tough decisions.

Now let's observe someone who has better delegation skills.

CASE STUDY

A Better Way to Delegate

Sheila Burke sat at her office desk looking out at the sunrise. She had left home even before her children had boarded the school bus so that she would get a few quiet moments to think about organizing her work before everyone else came in.

Sheila was Manager of Human Resources at Atlantic Corporation. Although most people considered that a fancy title for personnel manager, Sheila took the broader definition seriously. Her immediate concern was with the expansion program planned at the Connecticut plant. Not only was the total work force to be enlarged, but the number of job classifications was to be almost doubled. Many employees would be added, and others would become involved in supervision, quality control, cost control, and other line and staff positions.

The job specifications were to include objectives to be achieved in the next 12 months. These were to be used in end-of-the-year evaluations. The recruiting group had to match applicants with the specifications. Then there were training programs and evaluation procedures just being implemented. All this was Sheila's responsibility.

There was a lot to do. Although Sheila had been able to increase her staff by two, the individuals were inexperienced. Nonetheless, she had to delegate some key tasks and gradually develop her staff, or she would be forever writing job specifications and conducting evaluations (which she detested).

Maybe the job classifications and coordination with recruiting would be a good place to start. Sheila wrote down the names of the people on her staff: Jill, Cliff, Betty, Lee. She thought about their qualifications, personalities, and the extent and urgency of their other assignments. "Betty Hancock," she thought. "She doesn't have much experience, but she is likable and she has the quiet aggressiveness to get the information we need from department heads to draw up the specs. Most of them don't like to spend time on that— they must think we have a crystal ball or something. She's divorced with a couple of kids, mature, and seems ambitious. But she'll need some training, and I'll have to free her from some of the new employee orientations she's been doing."

With that, Sheila began writing a job assignment. She thought about the deadlines for having new personnel in place. This would mean a tight schedule of lead times for getting the specs put together. She set some reporting dates when she would want to review certain groups of specs,

progress with recruiting, and so forth. "How should I evaluate the results?" she asked herself, and jotted down several important performance criteria that could be reviewed. Finally, she noted several good references on job specifications that Betty should read and the possibility of her picking up a course at the nearby technical institute, if needed.

About that time, the staff began coming in. Sheila looked over the job description she had outlined. "Looks good," she thought. "I'll get it typed up and talk to Betty this morning." She walked out of her office and over to Betty's desk. "Betty, would it be convenient to get together to talk over some things about 10:30 this morning? I have something exciting to discuss with you." "Sure," Betty replied.

Questions

1. What things did Sheila do that would indicate effective delegation?

2. What additional things would need to be done?

3. Would you predict that this task will be successfully accomplished?

4. How would you characterize the relationship of Sheila and her staff based on this incident?

Discussion

1. Sheila was thoughtful and careful about selecting the best person for the job. In choosing Betty, she decided that the woman's personality, attitude, and aptitude compensated for her lack of experience. Sheila wrote down a definition of the job she was delegating, including results expected, deadlines, and criteria for evaluating performance. She made plans for her subordinate to acquire the additional background and training she would need—a reading list and a college course. She set a definite time to discuss the new assignment with Betty, and was prepared for that discussion with the typed job description. She increased Betty's motivation by initially presenting the assignment as an exciting opportunity.

2. When Sheila and Betty have their 10:30 appointment, Sheila will have to spell out how much authority Betty will have in carrying out the delegation. Then Sheila will have to notify her other staff members and the department heads of Betty's new responsibilities. If Betty does well, Sheila should reward her appropriately, possibly with a good merit raise and increased responsibility. And, of course, Sheila will have to keep to her part of the "contract," reviewing Betty's performance on the schedule she has set for herself.

3. I would. At least it's off to a good start.

4. Sheila seems to have a good understanding of the strengths and weaknesses of her staff members, and her communication skills are good. She is considerate of their time, and when she meets with them she is well prepared, having thought about what she wants to say and put the most important points in writing to prevent misunderstanding. Sheila also has confidence in the ability of her people to grow in their jobs, and she communicates this confidence to them.

Now it's your turn. Using Exercise 9.1 to help you, lay out some task you have decided to delegate. First, choose the right person. Pick someone who has the basic ability and interest in the task, and someone for whom you can make sufficient working time available. Define the task, including the scope of responsibility, key areas in which results are to be accomplished, and specific objectives for a particular time period. Try to make these objectives measurable (e.g., "reduce the average time of response to customer inquiries from five days to three days," or

The Process of Delegating

Task to be delegated, including specific objectives

Selection of the person

Abilities:

Training:

Interest/Motivation:

Time:

Instruction/training needed

Communications/feedback

From the person you delegate:

From you:

To others:

Responsibilities of delegator

Authority needed

Limits:

"complete market tests of new product Z by January 1, and submit recommendation by February 1").

Discuss the nature of the problem or task and the general approach to it with the person you select; make sure that the person understands what results are expected and has authority to go after those results. Provide training, if needed, and establish a method and timetable for reporting back to you. Above all, be patient!

VICTIMS OF POOR DELEGATION

Some of the most challenging time management problems are expressed by frustrated subordinates who are the victims of inept delegation.

"How can I manage my time when my boss keeps interrupting me with questions, problems, and new things to do?"

"I've been assigned so many projects, all important, that I can't do any of them well. How is time management supposed to work for me?"

"My superior keeps changing priorities on me. First this is top priority, then that, and then something else. How am I to plan by priority?"

"Everything I'm given to do is a crisis—A-1 priority. There is no such thing as working on the most important."

All of these are legitimate problems faced by subordinates to whom responsibilities have been delegated. Are your instructions causing this type of confusion and frustration? It would be nice if all of us were perfect delegators, but we're not. Often, the very people who complain about their superior's poor delegation delegate badly to their own subordinates.

Sometimes the problems just noted have causes that go beyond inept delegation, such as:

The organization has grown rapidly, with problems and opportunities growing beyond the management talent available to cope with them.

The organization has inflexible policies, such as the "open door," "answer and place your own calls," "service to the customer (at all costs)," or "fast reaction to changes."

The company has the policy of extracting as much hard work from employees as possible, getting its payroll dollars' worth by continually piling on the work.

A highly bureaucratic organization has heavy reliance on routine reports, decision by committee, the chain of command, and other red tape.

When faced with these conditions, many subordinates feel they have no choice but to go along—in effect, to be controlled by whimsical changes in priorities, by a suffocating overload, by unrelenting disruptions, and by the cumbersome red tape demands of a bureaucracy. There are alternatives, however, even under these difficult conditions. Time management principles can be applied with beneficial results, but careful analysis and decisive planning and techniques are even more crucial in such difficult situations. If our time management problems are simple, then our methods can be simple and informal. If our problems are tough, then our system must be more exacting and we must be more committed.

If your effectiveness as a manager is being impaired because of the conditions just noted, you have a responsibility to bring this to the attention of your superior. If your superior chooses to do nothing about it, so be it. But most managers will not knowingly perpetuate ineffectiveness. Most will welcome the information and take some steps to correct it.

In pointing out these matters to your superior, it's important to "build a case," so that you can clearly present the problem, supported by facts. Here are some methods that have been used successfully.

- Use your time log to analyze the problems. For example, Dwight found that in a typical day his boss interrupted him six times. Each interruption lasted about 15 minutes, then it took Dwight about 5 minutes to get back into the particular programming problem he was working on. All this amounted to over two hours a day. After finding out about this, Dwight's superior began accumulating items on a list, and they would go over them only once or twice a day. This time robber was cut in half, to less than one hour per day.

- If you have a lot of assignments to work on, try to estimate how long each will take and fit them into a daily schedule (or weekly or monthly schedule if the duration of the projects spans a longer term). Give yourself a little slack in case a problem comes up or you want to do something extra. If the schedule shows that there are more assignments than time available, go to your boss and ask for suggestions and help.

  For example, Jane and her two assistants in the creative art department of a small advertising agency plotted out the time required to fulfill the commitments to their clients over the next two months. If Jane and her group were to get out the material to meet the deadlines they would have to work almost 54 hours per week. When Jane showed this to the head of the agency, it was agreed that Jane's group would work every other Saturday during the two-month crunch and that two of the large jobs would be subcontracted outside.

- If rapidly changing or ill-defined priorities are giving you trouble, set up a meeting with your supervisor to discuss a list of your assignments—their progress, problems, and priorities. Sometimes a half hour at the beginning of the week will do it. Or, if priorities change during the week, a 5- or 10-minute session at midweek can clear up shifting priorities and most other problems.

- If you can make a case that the "open office" or "bull pen" arrangement is seriously interfering with your efforts to analyze the sales statistics or work with low-producing salespeople, maybe your superior will give you access to a conference room twice a week, or let you use the office of someone who's traveling.

Are there some "tough" situations you can analyze? Use Exercise 9.2 to put together a case. Present it to your superior. See if it doesn't have some positive results.

EXERCISE 9.2   **The Special Problem in My Subordinate Position**

What is the problem?

EXERCISE 9.2
(continued)

What supporting data do I have?

What?

When?

Who?

How much?

What impact does it have on job effectiveness?

Possible solutions

Information should be presented to:

Whom?

How?

References

To further increase your delegation skills, refer to the book by Robert B. Nelson, *Empowering Employees Through Delegation* (see Appendix III, "Recommended Time Management Resources," p. 309). Also in Appendix III are several references on teamwork through time management (p. 310).

SUMMARY

Ineffective delegation, whether because of fear, mistrust, or lack of ability, is among the worst time robbers. But the inept delegator does not create a problem that only he or she must solve. Bad delegation also adversely affects the performance of other members of the team—the ripple effect.

In this chapter, we have discussed the concepts of delegation, and how they apply to both family and work situations. Developing delegation skills will enhance both individual and team effectiveness. The effective time manager is also an effective delegator. In the next chapter, we will consider another important aspect of time management—running more effective, efficient meetings.

10 Improving Meetings: A Key to Effective Teamwork

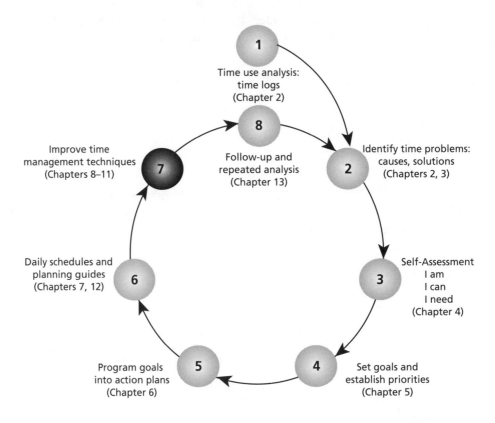

If, when you analyzed your time use in Chapter 2, you identified meetings as one of your major time robbers, you have plenty of company. Various estimates show that there are some 25 million meetings held in the United States every day. It has been estimated that middle managers spend one third of their working hours in meetings, and top managers may spend over one half. Many civic and service organizations, such as the PTA, churches, and clubs, are literally run by meetings.

Meetings are costly, not only in time but also in dollars. About 10 percent of total personnel costs of businesses are spent in meetings. If you call seven or eight middle managers to a meeting, their combined salaries and benefits are costing about three dollars a minute. Try computing the costs of your meetings.

I once worked with a group of plant managers from a large apparel manufacturing company. After keeping time logs for a week, they all reported that they were spending almost four hours a day in meetings. When asked how efficiently that time was used, and how effective the meetings were in achieving their purpose, the overall response of the group was 25 percent. The potential gain from controlling that one time robber was three hours per day! Typically, meeting goers will respond to "what percent efficient?" and "what percent effective?" questions with estimates in the range of 10 percent to 50 percent. As time robbers, meetings are among the worst.

As expensive and as time-consuming as meetings are, most organizations couldn't get along without them. We need meetings for communication, making group decisions, creative problem solving, building teamwork and commitment in the group, and accumulating knowledge and skills. But too often, meetings also produce frustration, tension, hostility, and conflict.

Review the situation in which Chet Craig called a meeting to decide about the purchase of a large press (pp. 2–4). The group did not add significantly to the decision process, and Chet ended up making the decision himself, at the last minute before running to catch a plane.

Question

Identify as many reasons as you can for the ineffectiveness of Chet's meeting.

Discussion

Chet's meeting was unscheduled, interrupting the already busy schedules of the people involved. It should not have been a crisis, because the need for and importance of the decision had been known for some time. But Chet had taken no action, and now the supplier was forcing a decision. Therefore, several key ingredients of good meetings were ignored:

1. The timing was all wrong: It was inconvenient; it conflicted with other commitments; it was at the end of the day, when people are usually tired. It was also rushed, with too little time available for such an important decision.
2. There was no advance preparation; for example, the necessary market, productivity, and cost data had not been gathered and circulated. If Chet had screened out interruptions from 2:30 to 4:45, he would perhaps have been able to do some of this advance preparation, at least enough to make the meeting partially effective.
3. There were no ground rules on how the decision would be made and no agenda specifying the issues to be covered.
4. The meeting was interrupted by Chet's secretary with messages and letters to sign and by a call from his wife.
5. The other managers could have contributed much more of their expertise if they had been better prepared and had had more time. Not all of their questions and objections were answered.

Think back on meetings you attended recently. Did any of them resemble Chet's? Did they fail to achieve their purpose? Were they timed poorly? Were they badly prepared for and frequently interrupted? On the other hand, were there meetings that were effective in fulfilling their objectives? Did they start and end on time? Did the meeting leader do a good job?

In Exercise 10.1, describe one or two meetings that were pretty much a waste of time and a couple that were relatively successful. Consider meetings at work as well as PTA, Chamber of Commerce, or volunteer organization meetings. Note the meeting's purpose, and identify some of the factors that contributed to success or failure.

In the next section, we will develop a framework for managing better meetings. Later, you can come back to this exercise and look for ways to improve the meetings that you call or attend.

EXERCISE 10.1   **Analysis of Meetings**

Ineffective Meetings—Time Robbers

Meeting	Purpose	Reasons for lack of success

Good Meetings

Meeting	Purpose	Reasons for success

A FRAMEWORK FOR EFFECTIVE MEETINGS

How can we make meetings more effective? Let's start with the following working definition. A meeting:

brings together a group of people
with a common interest
and with relevant knowledge and expertise,
to accomplish some purpose or goal
through a process of group interaction.

The definition provides us with some clues about the management of a meeting.

The purpose or goal should be well defined. If the purpose is to solve a problem, exactly what is the problem? Do we stop when we have found the causes of the problem, or do we go on to solutions or plans for implementation?

We must carefully select the people involved—those with a common interest as well as those who have relevant knowledge and expertise. Bringing these people together means preparation—setting the when, where, and how of the meeting, as well as completing any advance data gathering, research, and analysis.

The process of group interaction means establishing some ground rules, providing leadership, and encouraging creative thinking, openness, and communication. We also need to record and evaluate the actions of the group.

From this definition of a meeting, we can develop the elements of a five-part framework that will help us manage more effective meetings.

1. *Statement of the purpose or goal:* Why have a meeting? What are the objectives? What type of meeting?
2. *Selection of participants:* Who should be there? What is their interest? Their expertise? What should they contribute? What are possible attitude and personality problems? What effect will they have on the group process?
3. *Preparations for the meeting:* When should the session take place? Where? How long should it take? Are any special arrangements necessary? What ground rules should we employ during the meeting? How should the agenda items be ordered? How do we approach each one? Is there advance preparation the participants should do? Should there be presentations?
4. *Leadership of the group decision process:* How do we get everyone to bring their knowledge and expertise to bear on the issues? How do we foster an atmosphere of creative problem solving? How do we overcome personality problems?
5. *Recording and evaluating results:* What decisions were made? What action is to be taken? Who will do it? When? How do we follow up to make sure the action has been taken? What was the payroll cost of your meeting? Did the benefits exceed the costs?

Whenever you plan a meeting, you should consider these five elements. Obviously, some meetings require elaborate preparations, whereas others need little. A meeting intended to provide information will require much less thought about the group decision process than a meeting intended to solve a complex problem.

Nevertheless, if you check through these five elements, you can be sure that your meetings will not fail because of oversights in your planning and preparation. The following sections consider each of the five elements of our meeting framework.

Statement of Purpose or Goal

Meetings are called to accomplish one or more of the following objectives. They are intended to:

Plan
Make a decision
Implement a plan
Evaluate
Solve problems—find causes and/or solutions
Inform or train
Capitalize on the group's knowledge and expertise
Build cooperation and commitment
Provide involvement and support

When asked about the purpose of a meeting, people often say, "That's obvious. It's a budget meeting," or, "We're going to discuss late deliveries." Those are statements of subject matter and not purpose. Fuzzy statements of purpose often get us into trouble. For example:

> Sonny has just received a report that shows the overtime in his department last month was 50 percent over budget. He calls his supervisors together "to find out what the hell happened."
>
> Instead of preparing himself with a clear statement of purpose, Sonny rushes into the meeting, finds out that most of the excess overtime occurred in two of the supervisors' sections, and admonishes the two culprits with "Don't let it happen again. I don't like those kinds of surprises." The two supervisors leave the meeting grumbling. "That SOB wouldn't even listen. It's because of all those scheduling changes we got at the end of the month."

Sonny's purpose should have been to (1) find out the causes for the excessive overtime; (2) find ways to prevent it from happening again, or at least ways to anticipate it; (3) take any actions necessary to accomplish step 2; and (4) gain the commitment of the supervisors involved.

Has Sonny accomplished his purpose? It's doubtful. If the supervisors can't control the schedule changes, it's unlikely they will be able to keep the overtime down. Certainly Sonny's management style contributed to the poor outcome of the meeting, but the fuzzy statement of purpose provided no help.

On the other hand, observe Vicky:

> Vicky has made up her mind to introduce a new package size into the line of soap products for which she's responsible. She decides to call together her department heads to discuss the decision. She writes out her statement of purpose and specifies three objectives.
>
> Purpose: To discuss the introduction of the new six-ounce package with all the department heads involved.
>
> Specific objectives:
> 1. Communicate the decision to introduce the six-ounce package based on market research and cost studies. Answer any questions about who's responsible for what steps and assure interdepartmental coordination.
> 2. Get everyone's input on the best timing. Decide on a date for introduction.
> 3. Get everyone's commitment to make the program work.

Will Vicky's meeting be a success? Probably. Although things can still go wrong, she now knows precisely what she wants to accomplish, so she can make an orderly plan for getting there.

Now it's your turn. Refer back to Exercise 10.1. Choose one of the time-waster meetings you described there, and answer the following questions.

Was the meeting's purpose clearly stated?

Were the objectives specified?

If not, what problems did this cause in the progress and outcome of the meeting?

In the space here, write a clear statement of purpose with specific objectives for that meeting.

Next, think of a meeting you are about to call, at work or in the community, and in Exercise 10.2 write a statement of purpose and list specific objectives for that meeting.

EXERCISE 10.2	**Planning a Meeting**

Statement of purpose

Specific objectives

Sometimes, after you clarify your objectives, you may decide a meeting isn't required. Perhaps a written memo would do the job just as well, or it may be better to meet with people individually, rather than as a group. But once you decide a meeting is needed, you will want to communicate the purpose to the other participants when you announce the meeting.

Selection of Participants

Next, think about *who* should attend. In some types of meeting, the answer is obvious. At a meeting of the finance committee, probably only members of that committee would be present. At a school board meeting, the board members and the superintendent would participate, with staff members present to answer questions, and members of the public in attendance to bring specific matters before the board at a specified time. But, in many business meetings, the chairperson must decide who should attend and who need not. If you are chairing a meeting, try to keep down the size of the group—four to seven people is easiest to work with—but include everyone who has an important involvement or contribution to make. If the group is going to make an important decision, strive to get a good cross section of representatives from all areas affected. People will cooperate more fully in implementing a decision if they have had some input in making the decision. Groups of over 12 or 15 can solve problems and make decisions effectively, but often they work best if they are divided into smaller groups for specific functions.

Some people, even though they are involved and have a contribution to make, tend to stifle creativity and openness in others. People with high rank, or who flaunt their education or position, may cause others to clam up, become defensive, or be insincerely agreeable. Other people have strong biases, are overly aggressive in advancing their ideas, and mercilessly attack others' ideas.

Therefore, the person organizing a meeting should consider the participants from two aspects: (1) their interest, knowledge, and expertise related to the purpose of the meeting; and (2) their effect on the interrelationships of the group. The following questions should be answered: Who should participate in that meeting? What should be their contributions? What effect will he or she have on the interactions of the group?

The Participant Profile worksheet in Appendix I (p. 272) will help you analyze these questions as you select the people who will make your meeting most effective. Refer back to the meeting you planned in Exercise 10.2 and develop a profile of potential participants for that meeting.

Preparations for the Meeting

The next step is to prepare for the meeting: When? Where? What? How? The statement of purpose and the list of participants will help you determine where the meeting should be held and how long it should be. When people from a variety of organizations are meeting, it is often best to meet on "neutral" territory—in a conference room of a hotel or library, for example. If the subject is complex and sensitive and will require several hours, it may be best to hold a retreat outside the city where information and discussion sessions can be alternated with meals and recreation time.

Try to find a meeting room that suits the purpose of the meeting. For example, a long, narrow conference table is not a good arrangement for problem solving and group decisions (a round or square table is better), but it might be fine for an information meeting at which participants make presentations one at a time and a decision is made later.

The room and the seating arrangements do make a difference. Have you ever attended a meeting where two dozen people had to sit in fixed seats in a big auditorium, or a department meeting where 20 people were crammed into the boss's office, or a controversial meeting where hostile parties were eyeball-to-eyeball across a table? Try to find a room where people can be comfortable—where the heat or air conditioning can be adjusted, where people don't have to face the door and be distracted by late arrivals and early departures, where everyone can feel like part of the group and can hear and see any materials presented.

Drawing up an agenda sometimes seems like a waste of time, but a good, detailed agenda can be your most useful tool in achieving smooth and productive meetings. The agenda is like a road map; it tells participants what the meeting is expected to accomplish and how they're going to get there. It gives them the opportunity to prepare for their roles in the discussion. The meeting agenda should, of course, include the date, place, and starting time of the meeting, and it should also include the ending time. If a caller of a meeting you are to attend has failed to do this, ask. Open-ended meetings are an invitation to waste time. Meetings can drag on indefinitely if allowed to, and as they drag on the participants become restless, inattentive, and angry. Not many groups achieve much after two hours of unbroken meeting time, so plan breaks in your agenda accordingly.

When several items are to be included on the agenda, consider their order carefully. You may decide that you want to begin and end the meeting on a note of unity, and plan the controversial topics—items that may be divisive and cause heated discussion—for the middle. People are usually more energetic and alert in the early part of a meeting, so you might schedule problem-solving discussion ahead of the committee reports or other routine items. Large items of business should be subdivided (e.g., for a complex problem: review of information, causes, solutions, action plan, and follow-up steps). There is no "correct" way to order an agenda, but you should plan your agenda consciously, taking these factors into account, rather than haphazardly.

Imagine attending the meeting of a committee that spent 45 minutes discussing refreshments to be served at the open house and 7 minutes deciding how to use a $50,000 bequest, and you can appreciate the important of time limits for each agenda item. As a meeting organizer, you should decide how much time each item is worth, write it down, and stick to it. To keep clear in everyone's mind what the group is trying to accomplish, it is also useful to label each agenda item "for decision," "for discussion," or "for information."

One other useful item on an agenda is a procedure column. For each agenda item, this column contains a description of how the item is to be handled at the meeting. Sometimes the procedure is simply to open up the agenda item for discussion; in other cases, you may want to start with an analysis of a statistical report, or a report presentation. Perhaps the outcome you're looking for is a list of most likely causes of specific problems, or volunteers to investigate them further. It's helpful to indicate this on the agenda beforehand, so the participants can gear their thinking in those directions.

The agenda should be sent to participants several days before the meeting. It should be accompanied by any necessary background material—research reports, statistics, proposals, résumés, site plans, and so forth. The participants need this information to be effective in the meeting, but you should try to keep this information to a manageable length. In any case, do not waste valuable meeting time by introducing such materials at the meeting.

You also need to make clear how the meeting will be run. Participants need to know who's in charge and if the meeting will be a brainstorming session or will follow Robert's Rules of Order. They need to know if they are making decisions or recommendations. Are the decisions to be made by voting or by consensus (a compromise everyone can live with)? Does the boss have decision-making or veto power?

The Agenda and Preparation planning guide in Appendix I (pp. 273–274) will help you prepare for a meeting. Refer to the meeting for which you completed Exercise 10.2 and the Participant Profile in Appendix I (p. 272). Turn to Appendix I and fill in the Agenda and Preparation planning guide.

If the Agenda and Preparation guide seemed useful in planning a meeting, make copies of this planning guide, and use it regularly. If a different format or more items would work better for you, design your own. If others in your organization are not preparing adequately for meetings, refer the planning guide to them. A tactful approach should not offend. After all, no one enjoys chairing a time-waster meeting.

The Group Decision Process

The group process—an effective team of people working together to achieve a common goal—is fundamental to our modern society. Although we can do many things alone, many other things must be done through teamwork because of legal or organizational requirements, or for maximum effectiveness.

Meetings are the vehicle for the group decision process. We meet to communicate, solve problems, create new products. When the process works, we accomplish things we never could do alone.

Research indicates that over 90 percent of the millions of meetings held in the United States each day are for the purpose of making decisions or solving problems. Research has repeatedly demonstrated that a group of people who effectively bring their combined expertise and creativity to bear on a problem will usually make a higher-quality decision than can any individual member of the team.

A common way of demonstrating this is through an exercise developed by Jay Hall called "Lost on the Moon."* The essence of the exercise is that the group has just crash-landed a spacecraft on the moon's surface and is stranded 200 miles from the mother ship. Fifteen items have been salvaged. The group members are instructed to rank the 15 items in terms of their importance for survival.

First, each individual sets priorities. Then, teams of four to seven people are formed and are asked to rank the 15 items by voting on their importance. Next, the teams are instructed in group consensus rules. These rules require more fully exploring the points of view, objections, and expertise of each member of a team, because no decision is made until everyone can at least "live with the decision."

An important advantage of consensus decisions: There are no losers. Losers in a voting decision often withdraw their commitment. With the consensus rule, although some team members may feel the decision is not perfect, their important objections will have been answered, and they can live with it. This is a win/win decision, as opposed to the win/lose decisions produced by voting. A typical set of consensus decision rules, developed by Jay Hall and other behavioral scientists, is shown in Figure 10.1.

Once the teams are instructed in consensus rules, they are again asked to rank the moon survival items using the consensus process. Finally, both the individual and team decisions of the participants are scored against the rankings of experts from NASA (National Aeronautic and Space Administration). The team score arrived at by voting tends to reflect the average of the group. Sometimes a very assertive person influences the voting, with better or worse results. The consensus rankings, however, tend to improve on the teams' voting average, and often are

---

*Jay Hall's research was originally reported in *Psychology Today,* November 1971, p. 51.

When your group reaches the point where each person can say, "Well, even though it may not be exactly what I want, at least I can live with the idea and support it," then the group has reached consensus. This doesn't mean that all group members must completely agree, but all must at least minimally agree.

Consequently, any group member can block a decision. This is precisely why consensus decisions are both more difficult and more effective than other group decision methods, such as voting. They force the group to consider all aspects of the problem and objections to possible courses of action.

Treat differences of opinion as a way of (1) gathering additional information, (2) clarifying issues, and (3) forcing the group to seek better alternatives. If conflicts arise, try to deal with them immediately, so that they don't continue to hinder the group. Your willingness to take the risk and deal with personal conflicts can mean the difference between success or failure for the entire group.

Guidelines

1. Be wary of quick and easy agreements. Examine the reasons for the apparent agreement to be sure that a true consensus has been reached.
2. Try not to compete—even if you win, the group may lose in the long run.
3. Avoid arguing.
4. Avoid win/lose stalemates.
5. Avoid either/or propositions.
6. Avoid a compromise if you feel your position is the most reasonable—provided you have carefully listened to and answered the objections to your point of view.
7. Try not to settle an issue by voting—it will split the team into winners and losers.
8. Try to stick with the discussion even if somebody attacks you or your ideas.
9. Don't attack people—it only causes them to be defensive and therefore less effective.
10. Don't ignore conflict. Find out why it exists, so that it can be dealt with and resolved.
11. Listen and pay attention to what others have to say.

FIGURE 10.1
Consensus rules.

superior to even the best individual.* The teams can further learn from the exercise by exploring what went on during their interaction which helped or hindered their decision making.

Now look back to the meetings you noted in Exercise 10.1. Answer the questions in Exercise 10.3 about the group decision process at those meetings.

EXERCISE 10.3	**Analysis of Meetings**

In what ways did the group decision process work well?

In what ways did the process work badly?

What decision rules were employed (voting, consensus, the boss made the decision, etc.)?

If you found that the decision-making process of your team is not all that good, try the following exercise in creativity and consensus decision making.

First, think of a long-range objective that would really benefit your organization, such as a new product line, cost-cutting methods, improved services, or better working conditions. Some specific examples follow.

We would like to cut costs by 5 percent. What are some cost-cutting methods for achieving this?

Our goal is to increase sales by 10 percent. What promotional, advertising, and selling efforts could we undertake to accomplish that goal?

---

*If you want to experiment with "Lost on the Moon," refer to the Hall reference cited. Two other similar games you might wish to try are "The Desert Survival Problem," by J. C. Lafferty, P. M. Eady, and A. W. Pond, and "Lost at Sea: A Consensus-Seeking Task," in *The 1975 Annual Handbook for Group Facilitators* (La Jolla, Calif.: University Associates Publishers, Inc.).

What new or improved programs could our organization (church, school, welfare agency, YWCA, etc.) offer that would have greatest benefit to our public?

Write the long-range objective in Exercise 10.4.

Second, have each member of the team put forth at least two creative ideas for achieving that objective. Don't discourage any ideas, even those that are pretty far out. Keep it open and enjoyable. Write them down in Exercise 10.4.

Third, using the consensus rules in Figure 10.1, decide on the two or three best ideas. Some good ideas may have to be passed over, but make sure it's a consensus decision. Indicate the choices in the second column of Exercise 10.4, then write why such choices were made in the third column.

Fourth, evaluate what you have done. Have you generated some really neat ideas? Might they really benefit the organization in the long run? Did the group boil them down to the two or three best ideas? Is everyone able to live with the selections? What problems did the group

---

EXERCISE 10.4   **Creative Ideas and Consensus Decisions**

Important long-range objective

Creative ideas	*Accept 2 or 3— reject others*	*Reason for accepting or rejecting*

have with the consensus process? Can you find ways to overcome these difficulties in the future?

If your team is still having trouble with meetings, you may want to consider several other ideas. Many groups find it helpful to use a "facilitator" and a "recorder." Instead of the chairperson (often the boss, who has a heavy stake in the results) being captain and scorekeeper and referee all at once, a facilitator takes over some of these duties. The facilitator agrees to remain neutral and not to contribute his or her own ideas or evaulate those of others. As the servant of the group, the facilitator is present only to help the group members use the most effective methods for accomplishing their tasks.

Similarly, a recorder is assigned to be responsible for the group's short-term memory (aside from the long-term memory, usually represented by the minutes). Another neutral servant of the group, the recorder writes down, for the group to see, all the major points brought up by participants, often using felt-tip markers and large pieces of paper on a wall or stand in front of the group. This short-term memory kept by the recorder makes visible key information, alternative causes and solutions to problems, decisions, and so forth. This type of record alleviates confusion, cuts down on repetition of the same ideas, and helps everyone remember what they are talking about.

In my experience, the real challenge in leading a large group meeting is getting all of the participants to contribute. How often have you experienced a large group being dominated by three or four very vocal people? Or the discussion gets sidetracked as two parties persistently argue over a small issue, while others sit by frustrated.

There are two problems of getting reasonably even input from all participants in a large group (this is obviously much less of a problem in small groups of two, three, or four): (1) There is limited air time. If a group of 10 meets for an hour, the air time of each person is probably only about four minutes when you take out time for housekeeping tasks, telling a joke, getting started late, and so forth. (2) But how many of the 10 participants get their four minutes? Usually less than half. The aggressive, talkative ones dominate the air time, while the quiet, more timid members listen. Their potential contribution is lost. To overcome these problems, the meeting leader must be very skilled in eliciting input from all the participants, limiting those that are more talkative.

Often large groups meet for longer periods of time—a couple hours, or maybe a day-long retreat. But even then, usually there are people who have made only limited contributions and others who have talked too much. And often the number of issues resolved seems very meager beside the expenditure of time. One method of partially overcoming this is to utilize a methodology known as "delphi." Opinions and ideas are solicited via a series of written questionnaires and responses. That way everyone can provide input. When the group meets again, a full range of issues and ideas is on the table.

Interactive software is now available for doing this during meetings. All participants have input devices at their seats that feed into a central computer located in the center of the group, where the facilitator sits. The facilitator then has all the inputs in front of him or her. These can be displayed on an overhead projector as needed. As an example of how it works, the meeting facilitator may ask all participants to weigh or rank the solutions by entering them in their private input devices. The facilitator then displays the results and asks for discussion of the three most popular solutions. At this point, he or she may divulge the contributor and ask that person to present the pros and cons. After discussion, the facilitator may ask for another round of inputs. And so on. . . . This method can be very effective, but it does require an experienced facilitator.

Recording and Evaluating

The minutes are the long-term memory of a group meeting. Minutes should concentrate on decisions that were made, actions to be taken, by whom, and when, with follow-up steps noted. Extensive dialogue, personal opinions, and points of conflict generally should be avoided. Dick Lohr, in his videotape,* suggests making "one-minute minutes," which tends to keep them short and to the point.

In addition, evaluation of meetings is important to keep us thinking about ways to improve, rather than falling back into bad habits. Frequent use of the Record of Minutes and Evaluation form in Appendix I (pp. 275–276) will help you do this.

Some groups evaluate every meeting on three scales:

percent effective in achieving the purpose

percent efficient in the use of the time

payroll cost compared to benefits

These scales provide a way to "keep score" on the success of meetings.

*Dick Lohr, "Taking Control of Your Work Day," 1992.

References

For additional information on building skills to overcome this important time robber, turn to Appendix III, "Recommended Time Management Resources" (p. 310).

SUMMARY

Meetings are enormously important to the smooth functioning of a team. Yet time-waster meetings abound—they are a major time robber as well as being ineffective in achieving their purpose.

In this chapter, we have developed a framework for improving meetings and gaining more effective teamwork. In the next chapter, we will discuss one more frequent time robber—procrastination.

11 Procrastination

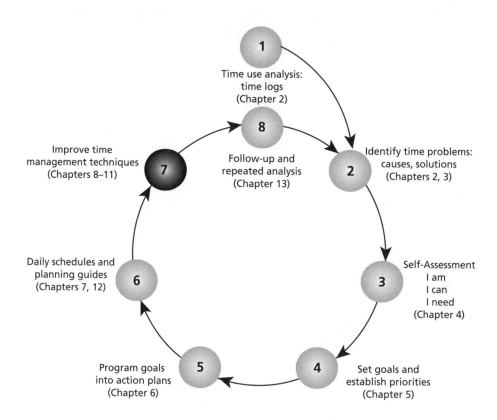

1 — Time use analysis: time logs (Chapter 2)

2 — Identify time problems: causes, solutions (Chapters 2, 3)

3 — Self-Assessment
I am
I can
I need
(Chapter 4)

4 — Set goals and establish priorities (Chapter 5)

5 — Program goals into action plans (Chapter 6)

6 — Daily schedules and planning guides (Chapters 7, 12)

7 — Improve time management techniques (Chapters 8–11)

8 — Follow-up and repeated analysis (Chapter 13)

Let's say you've set your goal, programmed it, and scheduled time to begin working on it at 8:45 a.m. Monday. The hour arrives, but you don't feel quite ready. "Think I'll have another cup of coffee first. That will help me really get rolling," you tell yourself. Fifteen minutes pass as you sip coffee and stare into space. You're still not up to beginning. You remember that you really should balance your checkbook to see if you can pay all your bills this month. You're not putting off the unpleasant, you tell yourself. After all, figuring out that checkbook mess is no fun either. More time passes. The phone rings and you talk for awhile. You look at your watch. It's 10:15. "There's not really time to get started on the project, with staff meeting coming up at eleven. Might as well use the dead time to go across the street and get a haircut."

There you are. You know just what you have to do, you know exactly how important it is, and you've allotted yourself time to do it. But you can't get started. You are up against one of the most universal and difficult of time problems—procrastination.

Are you a procrastinator? Rate yourself on the questions in Exercise 11.1.

EXERCISE 11.1	**Procrastination Quotient**			
		Strongly agree	*Mildly agree*	*Mildly disagree*	*Strongly disagree*
	1. I invent reasons and look for excuses for not acting on a tough problem.	_____	_____	_____	_____
	2. It takes pressure to get on with a difficult assignment.	_____	_____	_____	_____
	3. I take half measures that will avoid or delay unpleasant or difficult action.	_____	_____	_____	_____
	4. There are too many interruptions and crises that interfere with my accomplishing the big jobs.	_____	_____	_____	_____
	5. I avoid forthright answers when pressed for an unpleasant decision.	_____	_____	_____	_____
	6. I have been guilty of neglecting follow-up aspects of important action plans.	_____	_____	_____	_____
	7. I try to get other people to do unpleasant assignments for me.	_____	_____	_____	_____

	Strongly agree	Mildly agree	Mildly disagree	Strongly disagree
8. I schedule big jobs late in the day or take them home to do in the evenings or weekends.	_____	_____	_____	_____
9. I've been too tired (nervous, upset, hungover) to do the difficult tasks that face me.	_____	_____	_____	_____
10. I like to get everything cleared off my desk before commencing a tough job.	_____	_____	_____	_____
Total responses	_____	_____	_____	_____
X Weight	X 4	X 3	X 2	X 1
= Score	_____	_____	_____	_____

Total _____ Procrastination
score   quotient

If your procrastination quotient is below 20.	You are not a procrastinator; you probably have an occasional problem only.
If your quotient is 21–30:	You have a procrastination problem— but not too severe.
If your quotient is above 30:	You probably have frequent and severe problems of procrastinating.

The case of Martha Wagoner, a procrastinating public school principal, shows how easy it is to fool ourselves into believing we are being productive while we put off making progress on our most important goals. Read the case study that follows, and observe how Martha is very efficient at doing certain kinds of tasks, yet procrastinates badly when faced with others. By studying the causes and solutions for Martha's problem, perhaps we can learn some things about our own. After reading the case, try answering the questions that follow it.

CASE STUDY

Martha Wagoner, Public School Principal

Martha Wagoner knew that organization was her strong point. In college, she had taken excellent notes, kept orderly files, made outlines before writing exams and papers, and had the neatest room in the dorm. She had made the transition from college to marriage and teaching easily, carrying over her good habits. She was the envy of the other working wives she knew, never running out of salt or paper napkins or pantyhose. Her apartment was always presentable when guests dropped in. She managed the housework and marketing and errands efficiently because she made a schedule and stuck to it. And after the first year she managed her job with equal ease, setting aside regular hours for lesson preparation, grading, and conferences with students and parents.

After five years of marriage, she and her husband separated, and he remarried soon after their divorce. Though she was hurt and bewildered, Martha knew that her situation was not impossible. She was on her own financially, but was established in her career, and she and John had had no children.

During the year after her divorce, Martha reassessed her situation and decided she did not want to live forever on a teacher's salary. As a married woman, she had expected to be able to own a house, dine out often, hold season tickets to the local symphony and theater, take frequent skiing trips, and indulge her taste for good clothes and antique furniture. With only one income, and a pay scale that topped out at $26,500, that kind of life would not be possible.

Martha decided to get her master's degree and go into school administration. She enrolled in a two-year evening program and was hired as an administrative intern at Washington Elementary School, where she had taught sixth grade. She had expected to remain in that position for several years before being promoted, but during the summer after her first year the principal died suddenly of a heart attack and Martha was offered his job. At 33, she was the youngest principal in the system, but now it was the end of the first semester and Martha was having doubts about her executive ability. She often felt in over her head, and it seemed that none of her old methods of making things go smoothly worked very well in this situation. Martha, who was as critical of herself as she was of other people, knew that she sometimes shrank from using her authority.

One morning in January, Martha woke up full of determination to get moving on her two most important and urgent projects. She had to complete her evaluations of the teachers within the next week, and she wanted to launch an experimental reading program in the primary grades. As a teacher, Martha's greatest frustration had been trying to cope with sixth graders who couldn't read well enough to do sixth-grade work. For years, she had been developing in her mind a different approach to teaching reading that would involve some additional training for the teachers, a different use of aides and student teachers, a new role for the library staff, and some materials she had discovered at a teachers' convention. She had gotten the approval of the superintendent of schools in October to implement the program, but so far it existed only in her head and in the bulky file of notes and clippings she had compiled.

As she drove to school, she resolved to spend part of the morning ordering materials, setting up a timetable, and working on a staff presentation for the reading program, and then to spend part of the afternoon going over her evaluations with two teachers. Martha had already done evaluations on the maintenance people, the cafeteria workers, and her secretary, and she had filled out the forms for the teachers, but she dreaded the next part: meeting with each teacher to go over the evaluations. Several of them had been her co-workers two years ago and were older and more experienced than she was. Though she had done well in graduate school and felt pretty sure she had the respect and support of the teaching staff, she felt awkward about being in a position to judge them. But today she would face it, starting with two young, first-year teachers.

After her customary inspection of the school grounds and building to check for signs of vandalism, she walked into her office at 7:30. Two men were sitting in the outer office, one with a pair of cameras slung over his arm.

Sandra, the school secretary, called Martha aside to explain that the two were a reporter and photographer from the *Daily Courier.* They were checking a dozen schools in the city for cleanliness. At the school board meeting last night, a parent had complained about filthiness at the schools, and the newspaper had decided to make its own investigation by paying unannounced visits.

Martha felt her stomach tighten as she summoned the men into her office. They said they had come early so as not to disturb any classes, and they wanted to inspect the washrooms, the kitchen, the cafeteria, and the gym. Martha hesitated. She wondered if she ought to call the central administration building and ask for some direction. She knew that the reporter was within his rights and, from her own inspection this morning, that he wouldn't find anything amiss, but you never knew what the newspaper would do for a story. She wondered if she should let the reporter roam free, have Sandra give him the tour, or stick with him herself to keep better control of things? She decided to go around with him, though this would mean disrupting the schedule she had set for herself.

The tour took longer than she had expected—she had never met a man with more nosy and persistent questions—and when she got back to her office she found the mother of a second grader waiting for her. The woman, Mrs. Walker, had scheduled an 8 a.m. appointment in order to get to work on time. She seemed irritated at having been kept waiting for 10 minutes.

Martha apologized for the delay and listened to Mrs. Walker's complaints about her child's teacher. She interrupted twice to defend the teacher, but this seemed to infuriate the woman, who hinted that she might go to the superintendent with her problem. Martha was able to pacify her to some extent, but when Mrs. Walker left, Martha felt that nothing had really been settled. Mrs. Walker would be back, she was sure, and a confrontation with the teacher couldn't be put off indefinitely.

At nine, Martha began dictating correspondence and reports for Sandra to type. She enjoyed this part of her job because she knew she did it well. She had handled most of the paperwork last year as an intern and was quite comfortable with it. But when she glanced at the clock and saw that it was almost eleven, she felt a twinge of guilt at having spent the morning in what was essentially busywork. Sandra, who at this moment was doing nothing but screening phone calls, could easily have composed half of the letters herself, and Martha could have made better use of the morning by working up the timetable for the reading program. She picked up the phone and asked Sandra to schedule two of the teachers for evaluations this afternoon.

At eleven, Martha finished up the attendance reports and cleared off her desk as Sandra showed the officers of the PTA into her office. They had come to discuss the Family Fun Night planned for February, and the garrulous president went on and on about what kind of punch would be served, who was on the decorating committee, whether school tee shirts should be sold in the same booth with the pennants, and which merchants could be expected to donate door prizes. When they got up to leave, Martha saw that it was noon. A whole hour gone, and all she had needed to know was the time and date of the event, the parts of the building that would be used, and a brief rundown on the activities planned.

She didn't want to offend the PTA, but there must be a way of cutting these meetings down to a reasonable number and length of time. She berated herself for spending the whole morning in public relations and paperwork. She had faulted her predecessor for spending most of his time in administrative busywork and almost none of it on the instructional program, and she had been positive that when she got to be a principal she would keep her own priorities straight. She had been sure that she would be able to take care of the administrative work before and after school hours, and would spend all the classroom hours in work directly related to the classroom.

After lunch, she spent one class period observing for a few minutes in several classrooms, as she tried to do every day. When she got back to her office, she made notes on her observations. She was interrupted by Angie Hoffman, the third-grade teacher. Angie said her class was outdoors with the physical education specialist and asked if this would be a convenient time to talk. Martha glanced at her watch, decided that it wouldn't really hurt to put off one of the evaluations for another day, and asked Angie to come in. Angie had just found out she was pregnant and wouldn't be able to finish out the year. She wanted to know about maternity leave. Martha quickly found the policy in one of her manuals and read it to Angie. She poured coffee for both of them and talked to Angie about her plans for moving to a house, getting a baby sitter, and having the baby weaned by September. Martha knew she tended to be a little stiff, with adults anyway, so she felt pleased that Angie wanted to confide in her and sorry to bring their talk to a close when she saw that it was 2:30 and time to help get the children on the buses.

When she returned, the janitor was waiting for her. A drain in the boy's room was clogged, and he couldn't fix it himself. Martha called the administration building and asked to have a plumber sent over.

Jerry Evans, the first teacher she had chosen to evaluate, came in promptly at three. He was young, eager, and receptive to suggestions, and Martha was glad she had picked him first. After the evaluation, which turned out to be considerably less painful than Martha had expected, he stayed on and sipped a coke and told her about the progress he was making with a blind child in his class. Martha, who had taught several kinds of physically handicapped children, was interested in what he had to say. She offered him a number of ideas on how he could rearrange some things in the classroom to accommodate the child and how he could enlist the other children's support.

Martha was still thinking about her talk with Jerry as she drove to the administration building for a four o'clock meeting of the elementary school principals. Maybe the evaluations weren't going to be such a grisly chore after all. As a teacher, she had rather enjoyed the opportunity to discuss her own successes and her ideas with the principal. Probably most teachers felt the same way.

After the meeting, she dropped by the home of a child who had missed six weeks of school because of illness, and then she headed for the grocery store with a list she had made the night before. Why can't I be as organized in my work as I am in my personal life, Martha wondered?

She had always worked hard and demanded a lot of herself. She was putting in long days and doing more work in the evening at home. And she knew that she had good insights and ideas on how to improve the school, which, if the standardized achievement test scores were any indication, had a lot of room for improvement. But she never seemed to get down to the things that she knew were really important, and her energy was going into routine tasks.

Today had been a little better. She had finally started on the teacher evaluations, and the experience had been quite gratifying. Maybe now she could begin to stop worrying about criticism and conflicts and making mistakes, and start being the leader she was hired to be.

Questions

What tasks does Martha do easily and efficiently?

What tasks does she find difficult to do and procrastinate about?

Discussion

Martha obviously feels comfortable planning, following directions, and doing pencil-and-paper tasks. But she is bogged down when she must make decisions, help resolve conflicts, and exercise leadership with people she perceives as her equals in intelligence and experience.

It's hard to read about Martha without feeling some impatience. "Stop putting things off, stop rationalizing, stop kidding yourself," we want to tell her. Martha's problem is uncomfortably close to home for most of us. What can we learn from Martha? First, that procrastination isn't laziness. Most of us find it easy to do some kinds of tasks and very difficult to get going on others.

As another example, Eleanor found that she put off paying bills, balancing her checkbook, filling out her income tax return, measuring the windows in her apartment for curtains, and drawing up the budget for her division. The common element in all these tasks was working with numbers, which she was afraid of.

Take some time now to list tasks you have postponed in Exercise 11.2. Then analyze your list to see if there is a pattern to your procrastination.

Most people find that they postpone tasks that seem too big, too hard, or just plain unpleasant. But any complex project is made up of many little tasks, whether it's packing household items for a move or writing a thesis or adding a room onto the house. You may be overwhelmed by the idea of writing 50 pages or losing 50 pounds, but if you decide to write 5 pages today or lose 2 pounds this week, you have a

EXERCISE 11.2   Tasks that I am currently procrastinating about.

Other tasks that I can recall procrastinating about in the past.

Is there a pattern? Do certain types of tasks predominate?

manageable beginning. When you have taken that first small step, the project is never again going to be so awesome. Alan Lakein, in his book *How to Get Control of Your Time and Your Life,* refers to this as the "swiss cheese" approach to an overwhelming task. The idea is to punch holes in the overwhelming task and reduce it to bite-size pieces.

Break your project down into little steps, and start with the easiest. You might even set a timer to go off in 20 minutes, and commit yourself only to this amount of time. When the timer goes off, you can quit in good conscience. Often by then you'll have worked up some momentum and won't want to stop.

This technique could have helped Martha with her reading program. Instead of deciding that in one morning she was going to tackle the whole project by ordering materials, working up a staff presentation, and setting a schedule, she could have simply decided to do one of those tasks. Because she had set an unrealistic goal for one day, she ended up doing nothing on the reading program, though she had time to make a modest beginning.

If the project seems too hard, as doing the teacher evaluations seemed to Martha, you may be able to approach it by starting with the easiest part, as she did with one or two evaluations that were least threatening. When you succeed with the first step, you will be in a more positive frame of mind for tackling the more difficult steps.

Sometimes tasks seem hard because they are unfamiliar. If that's the case, don't hesitate to get some help. Read up on the subject, ask someone to teach you to operate the machine, or find out how others have solved similar problems. Use the resources that are available to you. Think of a project you have been putting off because it seems too hard, and make a list of all the people, agencies, printed material, or training opportunities that could help make it easier for you.

If you are postponing something because it is unpleasant, such as apologizing for a mistake or asking for a loan or sitting down to talk with an employee who isn't doing a good job, think about what will happen if you delay action. For example, you're going to go out of your way to avoid seeing Mary because you owe her an apology. The longer you procrastinate about apologizing, the guiltier you become, the more uncomfortable it becomes to do it, and eventually it may become impossible to even salvage the relationship. Similarly, if you delay telling Jake he isn't meeting your expectations in doing his job, the problem will continue and get worse. Because his performance will reflect badly on you, you will begin to resent him, and it will be increasingly difficult to have a constructive talk with him.

Avoiding unpleasant chores usually doesn't make them go away. You must deal with them sooner or later, and they tend to get more unpleasant and worrisome as time goes by. Being aware of the price of procrastination can often prod you into action. And whether the project is big, hard, or unpalatable, you can often "psych yourself up" by imagining how good you are going to feel when you have done it.

Martha could have used this approach to settle the conflict between the irate parent and the teacher. Sitting down with the two and helping them iron out their differences may be a grim experience, but Martha will be very relieved when it's over. She'll be able to answer her phone without the nagging worry that it's the parent or the superintendent putting blame on her, and she'll be able to look the teacher in the eye again.

So give yourself a pep talk. Tell yourself how great it'll be when the room is painted or when the wisdom teeth are gone or when the report is written. Hypnotists use this technique to help people lose weight, stop smoking, and overcome fears. They paint a vivid picture of how terrible things will be if the bad habit continues and how glorious will be the results of changing behavior. You can talk yourself into getting a job done the same way.

Here are some more ways to get yourself going when you think you can't:

- Make a commitment to someone else. It's harder to make excuses to another person for not getting the job done. Making a promise to someone else can be a goad to action.

- Arrange your environment to make it easier to keep going once you get started. Put yourself out of the way of distractions like the telephone, the television, the magazine rack, the refrigerator, or whatever it is that beckons irresistibly.

- Give yourself rewards along the way. Promise yourself that you'll work until eleven tonight and then sleep late tomorrow, or that you'll take an evening off and go to a movie when one step is completed. And promise yourself a big reward to look forward to at the end of the project, such as "after the thesis is written, I'll go to the beach for a week," or "when I've lost 30 pounds, I'll take $500 out of savings for some new clothes."

For many other good ideas on how to overcome procrastination, see Appendix III (p. 311), specifically, Susan Fowler Woodring's videotape, *Overcoming Procrastination*.

SUMMARY

Procrastination is a tough time robber to overcome. It is a real test of our commitment to apply sound management principles to a problem area. Using the first principle of time management, then, we must analyze what we procrastinate about, what interruptions and excuses we find to get out of doing that difficult or unpleasant task.

Second, we must set priorities and try to stick with them. Don't make the same excuses and fill in the time with the same self-imposed, less important interruptions.

Finally, we have to do a little planning, particularly if the task is large. Subdivide it into smaller segments. Get it organized in terms of information needs and people who must be involved. Delegate parts of it. Schedule it in a realistic time frame, and protect the blocks of time allocated to it. If it's a tough task, try to do it when your energy level is high.

In the next chapter, we will try to bring together all the time management principles we have learned by doing a comprehensive exercise. You should find it a real challenge to sort out a couple of typical days in the life of a busy manager.

12 Your Monday Morning In-Basket

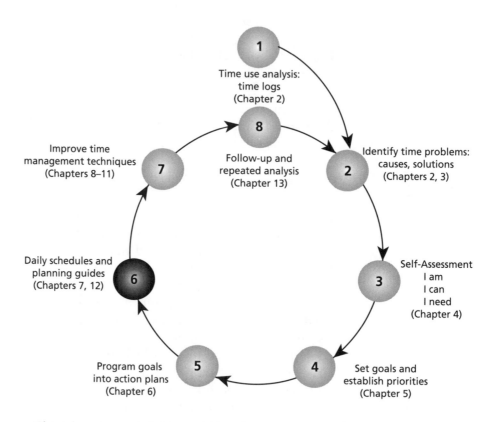

This chapter contains a simulated exercise in daily planning that will sharpen your skills in managing time over a one-week period. You will have to use a number of the time management concepts you learned in previous chapters:

Setting priorities
Organizing time in a weekly planning guide
Delegating
Planning a meeting
Accumulating similar tasks

Put yourself in the shoes of a more-or-less typical manager coming to work on Monday morning. You are the controller of Pacific Food Products Company. Last week you attended a workshop in Denver on computer networks and then took a long weekend with your spouse, Pat. As you left the house, you thought, "It's going to be a helluva busy week." Getting caught in a traffic jam on the freeway meant you didn't get the early start you had hoped for. After chatting with a couple of co-workers about the workshop, you finally get to your office, open your briefcase, and pull out a to-do list that you scribbled on the plane trip back from Denver. Clipped to it is a note from Pat urging you to talk with your daughter about college. You glance at your in-basket, which is piled high, and you decide to get a cup of coffee before tackling it. Upon returning, you find that your in-basket contains the following.

Your Weekly Planning Guide. The only entries in it are your weekly staff meeting, plane and motel reservations for an upcoming trip to several plants, and meetings with plant personnel that your secretary, Barbara Reed, arranged while you were away.

A "Current" file with phone messages, letters, notes, and memos (addressed to YOU). Barbara made hard copies of your voice mail and E-mail messages for ease of handling.

A "General Information" folder containing several interdepartmental memos, two lengthy reports, several business and trade magazines, and a pile of "junk" mail.

Your job is to sort out the tasks that face you, indicating the priority and disposition of each item. You should then organize these tasks in your planning guide. The complete "in-basket exercise," including instructions, is in Appendix II (pp. 277–308), perforated for easy handling. To make this time management simulation of greatest value to you, don't go on to the discussion that follows until you have worked through Appendix II.

Your effectiveness as a manager will depend on how well you use your time. Good luck!

DISCUSSION OF THE IN-BASKET EXERCISE

The real YOU, who occupied the controller's position at Pacific, started out a very busy week with about three quarters of an hour of planning, following the principles of time management. This brief period of planning enabled YOU to accomplish most of the important tasks that had to be done that week; those that could be deferred were scheduled for the following week.

Too often, when we're under the pressure of deadlines, we panic, rushing about from task to task—starting a lot, not finishing many, not doing them in order of priorities. When you feel yourself getting into this state of panic, pause a moment as YOU did. Take a "time out." Lean back and think about what you want to accomplish, what's most important, where you're going, and how you're going to get there. Then commit your plan to writing.

The plan may be a simple list, notes in a calendar, or a more complete planning guide—whatever seems most appropriate and fits your style. The important point is to take the few minutes to plan so that you are effective during the critical period you face.

The next four chapter sections consider how the real YOU planned and scheduled this critical week, in the following areas of time management activity:

    I. A- and AX-priority tasks
   II. Tasks that could be delegated
  III. Phone calls and memos to be accumulated and done at one time, using marginal replies
  IV. The daily schedule and use of the Weekly Planning Guide

I. A-Priority Tasks

Review what tasks you designated A priority and why, and what action you took. Then look at the following discussion.

A Priorities on the Job

The real YOU decided on the following A priorities in order of urgency.

AX-1 Task: The meeting to resolve the issues surrounding the loss of market share of cake mixes in the Southern California market.

This task appears important, urgent, and tough. It's important to the company not to lose market share in this region, and prompt action is required. You must try to handle it Tuesday and Wednesday before you leave for the plant meetings.

It's important to you because your boss is relying on you for a recommendation. Whatever you do is going to get visibility throughout the Pacific organization. It had better be good!

It's tough because information is conflicting and emotions seem to be running high. Arriving at a sound consensus decision may be difficult.

The action steps would include:

1. Collecting information, including:

   - Sales data from Scott Adams, including his evaluation of the San Diego sales office

   - Details of the $175,000 promotional program prepared by Marlene Bassett and Mike Ketchum

   - The advertising and promotion effectiveness study done by Janice Pope

   - Budget information, which might tell you where $175,000 could be squeezed out

2. Planning and preparation for the meeting, including:

   - An information packet, which should be out to participants Monday afternoon

   - Scheduling two meeting times—say, Tuesday afternoon and Wednesday morning—the first to discuss causes and ideas for solutions, the second to agree on a solution and take action steps

3. Attention to group interaction problems:

   - Are you the best meeting facilitator? If not, who is?

   - Who would be an effective recorder?

   - At what point do you get the VP's involved? Perhaps not immediately, because they may attempt to use their power before all the facts have been brought out.

Shown on page 205 is the Agenda and Preparation guide for the meeting, which the real YOU prepared.

At the end of the meeting, you will want a few minutes to brief your boss, Joe Black, on the results and give him your recommendations.

AX-2 Task The visit to the three plants with budget problems. Resolving problems in the area of budgets is what YOU get paid for. This task is urgent because the meetings are all set up and deadlines are probably approaching. Preparations include the following:

Briefing meeting with Jeff Hughes to go over relevant data he has collected

Key issues meeting with Joe Black

Miscellaneous files and other materials to take along

AX-3 Task Organizational and management problems in the controller's department—YOUR department. The most obvious problem is George Jarvis, and some immediate crises need attending to:

Martha Johnson

Computer repair

Errors in the payroll

These can be handled by a meeting with Jarvis to get facts and then some follow-up communication with Joe Black, Martha Johnson, and the computer company.

In the long term you will need to strengthen that department if you are to achieve your objective of integrating and networking the computer applications in Pacific.

AX-4 Task Integrate and network the computer applications. YOU designated this A4, not because it is less important, but because it can be deferred. This project is, in fact, probably the highest in terms of long-term value to Pacific.

YOU planned no action this week, but made notations in next week's planning guide—two segments of two hours each to develop a plan for achieving this goal.

MEETING AGENDA AND PREPARATION

Chairperson: YOU

Recorder: Marlene Bassett—good at summarizing

Participants:

Controller Dept.	Sales & Marketing
YOU	Marlene Bassett
Scott Adams	Mike Ketchum
Janice Pope	Kendal Sears
Charlie Horner	Dave Saul
Standby: Joe Black	Standby: Perry Biggs, Jim Hoch

Time—begin:	Tues. p.m.: 1:00	Wed. a.m.: 8:30
end:	4:00	11:30

Location:

Reserve Board Room—screen phone calls	Board Room—screen phone calls 8:00 coffee and doughnuts

Statement of Purpose: To determine the cause of loss of market share in the Southern California region and to take corrective action.

Specific Objectives:

1. Determine cause(s):　ineffective selling effort?
　　　　　　　　　　　ineffective promotion/advertising?
　　　　　　　　　　　aggressive competition?
　　　　　　　　　　　other?

2. Solution(s):　　$175,000 additional advertising/promotion?
　　　　　　　　　others?

3. Action to be taken

Advance Preparation:

Definite:	1. Southern California market analysis
	2. Proposed promotion/advertising program
Maybe: (in some form)	3. Janice Pope's advertising effectiveness report
	4. Scott Adams's selling effectiveness evaluation

Ground Rules:

1. Keep open mind on all possible causes
2. Creative approach to solutions
3. Early part of session: objective fact-finding session by staff
4. If possible, arrive at consensus recommendation by middle management to VPs
5. If not 4, then voting majority recommendation to VP bosses, based on as much factual info as possible.

AGENDA

Item		Procedure	Estimated time
Tues. p.m.	Causes	1. Factual presentations of information	Start 1:00
		a. market analysis	1:15
		b. proposed program	1:30
		c. selling effectiveness	1:45
		d. advertising effectiveness	2:00
		e. others	2:15
		2. Reach consensus on causes	3:15
	Solutions	3. Explore solutions—assign responsibility for information-gathering overnight	4:00
Wed. a.m.	Review	1. Review progress—causes	Start 8:45
		2. Discuss alternate solutions—presentations	
		a.	
		b.	
		c.	10:00
	Actions	3. Develop action plans	
		a. what	10:00
		b. who	10:45
		c. when	11:00
	Conclusion	4. Summarize decisions, action plans, who's responsible, timetable. Gain commitment	

Personal and Family A Priorities

A-1 Task The talk with Leslie. YOU decided to handle the talk with Leslie in two phases. First, you met for a pizza Monday evening to "think about things she would like to do when she graduates from high school" and to sign up for the SAT exams. Second, YOU scheduled some Sunday afternoon sailing to talk about some of her ideas.

A-2 Task The planning board meeting. YOU decided it would be necessary to defer the planning board activities until next week. YOU called the suburban manager and suggested a meeting on the following Wednesday. This was agreed to, and YOU blocked out time in next week's planning guide both for preparation time and the meeting.

II. Tasks to Be Delegated

Review what tasks YOU decided to delegate. Did you remember to allow adequate time for instruction as well as follow-up? Then look at the following discussion.

YOU made a list of items to be delegated and entered them in the planning guide.

Priority	
	Barbara (Secretary)
X	Write letters in answer to résumés—jotted notes in the margin of the résumés to guide her.
C	Get conference table.
X	File insurance claim, pencil in dates, doctor's name, etc., sign form.
AX	Look up correspondence files for plant visits, copy my trip plan in case someone needs to get hold of me.
X	Get security badge, write necessary authorizations for my people.
X	Call Phyllis Parker re United Way. May Williams is responsible. Cancel meeting—May will be in touch later this week.
	George Jarvis (Manager, Computer Services)
X	Get info on Martha Johnson—see her briefly Monday or Tuesday a.m.
AX	Develop history and source of errors in computer payroll—what can we do to correct it? Tell Joe Black I'll have an answer in two weeks.
X	Is letter from Technologies accurate? $32,750—fair price? Any alternatives? How can we schedule time?
	May Williams (Manager, Billing and Accounts Payable)
X	Responsibility for United Way campaign in department; contact Phyllis Parker.

Priority	
	<u>Charlie Horner</u> (Manager, Budget and Cost Analysis)
AX	Gather reports and info on cake mix problem.
AX	Ready materials to send out to participants some time Monday for advance study.
	<u>Helen Sinclair</u> (Budget and Cost Analysis, R&D Section)
X	Check on Irwin Huggins's memo re Carbohydrate Electroscope Analyzer. What is total installed cost? Are we committed? Where can we find it in the budget?
X	Analyze causes of excessive overtime in August.
	<u>Jeff Hughes</u> (Budget and Cost Analysis, Plant Operations Section)
X	Make study of increased accident rate—cause of increase in Workman's Compensation.
	<u>Pat</u>
X	Need help this week. How about making transfer and paying bills this time? Discuss Monday evening.

III. Accumulating Phone Calls and Writing Tasks

Review your response to the in-basket exercise. Which phone calls and writing tasks did you plan to accumulate and handle all at one time? Which writing tasks did you identify for handling with a simple marginal reply? Now compare your decisions with those of the real YOU.

YOU entered the following list of phone calls and writing tasks in YOUR planning guide. YOU planned to handle as many as possible—at least all the A's and X's—from 9:15 to 10:00 before Barbara came in.

Phone Calls

Priority	
A	Dennis Hamby: Try to get Planning Board meeting deferred to next Wednesday, September 21.
C	Ad in newspaper re sailboat, cover list of questions.
A	Call home and arrange to meet Leslie at Pizza Parlor at 6:30.
AX	Joe Black: Brief him on my plan to handle the cake mix situation. Schedule two-hour lunch meeting Wednesday. Recommendations on cake mixes, key budget issues with three plants, tell him I'll have answer on payroll errors in two weeks.
AX	Charlie Horner: Get together all the info and reports on cake mix problem. Send out info packet to meeting participants.
AX	Call Perry Biggs, VP Sales & Marketing. Advise him what I plan to do re meetings, ask him to be available Wednesday a.m., keep him away Tuesday if possible.

Priority	
A	Call my lawyer about house problem and Coastal Developers' letter. Probably better to defer until next week when I have more time. Put it in next week's planning guide.
	Note on phone calls: Everyone will ask about trip—keep socializing to a minimum.

Writing

Priority	
X	Memo to District Sales offices. New procedure. Stress complete info to satisfy Sara Myers.
C	Letter to American Accounting Association. Defer until next week if rushed.
X	Marginal reply on memo to Huggins re analyzer: Appreciate his need but require more info before approving—Helen Sinclair will be in touch.
X	Marginal reply on memo to Phyllis Parker re training program: Will attend October 10.
X	Another memo to Phyllis Parker: Ask her about Rhoda Lefkowitz's inquiry—appears to be sex discrimination. What do we do?
X	List agenda items for staff meeting. Give to Barbara and distribute before noon.

IV. The Schedule and Use of the Planning Guide

The planning guide developed by the real YOU is shown on pages 210 and 211. Compare it with yours, and then read the discussion that follows.

Monday, September 12

It was 8:30 when YOU, fortified with a cup of coffee, dug into the in-basket. Because of YOUR crowded schedule, the most important task was to plan the time available. YOU told the receptionist, Jean, to screen phone calls until 10:00 and closed the office door. The time from 8:30 to 9:15 was spent reviewing the in-basket and arranging tasks in the planning guide. From 9:15 to 10:05 YOU made A- and X-priority phone calls (especially urgent are the ones setting up meetings) and completed X-priority writing tasks. At 10:05 Barbara came in. By that time YOU had the key meetings scheduled and had filled in the planning guide.

YOU then spent a few minutes with Barbara going over the list of items to be delegated to her. YOU went over the planning guide with her and agreed on times to check back with each other. Before the meeting

MANAGER'S WEEKLY PLANNING GUIDE

To-Do List
(indicate priorities)

Key People	Key Projects	A-Priority Tasks	Writing	Meetings	Phone
Boss: AX Cake mix problem AX Plant visits AX Payroll errors	No. 1 AX 1. Cake mix problem: — preparations — select participants — info needs — brief Joe Black	Prep for cake mix meeting Talk to Leslie	X District sales offices X Huggins AX Agenda—staff meeting X Parker X Parker C Amer. Acctg. Assoc.	Staff meeting Charlie Horner Jeff Hughes	AX C. Horner AX J. Black AX P. Biggs A D. Hamby A Leslie X Lawyer X Newspaper
Secretary: AX Correpondence for plant tours X Amer. Airlines X Security badges X Call Parker— United Way X Answer résumés X Insurance claim C Conf. table	No. 2 AX 2. Plant visits — briefing with Jeff Hughes — files	Cake mix situation		Charlie Horner Cake mix meeting	
George Jarvis X M. Johnson AX Payroll errors X Computer repairs *May Williams* X United Way *Jeff Hughes* AX Budget info for plant visits X Accidents *Charlie Horner* AX Cake mix info *Helen Sinclair* X R&D analyzer *Pat* Transfer $800	Others: A 3. Organization — develop plan next week (4 hrs.) A 4. Computer integration and network project — put out fires — no LT action this week A 5. Planning board — defer key meeting until next week A 6. Leslie	Brief Joe Black Plant visits	Take on trip: — minutes — memos — 2 reports — 1 or 2 magazines	↓ Joe Black	
				Oakland Sacramento	
				Eugene, Ore.	
		Talk to Leslie			

Schedule

WEEK OF: _____

	Morning	Afternoon	Evening

Mon.
Sep.
12
___
Date
	7
	8 8:30–10:00 quiet hour
	   —plan, calls, writing
	9
	10 11:00 flexible time
	    — Barbara, mail
	11 11:15 Charlie Horner
		12 Lunch—Sales & marketing
		    people (?)
		1 *Controller Dept.*
		   staff meeting
		2
		3 4:30 Jeff Hughes—
		   plant budgets
		4 4:30 check with Charlie
			5
			6 6:30 Leslie — Pizza Parlor
			7
			8
			9

Tues.
 	
13
___
Date
	7
	8 Flexible time
	   — mail and calls
	   — prep for meeting
	9
	10
	11
		12
		1 4:00 cake mix meeting
		2
		3
		4
			5 Review cake mix meeting;
			   get Charlie's opinions
			6
			7
			8
			9

Wed.
 	
14
___
Date
	7
	8 11:30 cake mix meeting
	9
	10
	11
		12 12:30–2:00 lunch and
		    meeting with
		    Joe Black
		1
		2 3:00 last-minute crises
		3 *Depart for airport*
		4 *4:05 American #612 to*
		   Oakland
			5 *Buford White (plant mgr.)*
			   will pick you up—
			6 *dinner and discussion*
			   of key issues
			7
			8 *Ramada Inn Airport*
			9

Thurs.
 	
15
___
Date
	7
	8 *11:30 Meeting with*
	   plant staff
	9
	10
	11
		12 *YOU will be driven to*
		    Sacramento
		1
		2
		   2:30 meeting—
		3 *Sacramento*
		4
			5
			6 *Evening open for*
			   additional meetings
			7
			8
			9 *Sheraton Downtown*

Fri.
 	
16
___
Date
	7 *7:15 Northwest #176 to*
	   Eugene
	8
	9
	10 *Meeting scheduled to*
	    start at 10:30
	11
		12
		1
		2
		3
		4 *4:45 United #905 to L.A.*
			5
			6
			7
			8
			9

Sat. 17 ___ Date			
Sun. 18 ___ Date			

Note: Entries in italics were the original entries when YOU arrived in the office Monday morning (see p. 285).

with Charlie Horner, YOU used the remaining flexible time to answer phone calls, dispose of other items of mail, and talk to a project manager from R&D who dropped by to ask why her request for a budget increase had been turned down.

The session with Charlie broke up a little before noon. YOU decided to go down to the cafeteria a bit early, to try to find a couple of people from sales and marketing, and to use the lunch hour to get some informal scuttlebutt about the cake mix situation. YOU luckily ran into Kendal Sears (marketing director) and Jim Hoch (general sales manager) and gained several interesting insights into the problem during the lunchtime conversation.

YOU returned to the office a few minutes before one to pick up a couple of messages, then went to the conference room and started the staff meeting promptly at 1 p.m. It ran over the hour scheduled because of all the items YOU needed to cover. At the end, YOU asked George Jarvis to stay and discuss the three crisis items. YOU also took the opportunity to ask George to "think about objectives for the Computer Services Section for the coming year." YOU hoped this would help in deciding what to do about the long-term organization of that section.

The time from 3:00 to 4:30 was occupied by the briefing with Jeff Hughes. From 4:30 until it was time to leave to meet Leslie, YOU used as flexible time and checked back with Charlie and Barbara.

It was almost nine when Leslie and YOU got home after stopping to look at the sailboat. There was time to do a few chores and scan the newspaper and the new issue of *Business Week* before going to bed.

Tuesday, September 13

YOU used the morning as flexible time—fitting preparations for the meeting and a brief talk with Martha Johnson in between phone calls, the mail, drop-in visitors, and other such interruptions. A little before noon, YOU went off to a quiet restaurant with YOUR meeting guide and made last-minute notes on the meeting.

The meeting went reasonably well, and by 4 p.m. most of the objectives for the first session were met. YOU felt it was a good time to adjourn, since the group was getting tired.

The rest of the day YOU reviewed the meeting, checked with Barbara, and returned messages.

Wednesday, September 14

YOU arrived at the office at 7:20 and closed the door. This was earlier than usual, but it was important to organize the details and strategies of the meeting.

At a little after 11 a.m., the meeting broke up with pretty good agreement on solutions and action plans to handle the cake mix problem. In reviewing the meeting, YOU felt a sense of accomplishment in the outcome.

YOU had a good hour to handle incoming mail, messages, and other crises and interruptions before the luncheon meeting with Joe Black. Joe was pleased about the outcome of the meeting and the fact that he wouldn't have to do battle with Perry Biggs.

When YOU returned to the office, Barbara had the correspondence files and budget info organized in folders for the trip. YOU took the copies of minutes, the interdepartmental memos, the two reports, and copies of *Management Accounting* and *Supermarket Retailing* from the "General Information" file and stuffed them in a briefcase. YOU also told Barbara to sort through the junk mail and throw it away unless something happened to look interesting.

Barbara asked about the memo from the President, Peter Riley, which was still in the "Current" file. "I don't have any ideas; put it in my C-drawer," YOU responded.

YOU left for the airport at three o'clock sharp, feeling good about the week.

SUMMARY

In Chapter 7, we discussed ways to organize and schedule your time and how planning guides can help. In Chapters 8 through 11, we explored ideas for controlling the key time robbers—interruptions, crises, paperwork, delegation, meetings, and procrastination. In this chapter, you had the opportunity to practice these concepts with the in-basket exercise.

We are now ready to close the cycle on our total time management process. The next chapter focuses on the importance of repeated analysis and follow-up.

13 Completing the Cycle: Repeated Analysis and Follow-Up

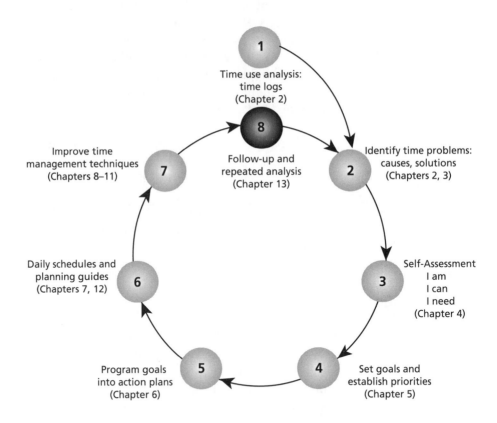

1. Time use analysis: time logs (Chapter 2)

2. Identify time problems: causes, solutions (Chapters 2, 3)

3. Self-Assessment
   I am
   I can
   I need
   (Chapter 4)

4. Set goals and establish priorities (Chapter 5)

5. Program goals into action plans (Chapter 6)

6. Daily schedules and planning guides (Chapters 7, 12)

7. Improve time management techniques (Chapters 8–11)

8. Follow-up and repeated analysis (Chapter 13)

You have now completed seven steps in the time management process. As you completed the worksheets and exercises, you identified your critical time problems, defined your A-priority goals, and developed long-range and daily plans. You should be on your way to using your time more effectively and efficiently.

But, like any other bad habit, poor time management habits are tough to break. You can easily slip back into your old time-wasting ways unless you carry on with step eight—repeated analysis and follow-up.

This step really completes the cycle of the time management process. This process is continuous—it doesn't end with reading a book or attending a seminar, but must become a routine part of your daily life.

The time management process has been illustrated as a circle, because there is no ending point. We must repeat the analysis of our time robbers to check our progress and find new ways to control them. We must also periodically reassess goals. As we change—and as our family, job, economic, and living situations change—we must set new priorities and plan new goals. Thus, the eighth step is perhaps the most important step of all.

Recall our discussion of goal programming in Chapters 5 and 6. We described as an example Bill, who planned a personal goal having to do with his church and religion. Let's visit Bill a year and a half later and see how he modifies his goal and his plans for achieving it.

> Bill has been at his plan for about a year and a half. He has become active in both the Outreach Programs and the Finance Committee. It's the time of the year when new committee assignments are being made. Bill is asked to chair the Finance Committee, which also puts him in a key role on the governing board.
>
> Bill first thinks, "This phase of the plan for my church-related goals is going faster than I expected." However, the Outreach Programs have really turned Bill on. They give him the feeling he is helping people instead of managing inanimate things, such as budgets, facilities, and procedures. The work on the Finance Committee is nowhere near as rewarding as Outreach Programs, and the position on the governing board looks like more of the humdrum organizational matters.
>
> Bill thinks, "Maybe I ought to reconsider some of this," as he pulls out his church involvement plan. Thus, Bill revises his plan: He will become more active in two of the Outreach Programs he believes are particularly valuable and reject the other appointments.

People have reported enormous payoffs from repeated analysis of a key time problem.

For example, after keeping a time log for a week, a hospital worker decided to do something about the four hours plus a day of routine interruptions. He adopted some of the ideas for controlling interruptions described in Chapter 8. After two months, he kept a log for a couple days on his "routine interruptions" and found he had shortened and reduced them to a little over three hours a day.

He talked with some of his co-workers and came up with additional ways to control these interruptions. After another two months, repeated analysis revealed a remarkable improvement—routine interruptions had been shortened to only two hours a day, what this manager considered an acceptable level. He continues to reanalyze interruptions every three or four months, however. "I like to see what new interruptions have crept in, so I can do something about them before they get out of control."

Reinforcement through teamwork can have real benefits, as the above example shows. If you want to learn more about how to work together with your work team for more effective time management, see Appendix III, "Recommended Time Management Resources" (p. 309).

In this book we have presented a framework for time management and, through the experiences of real people described in case studies, explored solutions to a great many time management problems. These time management ideas can work for you, too. In Chapter 1, on page 7, you wrote your objectives for improving your time management. Look back at those objectives and note them in Exercise 13.1. Then note what solutions you have found to your time management problems—the key ideas presented in this book that really work for you.

KEY IDEAS

The rest of this chapter lists key ideas for you to review. As you read them, fill in which key ideas apply to your objectives in Exercise 13.1. Include any other ideas which you feel you can use to improve your time management.

Three Steps to Better Time Management

1. *Analysis:*
   Keep a log of where your time goes.
   Analyze your key problems.
   Find solutions.

2. *Medium- and long-range planning:*
   Build action plans for accomplishing important goals.

3. *Short-range planning:*
   Develop the habit of daily planning—using planning guides, to-do lists, and other aids.

EXERCISE 13.1   **Objectives and the Means to Achieve Them**

My time management objectives   *Key ideas for accomplishing my objectives*

Analyzing Your Time Robbers

Keep a log or other record, to provide you with accurate data on how much time you are spending and other pertinent information about who, what, where, when, and so on. Analyze the data you have collected, and identify the worst time robbers.

Look for solutions:

Set better priorities.
Plan and organize better.
Delegate portions of task.
Shorten or eliminate the low-value tasks.
Find better ways of doing necessary tasks.

Repeat the analysis in a month or two to monitor what progress you've made.

Look for additional solutions; talk to other people in similar situations.

Repeat the analysis occasionally; keep score on yourself; follow up on new solutions.

Keep the solutions visible.

Time Management and Teamwork

Your work team is the people with whom you interact on an everyday basis.

Look around at your work team. It probably includes your boss, subordinates, and secretary; outsiders, such as customers and suppliers; and peers you work with daily across the organization.

Gather information from time logs on how you waste their time and how they waste your time.

Talk with them and find ways to save each other's time, cut down on interruptions, and make each other's job easier.

Repeat the analysis and follow up on solutions.

The Maldistribution Rule

The 80/20 maldistribution rule says:

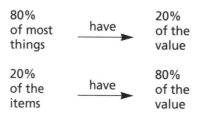

This is true of:

Our daily tasks and activities

Our goals

Interruptions, such as phone calls and drop-ins

Customers

Inventory items

Therefore:

Decide which are the high-value items.

Spend your time on those.

Minimize the time you spend on the other 80 percent.

Thirteen Key Time Savers

1. Learn to *set priorities* on things such as goals, tasks, meeting agenda items, interruptions.
2. *Start with A-priority tasks*—is it the best use of your time?
3. Fight *procrastination*—do it now if it's important.
4. Subdivide large, tough tasks into smaller, easily accomplished parts.
5. Establish a *quiet hour,* even though it requires willpower and may not always work.
6. Find a *hideaway*—the library or office of a co-worker who's traveling.
7. Learn to *say "no"* when you've something important to do.
8. Learn to *delegate*.
9. *Accumulate similar tasks,* and do them all at one time.
10. *Minimize* routine tasks—spend only the time they deserve.
    Shorten low-value interruptions.
    Throw away junk mail and other low-value paperwork.
    Delegate, shorten, or defer indefinitely the C-priority tasks.
11. Avoid *perfectionism*. Remember the 80/20 maldistribution rule.
12. Avoid *overcommitment*. Be realistic about what you can do in the time available.
13. Don't overschedule. Allow some *flexible time* for crises and interruptions.

The Goal-Programming Process

Part I: Four Steps in Analyzing Goals

1. Decide on a *goal.*

List your goals relating to work, family, community activities, and personal. Set priorities and start with the A-1 priority goal.

2. *List key tasks* required to achieve the goal.

3. Describe *measurable results* or outcomes for each of the key tasks.

4. *Test:* If steps 2 and 3 are accomplished, can you agree that the goal has been achieved?

Goals are abstract; you cannot do a goal. Goals must be defined in terms of tasks or activities for which we can measure the outcome.

Part II: Three Steps to an Action Plan

5. Place the tasks in the order or *sequence* they must be done.

6. Determine what *resources* (money, people, time, etc.) are needed to carry out the task.

7. Put everything in a *time frame.* Indicate milestone dates for the accomplishment of the tasks and the final achievement of the goal.

All tasks cannot be done at once—some can only be done after others have been completed.

Resources and goals are interdependent. Ready availability of resources will shorten the time.

Weekly Planning Guides

Planning guides have the objectives of:

Providing an "airplane view" of the week ahead

Scheduling A priorities before crises and interruptions press in

They should include:

Important activities—meetings, phone calls, writing tasks, etc.

Interaction with *key people* on your work team

Progress on *key projects*

Communicate the information with:

Your secretary

Key people

Your spouse

Don't forget to:

Do something to advance an A-priority goal

Build in a "quiet hour"

Take advantage of your biocycles—schedule important tasks when you are at your peak

Setting Priorities: Key to Daily Planning

A Priority

Key tasks that must be done to further your A-priority goals, in your discretionary time. They come from the goal-programming process described in Chapter 6. *These A's are yours, not someone else's.*

X Priority

Tasks that must be done because they are part of your job (system-imposed) or the boss tells you to (boss-imposed). X's are urgent, can't be deferred long, must be done today or now. Sometimes we need to schedule time for X tasks, or we simply need to allow plenty of flexible time to accommodate them if they arise as crises.

C Priority

Low-value, often routine tasks that can be deferred, delegated easily, or perhaps don't have to be done at all.

Controlling Interruptions

1. Analyze the interruptions. Keep a log for a couple days, including:
   Who or what
   Purpose
   Time spent
   A, X, or C priority
   Ways to shorten or eliminate

2. Accumulate interruptions of a similar type, and handle them:
   All at once
   During a low-priority time
   With a memo
   As delegated tasks
   In a group meeting
   By the person to whom they apply

3. Have your secretary, the receptionist, or a co-worker screen low- or medium-value interruptions during your quiet hour. Instruct this individual about:
   Priorities
   A call-back time
   Finding out the purpose of the calls
   Referring questions to someone else when possible
   Notifying callers to have background information ready when you call back

4. Use voice mail, e-mail, and answering machines as a means of communicating important messages when direct contact and meetings are inconvenient to arrange. Cut down on "telephone tag" by:
   Leaving more than your name and number
   Asking that important questions be answered on your voice mail or e-mail
   You may never have to speak directly with the other person.

5. During your quiet hour:
   Close the door when you have something important to do.
   Practice the open door policy, but within reasonable limits.
   Plan time when you will be available and time when you will limit your availability.

6. Learn to say "no" or "later" if you have something important to do.

7. Shorten less important interruptions—spend only the time on them they deserve. Some hints to achieve this:

   Time yourself with a clock or egg timer ("I'm only going to spend five minutes each on these phone calls").

   Have some favorite cut-off phrases for phone or drop-in interruptions.

Handling Paperwork

1. Sort your paperwork and mail in terms of priorities.

   A priority—items that are urgent and important.

   Information-type pieces such as minutes of meetings, interoffice memos, etc. Accumulate and scan them during an off time—maybe late in the day or while catching a bite to eat.

   C-priority paperwork—things that can be deferred, perhaps indefinitely, i.e., the need to handle them may disappear.

   Throw away junk mail and items that have little significance to you—don't keep or file them.

2. Get your secretary to help you sort your mail, to handle the more routine items, and to put before you only important matters.

3. Each time you handle a paperwork item, try to take care of it, or at least move it along to the next step. Avoid picking up a piece and putting it back down without taking some action on it.

4. Have your secretary, or someone else in the organization, designated as a librarian—to screen books, magazines, or articles that are relevant to your business and circulate them to the appropriate people in your organization.

5. Organize your paperwork and information flow using an appropriate filing system, with cross references, tickler files, and so forth. Invest the time to organize your paperwork.

6. Learn to skim background information. Scan the table of contents, chapter titles, headlines, key tables, and figures to get an overall understanding of the material. Take time to read in detail only if the material is important to you. If your reading speed is less than 300 words per minute, take a speed reading course (see Appendix III, page 310, for a reference on an audio cassette to improve reading speed and retention).

**Effective
Delegation**

Questions to ask yourself about when and what to delegate:

Is there someone else who can or should do this task—even though it may take longer or may not be done quite as well?

Is there someone who can do the task better than I can? Am I taking advantage of the abilities and experience of my people?

Is there someone who can do the task with less expense? Or with better timing?

Would this task contribute to the training and development of one of my subordinates?

**Steps in the
Delegation
Process**

1. Carefully *define the task* to be delegated. What are the expected results? What are the limits of authority? How should the task be approached?

2. Give some thought to the *selection of the person*. Does he or she have the ability? Training? Interest and motivation? The necessary time?

3. Plan for the *instruction or training* needed to carry out the task. What instruction is required? Is it available? Who will provide it? When?

4. Clearly *communicate the task* to the person as if you were entering into a contract:
   Scope of the job
   Specific results to be achieved
   Time schedule
   Authority needed to carry out the job
   A way of measuring performance

5. Consider the *human behavior aspects of motivation and trust*. What's your track record with this person? Have you been fair with evaluation and rewards? Have you been patient with past mistakes? Have you delegated the good as well as the dirty work and tiresome tasks?

6. Make sure you have delegated the *authority* to carry out the task as well as the responsibility. Have you informed other people in the organization?

7. Make sure you *follow up* on the results and give the person *feedback*. Try to keep your expectation consistent with the original agreement with that person. If the results are not satisfactory, or changes have to be made, discuss the matter with the person openly.

Meetings

A meeting brings together a group of people with a common interest and relevant knowledge and expertise to accomplish some purpose or goal through a process of group interaction.

Meetings are called to accomplish one or more of the following objectives. They are intended to:

Plan

Make a decision

Implement a plan

Evaluate

Solve problems—find causes and/or solutions

Inform or train

Capitalize on the group's knowledge and expertise

Build cooperation and commitment

Provide involvement and support

The vast majority of all meetings are called to make a decision or solve a problem.

Meeting Guidelines

1. Have a clear understanding of and be able to state the purpose or goal.
   Why have a meeting? What are the objectives? What type of meeting?

2. Carefully select participants.
   Who should be there? What is their interest? Expertise? What should they contribute? What are possible attitude and personality problems? How can you best facilitate the group decision process?

3. Prepare for the meeting.
   When should it take place? Where? How long should it take? Any special arrangements? What ground rules should you employ during the meeting? How should the agenda items be ordered? How do you approach each one? Is there advance preparation the participants should do? Presentations?

4. Provide skillful leadership of the group decision process.
   Get everyone to bring their knowledge and expertise to bear on the issues. Foster an atmosphere of creative problem solving. Overcome personality problems.

5. Record and evaluate results.
   What decisions were made? What action is to be taken? Who will do it? When? How do you follow up to make sure it's done?

Teleconferencing

Teleconferencing is another way to save time traveling to get to a meeting. It is not always necessary to have "face-to-face" meetings.

The Electronic Superhighway

Advancements in electronic and computer systems open up vast opportunities both for exchange of information and for human interaction. Many of us are already wired into global communication and information networks.

Howard Rheingold, in his book *The Virtual Community*, describes the "faceless culture" of the electronic networks.* He points out the promise and also the dangers of the global superhighway.

Beating Procrastination

1. Analyze what you procrastinate about.
   Keep a log and write down tasks that you are putting off.

   Is there a common pattern? Do you tend to put off tasks that involve figure work? Or interpersonal conflicts?

   Recognizing what you procrastinate about will signal you to begin applying solutions.

---

*Howard Rheingold, *The Virtual Community* (Reading, MA: Addison-Wesley, 1993).

2. Note your common "delay tactics."

   What kinds of excuses do you look for and find to put off doing that tough or unpleasant task?

   Recognizing those traps will help you avoid them.

3. Experiment with some solutions that will work for you.

   Subdivide that big, tough task into small pieces that can be done one at a time.

   Start with an easy or enjoyable piece to get going.

   Get someone to work with you—it will be less difficult and painful.

   Make a commitment to someone else or set a deadline—this will make it more difficult to put off.

   Get prepared for the tough task by having all the information available, and make sure you pick a time when you are rested and energetic.

   Block out distractions—close the door and have your secretary screen calls and visitors.

   Pick a place that's particularly conducive to accomplishing the task—if it's a creative project you may want a "retreat"-type structure:

   Reward yourself along the way.

Final Key

Remember to concentrate on effectiveness over efficiency. Efficiency is doing things right—the outcomes reflect the efforts you put in, as illustrated by the systems diagram below.

$$\text{Input efforts} \longrightarrow \boxed{\text{Your life}} \longrightarrow \text{Outcomes}$$

$$\text{Efficiency} = \text{Outcomes} \div \text{Input efforts}$$

Effectiveness is doing the *right things* right. This means the outcomes match up well with your *goals*:

$$\text{Effectiveness} = \text{Outcomes} \div \text{Goals}$$

Spend your time doing things which will advance your high-priority goals. Do the things you really want to do. After all, it's your life!

CONCLUSION

As we have noted throughout this book, the basic objective of time management is *not* to become super-efficient, super-productive, or super-busy, but to use our time in ways to achieve important personal goals.

As you manage your time, keep asking yourself, "Is this advancing my important goals?" or "Is this really what I want to be doing with my time?" Look again at the questions in Exercise 1.1, page 6. If you still are not satisfied with some of your answers, return to Chapters 4, 5, and 6 to reassess and replan your goals.

In Exercise 2.1, page 18, you compared how you would like to be spending your time versus how you are actually spending it. Was the gap large? Are you satisfied with your progress in closing the gap? If not, maybe you should go back to the chapters on planning guides, controlling interruptions, procrastination, or delegation, and commit yourself to making some changes. Pick up some of the references cited in Appendix III and increase your skill in areas of weakness.

Whatever your objectives may be, I hope this book will help you accomplish them.

Appendix I

Forms, Worksheets, and Planning Guides

This appendix contains the forms, worksheets, and planning guides that are used throughout this book and in your own personal time management program. The forms are described in the chapters indicated and located on the following pages.

You will find it most beneficial to use the pages here as a "master" set of worksheets. Photocopy the blank versions of the worksheets as many times as you need to use them.

TIME LOG CALENDAR

Date:_____

8:00 A.M.	P.M. 1:00
8:15	1:15
8:30	1:30
8:45	1:45
9:00	**2:00**
9:15	2:15
9:30	2:30
9:45	2:45
10:00	**3:00**
10:15	3:15
10:30	3:30
10:45	3:45
11:00	**4:00**
11:15	4:15
11:30	4:30
11:45	4:45
12:00	**5:00**
12:15	5:15
12:30	5:30
12:45	5:45

EVENING

6:00 P.M.	7:30
6:15	7:45
6:30	**8:00**
6:45	8:15
7:00	8:30
7:15	8:45

TIME LOG CALENDAR

Date:_____

8:00 A.M.	1:00 P.M.
8:15	1:15
8:30	1:30
8:45	1:45
9:00	**2:00**
9:15	2:15
9:30	2:30
9:45	2:45
10:00	**3:00**
10:15	3:15
10:30	3:30
10:45	3:45
11:00	**4:00**
11:15	4:15
11:30	4:30
11:45	4:45
12:00	**5:00**
12:15	5:15
12:30	5:30
12:45	5:45

EVENING

6:00 P.M.	7:30
6:15	7:45
6:30	**8:00**
6:45	8:15
7:00	8:30
7:15	8:45

TIME ROBBER ANALYSIS

1. Describe your worst time robber. _____

   _____

   _____

2. How bad is it?

   How many hours a day do you spend at it?_____ hours/day

   How many hours should you spend at it? _____ hours/day

   Estimate your effectiveness in using that time: _____ % effectiveness

   Estimate your efficiency in using that time: _____ % efficiency

3. On the next page list as many causes for the time robber as you can. Do you need to do some more analysis to better determine the causes?

4. Now look for solutions to the time robber. List them on the next page. Think creatively. List any solution, even if it sounds way out. Get a personal friend or co-worker to help you.

5. Set a target for yourself.

   How much would you like to reduce the time spent on the time robber?

   _____ hours/day

   How effective and efficient would you like to become?_____ % effective

   _____ % efficient

6. Commitment time! Commit right now to a target you think is realistic to achieve in the next 30 days:

   My target: _____

   Pick out the two or three solutions that are most likely to achieve that target and work at them:

   Solution 1 _____

   _____

   Solution 2 _____

   _____

   Solution 3 _____

   _____

7. Follow-up. In 30 days analyze your time robber to see if you've met your target. If not, why not? What got in your way? What additional solutions could you attempt to achieve or better your goal? Again, talk to a friend or a couple of co-workers to see what solutions they might come up with.

(continued)

TIME ROBBER ANALYSIS *(continued)*

Causes	Solutions
Internal	
External	

SELF-ASSESSMENT

Personal characteristics	Check (✓) 10 that best describe this person	Rank those 10 starting with 1 (strongest characteristic)	Check 5 characteristics that could be improved
1. Energetic and hardworking	_____	_____	_____
2. Accepts success gracefully	_____	_____	_____
3. Accepts defeat gracefully	_____	_____	_____
4. Takes responsibility for mistakes and errors in judgment	_____	_____	_____
5. Open to constructive criticism	_____	_____	_____
6. A good leader	_____	_____	_____
7. Good judge of character	_____	_____	_____
8. A good parent	_____	_____	_____
9. Recognizes own prejudices	_____	_____	_____
10. Trustworthy	_____	_____	_____
11. Likes to work on a team	_____	_____	_____
12. A loner	_____	_____	_____
13. Has a good sense of humor	_____	_____	_____
14. Takes pleasure in the accomplishment and successes of family, friends, and co-workers	_____	_____	_____
15. Keeps temper under control	_____	_____	_____
16. Highly motivated	_____	_____	_____
17. Doesn't need to get own way all the time	_____	_____	_____
18. Can accept people, including children and parents, whose values are different from own values	_____	_____	_____
19. Is growing, and accepts the pain and disruptions involved in the process of development	_____	_____	_____

(continued)

SELF-ASSESSMENT *(continued)*

Personal characteristics	Check (✓) 10 that best describe this person	Rank those 10 starting with 1 (strongest characteristic)	Check 5 characteristics that could be improved
20. Likes challenges, even at the risk of failure	_____	_____	_____
21. Well qualified for the present (or proposed) job	_____	_____	_____
22. Likes to work with people	_____	_____	_____
23. Not satisfied until having done his or her best on any given task	_____	_____	_____
24. Is creative in finding other solutions when one method doesn't work	_____	_____	_____
25. Asserts own needs and isn't victimized by others	_____	_____	_____
26. A "doer"—likes to get at what needs to be done	_____	_____	_____
27. Likes to carefully analyze and plan tasks to be done	_____	_____	_____
28. Works well under pressure	_____	_____	_____
29. Likes to work with reports, figures, data	_____	_____	_____
30. Prefers a lot of structure and organization	_____	_____	_____
31. Educational background is excellent	_____	_____	_____
32. Has much valuable experience	_____	_____	_____
33. Takes good care of own body and possessions	_____	_____	_____
34. Has a pleasing personality	_____	_____	_____
35. Knows what he or she wants and generally gets it	_____	_____	_____

SELF-ASSESSMENT AND GOALS

Self-Assessment Statements

Who am I?	I am	I can	I need
Physical/Health			
Emotional			
Intellectual/Education			
Professional/Career			
Social			
Spiritual/Moral/Ethical			
Other			

(continued)

SELF-ASSESSMENT AND GOALS *(continued)*
Goal Statements

	What I must do (commitments and constraints)	What I want to do (desires and goals)
Physical/Health		
Emotional		
Intellectual/Education		
Professional/Career		
Social		
Spiritual/Moral/Ethical		
Other		

GOALS

Job/Career Goals

Priority	General Goal	Subgoals	Specifics: How much? When?	Specific tasks and activities required to perform the goal
	Short-term job goals (Accomplishments in your work over the next 6 to 12 months that would signify a job done well to yourself and/or your boss.)			
	Longer-term job goals (Important accomplishments in your job over a period of several years.)			
	Personal career growth (Training, job expansion or new job, a change of careers, etc.)			
	Long-term career goals (What you would like to accomplish over the life of your career.)			

239

GOALS (continued)

Family Goals

Priority	General Goal	Subgoals	Specifics: How much? When?	Specific tasks and activities required to perform the goal
	Standard of living or lifestyle			
	Financial *Short-term* (The next six months to a year.)			
	Long-term (Insurance, education , retirement, etc.)			
	Family projects			

GOALS (continued)

Personal Goals

Priority	General Goal	Subgoals	Specifics: How much? When?	Specific tasks and activities required to perform the goal
	Personal growth (Reading, hobbies, arts and crafts)			
	Leisure-time activities			
	Health			
	Social			
	Spiritual			

Community Goals

Priority	General Goal	Subgoals	Specifics: How much? When?	Specific tasks and activities required to perform the goal

GOAL ANALYSIS

A-priority goal:

_____

General approach:

_____

Key tasks:	Measurable results:

Test: If the key tasks are completed with the indicated results, would most people agree that the goal has been achieved?

Yes _____   No _____

Are you sure?   Why not? What's the problem?

A-Priority Goal:

ACTION PLAN

Key performance tasks or activities (must be done to achieve the goal)	*Resources needed* (money, people, time, etc.)	*Time Frame:* Date I expect to begin: _____
1.		
2.		
3.		
4.		
5.		
6.		Time Line
7.		
8.		
9.		
10.		
11.		
12.		

Date I expect to achieve my goal: _____

MANAGER'S WEEKLY PLANNING GUIDE

Name: _____

Address _____

_____

Date: _____

Five Highest Priority Tasks for This Week

A-1: _____
A-2: _____
A-3: _____
A-4: _____
A-5: _____

MANAGER'S WEEKLY PLANNING GUIDE					
To-Do List (indicate priorities)					
Key People	Key Projects	A-Priority Tasks	Writing	Meetings	Phone
Boss:	No. 1				
Secretary:	No. 2				
Others:	Others:				

WEEK OF: _____   **Schedule**

	Morning	Afternoon	Evening
Mon. ____ Date	7 8 9 10 11	12 1 2 3 4	5 6 7 8 9
Tues. ____ Date	7 8 9 10 11	12 1 2 3 4	5 6 7 8 9
Wed. ____ Date	7 8 9 10 11	12 1 2 3 4	5 6 7 8 9
Thurs. ____ Date	7 8 9 10 11	12 1 2 3 4	5 6 7 8 9
Fri. ____ Date	7 8 9 10 11	12 1 2 3 4	5 6 7 8 9
Sat. ____ Date			
Sun. ____ Date			

Time Use Analysis: Weekly Summary

Planning and Priorities	Did I plan regularly? Did I set priorities? Did I stick with them?	A Priorities Number achieved _____ Problems: Some progress _____ Solutions: No action _____ % Effective _____
#1 Time Robber:	What was it? Who? How much? Causes Solutions	Hours/Day axis: 3, 2, 1 — x-axis: 4 3 2 1 — Prior Weeks / This Week
Discretionary time: Most productive time: Did I set a quiet hour?	When did it come? What did I do?	

Meetings: I ran Someone else's	% Effective	% Efficient	Problems Solutions

Procrastination	What? Why? Possible Solutions
Interruptions	Who/What? Purpose? How long? Ways to cut down or eliminate
Delegation	What did I delegate? How effective What else could I delegate?
Paperwork	How much paper shuffling? Ways to improve
Teamwork	How I wasted their time? How they wasted my time? Possible solutions

SALESPERSON'S WEEKLY PLANNING GUIDE

Name: _____

Address _____

_____

Date: _____

Five Key Selling Tasks for This Week

A-1: _____

A-2: _____

A-3: _____

A-4: _____

A-5: _____

SALES PLANNING GUIDE					
Call Plan					
Customer	Objective of Call	Priority	Route	Alternative	Expenses
					Travel: Lodging: Meals: Other:
					Travel: Lodging: Meals: Other:
					Travel: Lodging: Meals: Other:
					Travel: Lodging: Meals: Other:
					Travel: Lodging: Meals: Other:

Schedule

WEEK OF: _____

	Morning	Afternoon	Evening
Mon. ____ Date	7 8 9 10 11	12 1 2 3 4	5 6 7 8 9
Tues. ____ Date	7 8 9 10 11	12 1 2 3 4	5 6 7 8 9
Wed. ____ Date	7 8 9 10 11	12 1 2 3 4	5 6 7 8 9
Thurs. ____ Date	7 8 9 10 11	12 1 2 3 4	5 6 7 8 9
Fri. ____ Date	7 8 9 10 11	12 1 2 3 4	5 6 7 8 9
Sat. ____ Date			
Sun. ____ Date			

Time Use Analysis: Weekly Summary

Planning and Priorities	Did I plan regularly? Did I set priorities? Did I stick with them?	A Priorities Number achieved _____ Problems: Some progress _____ No action _____ Solutions: % Effective _____

#1 Time Robber:

What was it?

Who?   How much?

Causes

Solutions

Hours/Day
3
2
1

4   3   2   1

Prior Weeks   This Week

Discretionary time:
Most productive time:
Did I set a quiet hour?

When did it come?   What did I do?

Meetings:

I ran

Someone else's

% Effective	% Efficient	Problems Solutions

Procrastination

What?   Why?   Possible Solutions

Interruptions

Who/What?   Purpose?   How long?   Ways to cut down or eliminate

---

Delegation

What did I delegate?   How effective   What else could I delegate?

Paperwork

How much paper shuffling?   Ways to improve

Teamwork

How I wasted their time?   How they wasted my time?   Possible solutions

HOMEMAKER'S WEEKLY PLANNING GUIDE

Name: _____

Address _____

_____

Date: _____

Five Highest Priority Tasks for This Week

A-1: _____

A-2: _____

A-3: _____

A-4: _____

A-5: _____

HOMEMAKER'S PLANNING GUIDE				
Spouse/Children	Just for Me	Household Chores	Shopping	Driving

WEEK OF: _____ Schedule

	Morning	Afternoon	Evening
Mon. _____ Date	7 8 9 10 11	12 1 2 3 4	5 6 7 8 9
Tues. _____ Date	7 8 9 10 11	12 1 2 3 4	5 6 7 8 9
Wed. _____ Date	7 8 9 10 11	12 1 2 3 4	5 6 7 8 9
Thurs. _____ Date	7 8 9 10 11	12 1 2 3 4	5 6 7 8 9
Fri. _____ Date	7 8 9 10 11	12 1 2 3 4	5 6 7 8 9
Sat. _____ Date			
Sun. _____ Date			

TRIP PLAN

Name: _____

Address _____

_____

Date: _____

Highest-Priority Objectives of This Trip

A-1: _____

A-2: _____

A-3: _____

A-4: _____

A-5: _____

TRIP PLAN			
Business to Be Transacted			
Who to See	Purpose	Information Needs	Expenses
			Travel: Lodging: Meals: Other:
			Travel: Lodging: Meals: Other:
			Travel: Lodging: Meals: Other:
			Travel: Lodging: Meals: Other:
			Travel: Lodging: Meals: Other:

WEEK OF: _____   Schedule

	Morning	Afternoon	Evening
Mon. ____ Date	7 8 9 10 11	12 1 2 3 4	5 6 7 8 9
Tues. ____ Date	7 8 9 10 11	12 1 2 3 4	5 6 7 8 9
Wed. ____ Date	7 8 9 10 11	12 1 2 3 4	5 6 7 8 9
Thurs. ____ Date	7 8 9 10 11	12 1 2 3 4	5 6 7 8 9
Fri. ____ Date	7 8 9 10 11	12 1 2 3 4	5 6 7 8 9
Sat. ____ Date			
Sun. ____ Date			

JANUARY

SUNDAY	MONDAY	TUESDAY	WEDNESDAY	THURSDAY	FRIDAY	SATURDAY

FEBRUARY

SUNDAY	MONDAY	TUESDAY	WEDNESDAY	THURSDAY	FRIDAY	SATURDAY

MARCH

SUNDAY	MONDAY	TUESDAY	WEDNESDAY	THURSDAY	FRIDAY	SATURDAY

APRIL

SUNDAY	MONDAY	TUESDAY	WEDNESDAY	THURSDAY	FRIDAY	SATURDAY

MAY

SUNDAY	MONDAY	TUESDAY	WEDNESDAY	THURSDAY	FRIDAY	SATURDAY

JUNE

SUNDAY	MONDAY	TUESDAY	WEDNESDAY	THURSDAY	FRIDAY	SATURDAY

JULY

SUNDAY	MONDAY	TUESDAY	WEDNESDAY	THURSDAY	FRIDAY	SATURDAY

AUGUST

SUNDAY	MONDAY	TUESDAY	WEDNESDAY	THURSDAY	FRIDAY	SATURDAY

SEPTEMBER

SUNDAY	MONDAY	TUESDAY	WEDNESDAY	THURSDAY	FRIDAY	SATURDAY

OCTOBER

SUNDAY	MONDAY	TUESDAY	WEDNESDAY	THURSDAY	FRIDAY	SATURDAY

NOVEMBER

SUNDAY	MONDAY	TUESDAY	WEDNESDAY	THURSDAY	FRIDAY	SATURDAY

DECEMBER

SUNDAY	MONDAY	TUESDAY	WEDNESDAY	THURSDAY	FRIDAY	SATURDAY

ANALYZING INTERRUPTIONS
Phone Calls

Priority	Who	Purpose/Accomplishment	Elapsed time	Ways to shorten or eliminate

ANALYZING INTERRUPTIONS
Drop-In Visitors

Priority	Who	Purpose/Accomplishment	Elapsed time	Ways to shorten or eliminate

ANALYZING INTERRUPTIONS
Unscheduled Meetings

Priority	Who	Purpose/Accomplishment	Elapsed time	Ways to shorten or eliminate

ANALYZING INTERRUPTIONS

Other Causes

	Priority	Causes	Solutions
Unexpected Crisis			
Noise and Visual Distractions			
Self-Interruptions			

ANALYZING INTERRUPTIONS
Routine Paperwork

Priority	Item	Use or Purpose	Elapsed time	Ways to shorten or eliminate

MEETING PARTICIPANT PROFILE

Names of Participants (if more than six, use extra sheets.)

	1.	2.	3.	4.	5.	6.
What is their interest?						
What is their knowledge and expertise?						
What contributions should they make?						
Is their attitude toward the meeting supportive or antagonistic?						
Is their presence stifling?						
Are they open and creative?						
Do they have strong biases?						
Are there personality or other conflicts?						
Are they overly quiet or talkative?						
Do they have other disruptive traits?						
Is their presence really needed?						

MEETING AGENDA AND PREPARATION

Chairperson:

Recorder:

Participants:

Time—begin:
        end:

Location:

Statement of Purpose:

Specific Objectives:

Advance Preparation:

Ground Rules:

AGENDA

Item	Procedure	Estimated Time

RECORD OF MINUTES AND EVALUATION

Agenda Items:

Background/Comments:

Decisions: *Actions:*   *By Whom:*   *When:*

Follow-up:

EVALUATION

_____ % effective in achieving the purpose

_____ % efficient in the use of time

How well did the chairperson or facilitator:	Good	Average	Poor
establish the purpose and objectives?	_____	_____	_____
select the participants?	_____	_____	_____
establish ground rules?	_____	_____	_____
prepare in advance?	_____	_____	_____
set the agenda?	_____	_____	_____
begin on time?	_____	_____	_____
end on time?	_____	_____	_____
keep the meeting moving toward the tasks at hand?	_____	_____	_____
keep the group interaction smooth?	_____	_____	_____
encourage openness and creativity?	_____	_____	_____
gain consensus on decisions?	_____	_____	_____
obtain commitment by participants?	_____	_____	_____

How well did the recorder keep the group memory?	_____	_____	_____

How well did the participants:			
contribute their knowledge and expertise?	_____	_____	_____
offer positive/creative ideas?	_____	_____	_____
keep disruptive actions down?	_____	_____	_____
work to arrive at consensus?	_____	_____	_____

Appendix II

In-Basket Exercise

SITUATION

You are the controller of Pacific Food Products Company, a medium-sized producer of packaged foods. Some of these products are sold as store brands to retail food chains; others are advertised and marketed under a "Sunny Pacific" label, which is especially strong in the California markets. Pacific has several manufacturing and packaging plants in California and other western states; district sales offices are located in central market areas.

During the five years you've been with the company, Pacific has achieved healthy profits and above-average growth in its markets. As a medium-sized, regional company, however, Pacific sometimes finds it difficult to compete against the national giants.

You are 42, married to Pat, with a daughter Leslie, a senior in high school, and a twelve-year-old son Kevin. You learned accounting in a community college at night and have worked hard to advance in your job, becoming controller a little less than a year ago. You'd like to know all the latest wrinkles about how computer technology can be applied to your business, which is why you attended the Denver workshop. In your last evaluation, you and your boss set an objective to integrate, through a network system, a number of the accounting, production, and marketing functions—important given Pacific's growth.

You enjoy your family and life in a nice home in a Los Angeles suburb. You are active in the local planning board which is wrestling with rezoning issues. You enjoy sailing, but don't get much time for it.

The organization of Pacific is shown on the next page. The president, Peter Riley, in his late fifties, is very concerned about public and investor relations.

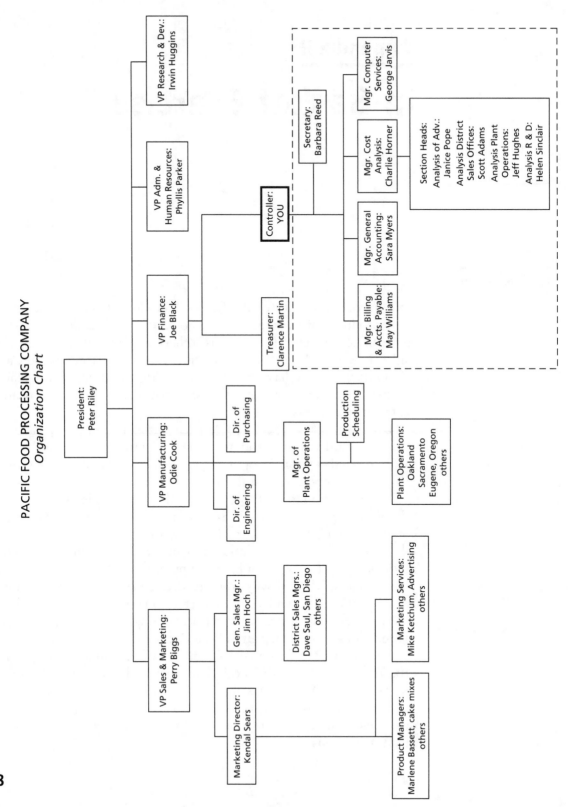

PACIFIC FOOD PROCESSING COMPANY
Organization Chart

President: Peter Riley

VP Sales & Marketing: Perry Biggs

VP Manufacturing: Odie Cook

VP Finance: Joe Black

VP Adm. & Human Resources: Phyllis Parker

VP Research & Dev.: Irwin Huggins

Marketing Director: Kendal Sears

Gen. Sales Mgr.: Jim Hoch

District Sales Mgrs.: Dave Saul, San Diego others

Product Managers: Marlene Bassett, cake mixes others

Marketing Services: Mike Ketchum, Advertising others

Dir. of Engineering

Dir. of Purchasing

Mgr. of Plant Operations

Production Scheduling

Plant Operations: Oakland Sacramento Eugene, Oregon others

Treasurer: Clarence Martin

Controller: YOU

Secretary: Barbara Reed

Mgr. Billing & Accts. Payable: May Williams

Mgr. General Accounting: Sara Myers

Mgr. Cost Analysis: Charlie Horner

Mgr. Computer Services: George Jarvis

Section Heads:
Analysis of Adv.: Janice Pope
Analysis District Sales Offices: Scott Adams
Analysis Plant Operations: Jeff Hughes
Analysis R & D: Helen Sinclair

Your boss, Joe Black, is fifty, a CPA, and had worked for one of the big accounting firms before joining Pacific. He's a strong advocate of accurate records and tight controls, and keeps the pressure on you.

Your secretary, Barbara Reed, has been with the company several years and has the reputation of "running the office."

All of the department heads who report to you were in their positions when you took over as controller. You are not altogether satisfied with the performance of some of them, but haven't decided to make any personnel or organizational changes as yet.

In general, the Pacific organization is aggressive and responsive to changes in market conditions.

The month is September, and the week for this exercise is blocked on the following calendar.

September

S	M	T	W	T	F	S
				1	2	3
4	5	6	7	8	9	10
11	12	13	14	15	16	17
18	19	20	21	22	23	24
25	26	27	28	29	30	

On Wednesday afternoon, you will begin a three-day trip to Pacific's plants in Oakland, Sacramento, and Eugene, Oregon. You are responsible for preparing plant operating budgets, and these three plants have problems with costs and meeting budget objectives. You've decided that the best way to resolve the difficulties is to visit the plants and get a first-hand view of what's going on.

On the following pages are a to-do list, messages, memos, and so forth. Read the instructions below, then assume that you have just arrived on a Monday morning to find these materials in your in-basket.

Instructions

1. Look over the organization chart and Weekly Planning Guide. Look over the to-do list and in-basket items quickly to get a feeling of the tasks to be done.
2. Indicate priorities of items on your to-do list, and note how you would handle each item. (Assign priorities using whatever code

works best for you; you may want to use the A, AX, X, and C method suggested in Chapter 7.)

3. Sort the in-basket items according to priorities, and note how you would dispose of each item.

4. Take the Weekly Planning Guide and schedule the tasks you have before you. Be realistic about how long the tasks will take. Don't overschedule—give yourself "flexible time" to handle other interruptions and crises that come up.

5. You estimate that the materials you would like to read in your "General Information" folder will take several hours. In the space provided on the list (as the final item), indicate how you would handle this reading time.

6. If you decide to call a meeting on the cake mix problem (see the memo, Item 4), use the Meeting Agenda and Preparation worksheet to plan it. Because of the complexity of the problem, you should plan five or six hours of meeting time.

7. After you have set the priorities, determined the disposition of all items, and scheduled your time using the planning guides, turn back to Chapter 12 (p. 202) for a discussion of the in-basket exercise. To get maximum value from this exercise, however, don't cheat and turn to the discussion until you complete pages 280 to 308.

THINGS TO DO		
Item	Priority	Disposition
1. Transfer $800 from savings account Pay bills: utility, telephone, insurance, other small items.		
2. Get a haircut		
3. My department—not performing as well as I would like. Need to make a careful analysis—talk to George Jarvis.		
4. Integrate computer system and network		

(a) Functions (currently only payables, receivables, and payroll on line).
    by end of year: general ledger
                  sales analysis and
                  forecasting		

Item	Priority	Disposition

next year: inventory control
production scheduling

longer range: personnel records
corporate planning
model

(b) Investigate larger system: IBM, Hewlett-Packard. Decision by first of next year.

(c) Personnel needs—need plan.

(d) Need thorough study of information system—get consultant help.

5. Write letters to people who sent in resumes—Redman looked good for cost job, Osburn and Parnell did not.

6. Call Dennis Hamby, suburban manager: When should we schedule the next meeting of the Planning Board? Need a quick update.

7. Need to get brought up to date with everyone.

(a) Department heads:

Sara Myers—when will trial balance be ready? New bookkeeping equipment arrived?

Charlie Horner—does he have cost analysis ready for the plants I'm visiting?

George Jarvis—did he get computer report reconciled with Sara's receivable records?

May Williams—is billing up to date?

(b) Joe Black—go over list of critical budget items for three plants (may take 2 hours).

(c) Barbara Reed—mail and phone calls. Did she get out report on sales variances?

8. Write memo to district sales offices regarding change in expense reports.

9. Check around for a small conference table for my office.

10. Get the insurance claim filed for Kevin's broken arm.

Item	Priority	Disposition
11. Call and get info about sailboat advertised for sale in newspaper—maybe get it for Kevin's birthday.		
12. Write American Accounting Association— need a speaker for our chapter meeting in November.		
13. Check with Irwin Huggins—why the large amount of overtime last month?		
14. Collect correspondence files for plant visits.		

Dear YOU,

Just a reminder note. I know you've got a busy week, but you must talk to Leslie about college. As I mentioned, she seems to have lost interest. She hasn't signed up for the SAT entrance exams, and the deadline is coming up. I think she'll listen to you.

Love,

Pat

MANAGER'S WEEKLY PLANNING GUIDE					
To-Do List (indicate priorities)					
Key People	Key Projects	A-Priority Tasks	Writing	Meetings	Phone
Boss:	No. 1				
Secretary:	No. 2				
Others:	Others:				

Schedule

WEEK OF: _____

	Morning	Afternoon	Evening
Mon. Sep 12 ___ Date	7 8 9 10 11	12 1 Controller Dept. 2 staff meeting 3 4	5 6 7 8 9
Tues. 13 ___ Date	7 8 9 10 11	12 1 2 3 4	5 6 7 8 9
Wed. 14 ___ Date	7 8 9 10 11	12 1 2 3 Depart for airport 4 4:05 American #612 to Oakland	5 Buford White (plant mgr.) 6 will pick you up—dinner and discussion of key 7 issues 8 Ramada Inn Airport 9
Thurs. 15 ___ Date	7 8–11:30 Meeting with plant staff 9 10 11	12 YOU will be driven to 1 Sacramento 2 3 2:30 meeting, Sacramento 4	5 6 Evening open for 7 additional meetings 8 9 Sheraton Downtown
Fri. 16 ___ Date	7 7:15 Northwest #176 to Eugene 8 9 10 Meeting scheduled to 11 start at 10:30	12 1 2 3 4 4:45 United #905 to L.A.	5 6 7 8 9
Sat. 17 ___ Date			
Sun. 18 ___ Date			

MEETING AGENDA AND PREPARATION

Chairperson:

Recorder:

Participants:

Time—begin:
       end:

Location:

Statement of Purpose:

Specific Objectives:

Advance Preparation:

Ground Rules:

	AGENDA	
Item	Procedure	Estimated Time

To **You**

Date **Sept 12**   Time **8:01**   A.M. ☑   P.M. ☐

WHILE YOU WERE OUT

M **Martha Johnson**

of _____

Phone _____
      Area Code   Number   Extension

TELEPHONED		PLEASE CALL	
CALLED TO SEE YOU		WILL CALL AGAIN	
WANTS TO SEE YOU	✓	**URGENT**	✓
RETURNED YOUR CALL			

Message **She wants to talk with you. Says it's important.**

Operator **Jean**

HOP
161P

Item 1

Priority:

Action you would take:

To **You**

Date **Sept 12** Time **8:12** A.M. ☑ P.M. ☐

WHILE YOU WERE OUT

M **Barbara Reed**

of **Your secretary**

Phone_____
Area Code   Number   Extension

TELEPHONED	✓	PLEASE CALL	
CALLED TO SEE YOU		WILL CALL AGAIN	
WANTS TO SEE YOU		**URGENT**	
RETURNED YOUR CALL			

Message **She will be in at 10:00 a.m. She and her husband are closing the mortgage on their new house. Says she is sorry— the only time they can do it.**

Operator **Jean**

HOP
161P

Item 2

Priority:

Action you would take:

To _You_

Date _Sept 12_ Time _8:15_ A.M. ☑ P.M. ☐

WHILE YOU WERE OUT

M _Ms. Cameron_

of _American Airlines_

Phone _____
Area Code   Number   Extension

TELEPHONED	✓	PLEASE CALL	✓
CALLED TO SEE YOU		WILL CALL AGAIN	
WANTS TO SEE YOU		**URGENT**	
RETURNED YOUR CALL			

Message _There seems to be some trouble with your reservations for Wednesday._

_____

_____

_____

Operator _Jean_

HOP
161P

Item 3

Priority:

Action you would take:

PACIFIC FOOD PRODUCTS COMPANY
MEMORANDUM

TO: YOU   **Date:** September 8

FROM: Joe Black

SUBJECT: San Diego situation re cake mixes

While you were away, Marlene Bassett (product manager, cake mixes) called and said $175,000 would have to be added to the advertising budget for special promotions in the Southern California market, principally for cake mixes. Seems we're losing market share there because of intense competition from one of the biggies. The $175,000 was a program she had worked out with Mike Ketchum (advertising) and Dave Saul (San Diego district sales manager).

I told her that was a lot of money that wasn't in the budget. Also that the president was trying to cut down on end-of-year expenditures. He wants to show as much profit as possible because we're going to have to raise capital next year.

Then Dave, the San Diego manager, called to cry about how they're getting killed in the cake mix market because General Food Products had launched a major campaign.

I checked around your office, and Janice Pope said a lot of money had already been spent in the San Diego market and she didn't think it was that effective. Scott Adams also said that he had just done a major study of selling effectiveness and the San Diego district looked weak.

Later in the day, Perry Biggs stopped by and tried to talk me into approving the $175,000. I told him I couldn't without getting all the facts. He suggested getting everyone together. I told him I'd prefer to wait until you returned because this was your area of expertise and responsibility and I wanted you to handle it.

We tentatively set a meeting for you for Tuesday afternoon and/or Wednesday morning. Dave Saul will be around as of noon Tuesday. He wants to be at the meeting.

I'll want your recommendation Wednesday afternoon. This one may have to go the the president if we decide against it. I don't like this kind of surprise.

Item 4

Priority:

Action you would take:

PACIFIC FOOD PRODUCTS COMPANY

MEMORANDUM

TO: YOU   **Date:** Sept. 6

FROM: Barbara Reed

SUBJECT: United Way Campaign

I set up a meeting for you at 2:00 p.m., Monday, September 12 in her office.

To ___You___

Date ___Sept 6___   Time ___3:15___   A.M. ☐ P.M. ☒

WHILE YOU WERE OUT

M ___Phyllis Parker___

of ___VP Admin. & Human Resources___

Phone _____

    Area Code   Number   Extension

TELEPHONED	X	PLEASE CALL	
CALLED TO SEE YOU		WILL CALL AGAIN	
WANTS TO SEE YOU		**URGENT**	
RETURNED YOUR CALL			

Message ___Wants to talk to you about___ ___the United Way campaign in your___ ___department--very important to meet___ ___goal.___

Operator ___Barbara___

HOP
161P

Item 5

Priority:

Action you would take:

To **You**

Date **Sept 12** Time **8:20**   A.M. ☑ P.M. ☐

WHILE YOU WERE OUT

M **Martha Johnson**

of _____

Phone_____
    Area Code   Number   Extension

TELEPHONED		PLEASE CALL	
CALLED TO SEE YOU		WILL CALL AGAIN	
WANTS TO SEE YOU	✓	**URGENT**	
RETURNED YOUR CALL			

Message **Very anxious to talk with you. Says she'll keep calling.**

Operator **Jean**

HOP
161P

Item 6

Priority:

Action you would take:

PACIFIC FOOD PRODUCTS COMPANY
MEMORANDUM

TO: YOU   **Date:** September 9

FROM: Irwin Huggins, Vice President Research and Development

SUBJECT: Carbohydrate Electroscope Analyzer

I know it's not in the budget, but we absolutely cannot do without this very useful equipment. It will enable us to carry out two extremely interesting development programs with much greater accuracy. The cost is $65,000 less whatever discount we get. We'll also need some heat and humidity controls to go along with it, which shouldn't cost much.

Item 7

Priority:

Action you would take:

PACIFIC FOOD PRODUCTS COMPANY
MEMORANDUM

TO: YOU   **Date:**   9/9

FROM: Barbara

SUBJECT:

Found out that one of the people May is recommending is moving to the East Coast the first of the year.
We'd be wasting company money to let her go to the course.

Told May you'd talk to her about it on Monday.

To_____You_____

Date___Sept 9_____ Time_____2____   A.M. ☐
                                         P.M. ☒

WHILE YOU WERE OUT

Mˢ   May Williams_____

of___Billing & Accts. Payable_____

Phone_____
       Area Code   Number   Extension

TELEPHONED	X	PLEASE CALL	X
CALLED TO SEE YOU		WILL CALL AGAIN	
WANTS TO SEE YOU		**URGENT**	
RETURNED YOUR CALL			

Message__May and two others in her
dept. want to enroll in Acctg. course.
Means leaving early Thurs. afternoons
all fall. Needs your approval for
time off and tuition reimbursement
by Monday PM (9/12)

                          Operator   Barbara

HOP
161P

Item 8

Priority:

Action you would take:

PACIFIC FOOD PRODUCTS COMPANY
MEMORANDUM

TO: YOU   **Date:** Sept. 7

FROM: Joe Black, Vice President Finance

SUBJECT: Computer Processing Unit

We've had several complaints on the computer processing unit from personnel. Errors in running the payroll have been increasing. Check into this and let me know what the problem is.

Item 9

Priority:

Action you would take:

PACIFIC FOOD PRODUCTS COMPANY
MEMORANDUM

TO: All Personnel   **Date:** Sept. 5

FROM: Peter Riley, President

SUBJECT: Public Relations

     I continue to be concerned about our public image in California and other states where we do business. Our plants are continuously accused of discharging organic materials and causing stream pollution. The enormous amounts we spend to control this seem to go unnoticed.

     I also feel that the large payroll to support families in these communities, the taxes we pay, and other support of community activities should be recognized by the press and public.

     If any of the personnel of this company have any ideas as to how to combat the bad publicity we are getting, send your suggestions directly to me. It is important that the public understand what an enormous contribution this company makes to the economy of this region.

Item 10

Priority:

Action you would take:

Computer Technologies and Software, Inc.

SUITE A, FEDERAL BUILDING
LOS ANGELES, CALIFORNIA 95401

September 5

Dear YOU:

This is to advise you that your present computer equipment is in need of some major repair work. Our last inspection indicated several potential problems.

Our estimated cost for this repair is $32,750. The system will have to be down about three days while this work is being done.

We recommend this work be done as soon as possible to avoid possible unscheduled downtime. We have talked to George Jarvis about this and he said you would have to make the decision on this size expenditure.

Respectfully yours,

Stanley Rosen

Stanley Rosen
Vice President

Item 11

Priority:

Action you would take:

PACIFIC FOOD PRODUCTS COMPANY
MEMORANDUM

TO: YOU   **Date:**   September 8

FROM: Charlie Horner, Mgr. Budgets and Cost Analysis

SUBJECT: Setting Objectives

As you recall my section was one of the groups in the pilot program on TQM (Total Quality Management). I have worked out several objectives with the supervisory people in my section, and have a meeting scheduled with Phyllis Parker on Friday, September 15. Would you like to review these before that meeting?

Item 12

Priority:

Action you would take:

PACIFIC FOOD PRODUCTS COMPANY
MEMORANDUM

TO: All Supervisors   **Date:**   Sept. 9

FROM: Phyllis Parker, Vice President Administration and Human
Resources

SUBJECT: Supervisors' Training Program

    Please submit a copy of your schedule of activities,
appointments, meetings, etc. to Al Hanson, our Training Director,
by 9 a.m. Monday, September 19. We need to schedule management training sessions for all supervisors.

    Sessions will begin September 26. They will be conducted
from 8:30—11:30 each morning for one week. With the number
of supervisors we have, we will conduct six separate sessions,
beginning on each Monday following the initial session.

Item 13

Priority:

Action you would take:

NORTHERN PACIFIC INSURANCE COMPANY

2000 OCEAN BOULEVARD
PALO ALTO, CALIFORNIA 95607

September 5

Dear YOU:

Attached is your Workman's Compensation report for the past six months. There has been a rather substantial increase in the incidence and severity of accidents. The statistical section of the report shows an upward trend over the past three years.

As a result of the larger claims, your rate has been increased 22% effective September 1. It is in your interest to determine why the incidence of accidents has increased and take whatever action possible to reduce it.

Very truly yours,

Roy Bishop

Roy Bishop

Item 14

Priority:

Action you would take:

PACIFIC FOOD PRODUCTS COMPANY
MEMORANDUM

TO: YOU

FROM: George Jarvis, Computer Services

SUBJECT: Discharge of employee

Date: 8:20
September 12

For your information:

I've given Martha Johnson two weeks' notice effective today. She's been a troublemaker ever since I took over the section. I didn't discuss this with you before, since I felt it was a problem I should handle myself.

Item 15

Priority:

Action you would take:

PACIFIC FOOD PRODUCTS COMPANY
MEMORANDUM

TO: YOU   **Date:** September 9

FROM: Sara Myers, General Accounting

SUBJECT: Expense Reports: District Sales Office

     I am completely fed up arguing with the Sales Offices about their expense reports. This bickering never seems to stop. Why can't they get all the information in the first time without making us call back for more every time? What can be done about this?

Item 16

Priority:

Action you would take:

PACIFIC FOOD PRODUCTS COMPANY
MEMORANDUM

TO: All Supervisors   **Date:**   September 7

FROM: Chief Security Officer

SUBJECT: Access to Company Buildings

This will serve to notify you that effective Tuesday, September 13, at 8:00 a.m., no one will be allowed access to the buildings without an authorized security badge. Please be advised that no exceptions will be made to this regulation. The above described regulation will also apply to all visitors.

Employees may pick up their badges from 8:00 to 10:00 a.m. and 1:00 to 3:00 p.m., Monday, September 12. Badges will not be issued, however, without written authorization from the respective supervisors.

Item 17

Priority:

Action you would take:

PACIFIC FOOD PRODUCTS COMPANY
MEMORANDUM

TO: YOU   **Date:** September 12

FROM: Rhoda Lefkowitz

SUBJECT: Salary

     Ms. Myers, my supervisor in general accounting, said it would be all right for me to contact you directly on this.

     I'm not complaining—I like my job O.K., but I'm a college graduate who has worked here for four years. I'm now making $1,920 a month, and our office just hired two men fresh out of college at $2,100 a month. Does this seem fair to you?

Item 18

Priority:

Action you would take:

PACIFIC FOOD PRODUCTS COMPANY
MEMORANDUM

TO: YOU   **Date:**

FROM: Perry Biggs, Vice President Sales and Marketing

SUBJECT: San Diego District, Cake Mix Situation

     Please advise me what you set up on the meeting. I'm going to try to be present part of the time. If I can't make it, Jim Hoch will.

     I hope you realize how important this is to our sales and marketing efforts.

Item 19

Priority:

Action you would take:

COASTAL DEVELOPERS
1671 Central Avenue
Los Angeles, California 95401

September 5

Dear YOU:

This is in reply to your complaint that there is severe erosion around the basement where the hill drops off. Since you have accepted the house and title has transferred, we do not feel that it is our responsibility. If we do the work we will have to charge you about $3,800. Please advise if you wish to have us do the work. We will need the payment in advance.

Sincerely yours,

Mort Simons

Mort Simons

Item 20

Priority:

Action you would take:

General Information Folder

1. Should review minutes of three meetings held last week—3/4 of an hour.

2. Interdepartmental memos: Require no action, but should be read for information; total of 16 memos. Will take an hour.

3. Two detailed reports which should be studied this week for possible action:

a. Two-year analysis and long-range forecast by product line
b. Product cost study showing how several products could be produced more economically outside by other companies

Will require an hour each.

4. Twelve news and trade papers and magazines—two to three hours reading.

5. About 25 pieces of junk mail—1/2 hour to review.

Appendix III

Recommended Time Management Resources

Books

Computers and Personal Organization

Jeffrey J. Mayer, *Winning the Fight Between You and Your Desk*. New York: Harper Business, 1993. *A comprehensive guide to using the computer to organize your time.*

Howard Rheingold, *The Virtual Community*. Reading, MA: Addison-Wesley Publishers, 1993. *A futurist discussion of the opportunities and dangers of electronic communication.*

Delegation

Robert B. Nelson, *Empowering Employees Through Delegation*. Homewood, IL: Irwin Professional Publishing, 1994. *Contains sections on the delegation process, many helpful ideas, and a delegator's checklist.*

General Time Management

Roy Alexander, *Commonsense Time Management*. Amacom Publishers, 1992.

Robert M. Hochheiser, *Time Management*. Barron Publishers, 1992.

Lauren R. Januz, *Time Management for Executives*. Smith Collins, 1992.

J. Serwert Lather, *Time Is Money: Save It*. Homewood, IL: Dow Jones-Irwin, 1989. *The author is a German consultant. Both German and English versions are available.*

Goals

Amy E. Dean, *Lifegoals: Setting and Achieving Goals to Chart the Course for Your Life*. Dan Olmos, ed. Hay House Publishers, 1991.

Eileen Dorsey, *Lifetime Strategies: How to Achieve Your Financial Goals*. Dorrance Publishers, 1993.

Sonya Friedman, *On a Clear Day You Can See Yourself: Turning the Life You Have into the Life You Want*. Little Publishers, 1991.

Tim Holt, *Achieve Your Goals: Create Your Best Future*. Info Publishers, 1992.

Eleanor Jacobs, *You Can Be Successful: How to Achieve Your Goals in 10 Easy Steps*. Jacobs House Publishers, 1991.

Elizabeth Jones, *You Can Get There from Here*. Washington Publishers, 1991.

Zig Ziglar is a guru on goal setting. He has written several books and produced audio- and video-training programs. Carrollton, CA: Zig Zigler Corporation.

Meetings

Karen Anderson, *The Busy Manager's Guide to Successful Meetings*. Career Publishing, 1993.

Richard Chang and Associates, *Meetings That Work!: A Practical Guide to Shorter and More Productive Meetings*. R. Chang Associates Publishing, 1993.

William R. Daniels, *Orchestrating Powerful Regular Meetings: A Manager's Complete Guide*. Pfeiffer & Company, 1993.

Michael Doyle, *How to Make Meetings Work*. Berkeley Publishing, 1993.

Sharon M. Lippincott, *Meetings: Do's, Don'ts, and Donuts: The Complete Handbook for Successful Meetings*. Lighthouse Publishers, 1994.

Three M Meeting Management Team Staff, *How to Run Better Business Meetings: A Reference Guide for Managers*. New York: McGraw-Hill, 1992.

Workteams

Merrill E. Douglass and Donna N. Douglass, *Time Management for Teams*. Amacom Publishers, 1992.

Alec R. MacKenzie, *New Time Management Methods for You and Your Staff*. Dartnell Corporation, 1990.

Alec R. MacKenzie, *Teamwork Through Time Management: New Time Management Methods for Everyone in Your Organization*. Dartnell Corporation, 1991.

Audio and Video Tapes

Susan Freeman, *Managing Your Time*. Boston, MA: INC. Magazine, Goldhirst Group, Inc., 1992. *Solutions to important time robbers, including procrastination and interruptions.*

Susan Fowler Woodring, *Overcoming Procrastination*. Boulder, CO: Career Track, Inc., 1992.

Verne Harmish, *Controlling Interruptions*. Boulder, CO: CareerTrack, Inc., 1992. *Practical ideas for controlling one of the worst time robbers.*

Learn Incorporated, *Speed Learning*. Mt. Laurel, NJ: Learn Inc. *An audio cassette course to improve reading speed and retention.*

Electronic Calendars, Personal Organizers, and Goal-Setting Software

Agenda and *Lotus Organizer*. Cambridge, MA: Lotus Development Corporation. *Personal organizers for use with Windows.*

Ascend and *Values Quest*. Salt Lake City, UT: Franklin Value Quest Company. *Software packages for answering the question, "What do I want to do when I grow up?" Integrating goals with daily activities, and many other features.*

Calendar Creator Plus. San Mateo, CA: Power Up Software. *A computer software package for customizing your own calendar to organize your time and activities.*

HP 100LX Palmtop. Portland, OR: Hewlett-Packard. *A portable approach to a personal organizer.*

Scan Card®. Columbus, OH: Executive Scan Card Systems. *A system for better organizing projects and activities. Available for both manual and computer operation.*

WordPerfect Office. Orem, VT: Word Perfect Corporation. *A software package that works on a local area network. Useful in organizing work groups.*

Index